"At last, a practical guide to th[...]
Sanders shows us how the Trin[...]
our faith is built, the hidden skeleton that gives shape and meaning to
the flesh and blood of daily experience. Highly recommended!"
Gerald Bray, Research Professor, Beeson Divinity School;
author, *Biblical Interpretation: Past and Present*

"Sanders has a gift for making the deep things of theology—in this case,
the doctrine of the Trinity—clear and compelling rather than shallow
and simplistic. Every evangelical should be able to explain how the
gospel is Trinitarian and the Trinity a summation of the gospel, and
Sanders shows us how. He makes a convincing case that there is nothing
wrong with the evangelical church in North American that a good dose
of Trinitarian theology, if absorbed into the bloodstream of the body
of Christ, could not cure. So take, drink, and prepare to be edified."
Kevin J. Vanhoozer, Blanchard Professor of Theology,
Wheaton College Graduate School

"Sanders's book should be required reading for anyone involved in the
work of the gospel. It will help readers catch a fresh vision of the depths
of the message they strive to proclaim and foster a renewed sense of the
grandeur of the Christian life they invite people to enjoy."
Mark Hopson, Regional Director, The California School Project

"Anyone who wants to know their great God better will be blessed by
meditating on the scriptural and practical truth in this book. Christian
leaders who want to ground their local congregations in the life of the
Three-in-One God will find both biblical depth and devotional insight
to help. Sanders makes clear what we tacitly know—that 'the gospel is
Trinitarian and the Trinity is the gospel.' It is my prayer that the whole
church will embrace *The Deep Things of God* and celebrate our relationship to the Trinity in the life of the church."
Scott Carpenter, Elder, Grace Fellowship Church,
Costa Mesa, California

"There simply aren't enough superlatives to describe how important and timely this book is. Sanders demonstrates how the Trinity is at the heart of the gospel and the foundation of the Christian life, and he makes his case by bringing forward distinctly evangelical voices. But this is no book of abstract theology. Sanders's work is lively, engaging, and accessible. He brings the Trinity out of the cloistered walls of academia and into the living room, explaining in terms anyone can understand that we are immersed in the reality of the triune God. There is no better guide I know of to explore the deep things of God than this book, and it deserves a wide and serious hearing by pastors, theologians, and laymen alike."

Matthew Lee Anderson, author, *Body Matters: Overcoming the New Gnosticism of Young Evangelicals*

"*The Deep Things of God* is a fascinating exploration of the Trinitarian heartbeat of the gospel that underlies the rich (though often ignored) practices of evangelicalism. Sanders wears his considerable learning lightly; this is a book I'm going to buy for my parents and recommend to my fellow doctoral students."

Ben Rhodes, PhD candidate in Systematic Theology, Kings College, University of Aberdeen

THE
DEEP THINGS
OF
GOD

how the **TRINITY**

CHANGES EVERYTHING

FRED SANDERS

CROSSWAY

WHEATON, ILLINOIS

To Susan,
relentless encourager,
who understands.

The Deep Things of God: How the Trinity Changes Everything

Copyright © 2010 by Fred Sanders

Published by Crossway
>
> 1300 Crescent Street
> Wheaton, Illinois 60187

Cover design: Faceout Studio, www.faceoutstudio.com

First printing 2010

Printed in the United States of America

Trade paperback ISBN: 978-1-4335-1315-2

PDF ISBN: 978-1-4335-1316-9

Mobipocket ISBN: 978-1-4335-1317-6

ePub ISBN: 978-1-4335-2414-1

Library of Congress Cataloging-in-Publication Data

Sanders, Fred (Fred R.)
    The deep things of God : how the Trinity changes everything /
Fred Sanders.
        p. cm.
    ISBN 978-1-4335-1315-2 (tpb)
    1. Trinity. 2. Evangelicalism. 3. Spiritual life—Christianity. I. Title.
BT111.3.S27   2010
231'.044—dc22   2010003951

Crossway is a publishing ministry of Good News Publishers.

VP		19	18	17	16	15	14	13
14	13	12	11	10	9	8	7	6	5

CONTENTS

LIST OF CHARTS AND DIAGRAMS

INTRODUCTION
EVANGELICALS,
THE GOSPEL,
AND THE TRINITY

(Or, How the Trinity Changed Everything for
Evangelicalism and Can Do It Again)

> I write to you, not because you do not know the truth, but because
> you know it. . . . Let what you heard from the beginning abide in
> you. If what you heard from the beginning abides in you, then you
> too will abide in the Son and in the Father.
> 1 JOHN 2:21–24

> The religious terrain is full of the graves of good words which
> have died from lack of care . . . and these good words are still dying
> all around us. There is that good word "Evangelical." It is certainly
> moribund, if not already dead. Nobody any longer seems to know
> what it means.
> B. B. WARFIELD (1916)

The doctrine of the Trinity has a peculiar place in the minds and hearts
of evangelical Christians. We tend to acknowledge the doctrine with
a polite hospitality but not welcome it with any special warmth. This
book shows why we ought to embrace the doctrine of the Trinity
wholeheartedly and without reserve, as a central concern of evangelical
Christianity.

How has it come about that so many evangelicals today are cold toward the doctrine of the Trinity, confused about its meaning, or noncommittal about its importance? Even though solid biblical and theological teaching on the subject is available, the doctrine of the Trinity continues to be treated as an awkward guest in the evangelical household. The very terminology of Trinitarianism sounds vaguely Roman Catholic to our ears: isn't Trinity, after all, a Latin word not found in the Bible but devised sometime in the Dark Ages? And though it was assembled (so the story goes) by clever theologians rather than apostles, isn't it of dubious status as a specimen of logic? Above all, isn't it a speculative distraction from the serious business of the gospel?

Doubts like these are hardly dispelled by the haunting thought that it is mandatory for Christians to believe it at peril of damnation. Perhaps you have heard the frightful admonition:

The
Trinity:
Try to understand it
and you'll lose your mind;
try to deny it and you'll lose your soul![1]

Heavy-handed theological pressure like that is about as helpful, in the long run, as tying shoelaces tighter to make up for a bad-fitting shoe. Wherever this pressure is felt, it turns us from negligent Trinity-ignorers to motivated Trinity-phobes. If we know nothing else about the Trinity, we at least know that explicitly denying it will put a church on the list of non-Christian cults. To many evangelicals, the stakes of thinking about the Trinity seem too high and the payoff too low—and we are not gamblers. No wonder the word *Trinitarian* is conspicuously absent from the list of adjectives that leap to mind to describe the theological character of evangelicalism. No wonder many of our congregations drift from year to year with only the vaguest apprehension of the fact that their Christian life is one of communion with the Father in the Son and Spirit. No wonder we have become so alienated from the roots of our existence as evangelicals: our Trinitarian roots.

TRINITARIAN DEEP DOWN

Evangelicals do have Trinitarian roots, after all, and those roots reach deep; not just into the history of the movement but into the reality of who we are in Christ. Deep down it is evangelical Christians who most clearly witness to the fact that the personal salvation we experience is reconciliation with God the Father, carried out through God the Son, in the power of God the Holy Spirit. As a result, evangelical Christians have been in reality the most thoroughly Trinitarian Christians in the history of the church. This is a strong claim and one not often heard these days, but I hope to make good on it in the course of this book. The characteristic beliefs, commitments, practices, and presuppositions of evangelicalism were all generated by a spiritual revolution: an applied Trinitarian theology which took more seriously than ever before in Christian history the involvement of Father, Son, and Spirit in the Christian life.

Nothing we do as evangelicals makes sense if it is divorced from a strong experiential and doctrinal grasp of the coordinated work of Jesus and the Spirit, worked out against the horizon of the Father's love. Personal evangelism, conversational prayer, devotional Bible study, authoritative preaching, world missions, and assurance of salvation all presuppose that life in the gospel is life in communion with the Trinity. Forget the Trinity and you forget why we do what we do; you forget who we are as gospel Christians; you forget how we got to be like we are.

The central argument of this book is that the doctrine of the Trinity inherently belongs to the gospel itself. It is not merely the case that this is a doctrine that wise minds have recognized as necessary for defense of the gospel,[2] or that a process of logical deduction leads from believing the gospel to affirming the doctrine of the Trinity, or that people who believe the gospel should also believe whatever the God of the gospel reveals about himself. No, while all those statements are true, they do not say enough, because there is a Trinity-gospel connection much more intimate than those loose links suggest. Trinity and gospel are not just bundled together so that you can't have one without the other. They are internally configured toward each other. Even at risk of being misunderstood before the full argument emerges in later chapters, let me say it as concisely as possible: the gospel is Trinitarian, and the Trinity is the gospel.[3] Christian salvation comes from the Trinity, happens through the Trinity, and brings us home to the Trinity.

Because the gospel is Trinitarian, evangelicals as gospel people are by definition Trinity people, whether or not they think so. It only makes sense that if the gospel is inherently Trinitarian, the most consistently and self-consciously Trinitarian movement of Christians would be the movement that has named itself after the gospel, the *evangel*: evangelicalism. This is not the conventional wisdom we usually hear. We are more likely to hear the kind of lament this introduction began with, the lament that evangelicals have at best a precarious and tentative grip on the Trinity. But the lamentations and warnings derive their force from the fact that our recent poor performance as Trinitarians stands in such stark contradiction to our actual existence as Christians who are in fellowship with the Trinity. Evangelicals are too Trinitarian to be so un-Trinitarian!

Although not everybody knows that evangelicals are Trinitarian deep down, it has not been a complete secret. One of the theologians who has, in recent decades, most faithfully and articulately insisted on the essentially Trinitarian character of evangelicalism is Gerald Bray, who says that "the belief that a Christian is seated in heavenly places with Christ Jesus (Eph. 2:6), sharing with Him in the inner life of the Godhead, is the distinctive teaching of Evangelical Christianity." No matter how much the doctrine may have become nonfunctional in the self-understanding of contemporary evangelicals, a robustly Trinitarian view of salvation has been the core, "the distinctive teaching" of the historic evangelical faith, according to Bray. In fact, though we have no grounds to be smug or triumphalist about it, we ought to testify clearly to our distinctively evangelical Trinitarian roots:

Without pride in our own tradition or prejudice against other forms of Christianity, we must surely proclaim that the experience of a personal relationship with God, sealed by the Spirit in the finished work of the Son from Whom He proceeds, is a deeper and more satisfying faith than any other known to man. . . . Evangelical Protestants are not wrong in insisting that theirs is a deeper, more vital experience of Christ than that enjoyed by Christians of other traditions. We have not received the grace of God in vain and we must not be ashamed to own the Christ we know as the only Lord and Saviour of men.[4]

Bray is a historian of ideas, so he is taking the long view of evangelical history. When he says that evangelical experience is marked by "a deeper and more satisfying faith than any other known to man," he is thinking in terms of five centuries of evidence, not the most recent five decades. He is not reporting current events but history; not today's headlines but the volumes and volumes of spiritual theology that fill well-stocked Protestant bookshelves. Similarly, the argument of this book is that evangelicalism is Trinitarian deep down, even if surface appearances are less promising.

OUR RELATED PROBLEMS: WE ARE SHALLOW AND WEAKLY TRINITARIAN

Anybody who stays on the surface of contemporary evangelical Christianity is unlikely to encounter profound Trinitarianism, either in teaching or in spirituality. Though most of this book will be about what evangelical churches do well, perhaps it's best to start by admitting two problems that any observer could see. First, evangelicals are not currently famous for their Trinitarian theology. Second, the evangelical movement is bedeviled by a theological and spiritual shallowness.

First there is evangelical coldness toward the Trinity. Above, I said that everything about evangelicalism presupposes that life under the gospel is life in communion with the Trinity, and that if you forget the Trinity, you forget why we do what we do, who we are as gospel Christians, and how we got to be like we are. Forgetfulness on that scale is, however, both possible and widespread. Forgetting where our evangelical commitments and practices originated, our churches are in constant danger of forgetting why we do any of the things we do. Our beliefs and practices all presuppose the Trinity, but that presupposition has for too long been left unexpressed, tacit rather than explicit, and taken for granted rather than celebrated and taught. We have systematic theology books that argue for the fact that God is Father, Son, and

Holy Spirit, but that fact seems like an item on a list, one of the many affirmations we make when summarizing the Bible. In every area of evangelical existence, our tacit Trinitarianism must be coaxed out, articulated, and confessed. We may be the most consistently Trinitarian Christians in the world, but it does us little good if we continue to be radically Trinitarian without knowing it. We are at risk of denying in our words and actions the reality that our lives are based on. We are at risk of lapsing into sub-Trinitarian practices and beliefs, of behaving as if we serve a merely unipersonal deity rather than the Father, Son, and Holy Spirit of the Bible. We are at risk of staying in the shallows when God calls us to the deep things.

This brings us, second, to evangelical shallowness. The evangelical movement is booming, but it often seems to be ten miles wide and half an inch deep. This shallowness is not only how things look from the outside, to the cultured despisers of evangelical religion. It also describes the way many evangelicals feel about their own churches and spiritual lives. Many evangelicals seem haunted by a sense of not being about anything except the moment of conversion. When they stop to ask themselves where they are taking their converts, they fear that when they get there, there will be no *there* there. When they sense that God is calling them to a deeper communion with him, they are unable to say what that would be. After all, you can't get any more saved than saved. When serious-minded evangelical Christians feel the desire to go deeper into doctrine or spirituality, they typically turn to any resources except for their own properly evangelical resources. A strange alienation of affections sets in. They cast about for something beyond what they already have, which leads them to look for something beyond the gospel. What sounded like such glad, good news at the outset (free forgiveness in Christ!) begins to sound like elementary lessons that should have been left behind on the way to advanced studies. What they embraced as the sum of wisdom when they first turned to God ("cultivate a personal relationship with Jesus by reading your Bible, praying, and going to church") begins to sound like Sunday school answers that never quite address the right questions. What has gone wrong when evangelicalism not only looks shallow from the outside but feels shallow from the inside?

These two problems, our forgetfulness of the Trinity and our feeling of shallowness, are directly related. The solutions to both problems converge in the gospel, the *evangel* which evangelicalism is named after, and which is always deeper than we can fathom. Our great need is to be led further in to what we already have. The gospel is so deep that it not only meets our deepest needs but comes from God's deepest self. The salvation proclaimed in the gospel is not some mechanical operation that God took on as a side project. It is a "mystery that was kept secret for long ages" (Rom. 16:25), a mystery of salvation that goes back into the heart of God, decreed "before the foundation of the world" (Eph. 1:4; 1 Pet. 1:20). When God undertook our salvation, he did it in a way that put divine resources into play, resources which involve him personally in the task. The more we explore and understand the depth of God's commitment to salvation, the more we have to come to grips with the triunity of the one God. The deeper we dig into the gospel, the deeper we go into the mystery of the Trinity. The puritan theologian Thomas Goodwin taught that the proclamation of the gospel was the "bringing forth and publishing" of a mystery that God had treasured from all eternity and that "the things of the gospel are depths—the things of the gospel . . . are the deep things of God."[5]

If the two problems of weak Trinitarianism and shallowness are related, there is also a single solution: we must dig deeper into the gospel itself. Instead of staying on the surface of it, satisfied with its immediate benefits to us and its promises of future blessedness, we can look into the essence of the gospel and find much more contained within it. Inevitably, what we will find in the depths of the good news is the character of God as Father, Son, and Holy Spirit. When we call to mind how the gospel is inherently Trinitarian, we will find that we are being called back to the depths of the encounter with God that brought about the movement called evangelicalism. The more deeply Trinitarian we become, the more Trinitarianly deep we become. We are who we are because of the triune God's work for our salvation, and it is high time for us to grasp this truth more firmly and bind to ourselves the strong name of the Trinity.[6]

EMPHATIC EVANGELICALISM

This chapter opened with the question, "How has it come about that so many evangelicals today are cold toward the doctrine of the Trinity, confused about its meaning, or noncommittal about its importance?" If evangelicalism is really Trinitarian deep down and came into existence because of a deep encounter with the gospel of the Trinity, its alienation from those Trinitarian roots is especially puzzling. But I think it can be explained by noting one of evangelicalism's primary characteristics: evangelicalism is emphatic.

Protestant evangelicals stand in a great tradition of Christian faith and doctrine: we are surrounded by a cloud of witnesses to the one Lord, one faith, and one baptism—the things that make Christianity Christian. No matter how defective your contemporary evangelical church experience may be, you can start there and pick up a trail to the great, confident evangelicalism of the nineteenth century and follow it back through the Wesleyan revivals and the Puritans, to the Reformation and its grounding in medieval Christendom, and behind that to the first heirs of the apostles, the earliest church fathers. All this is ours. Evangelicalism, in all its denominational manifestations, is an expression of that great tradition, and while it has nothing that is absolutely unique to offer, it does have distinguishing features. Chief among its distinguishing features is that it is emphatic. It has made strategic choices about what should be emphasized when presenting the fullness of the faith.

J. C. Ryle, the Anglican bishop of Liverpool, tried to put his finger on this distinctive trait in a tract called "Evangelical Religion." First he presented a list of the various doctrines that characterized the evangelical side of the Anglican tradition: the supremacy of Scripture, the depth of sin, the importance of the work of Christ, and the necessity of both an inward and outward working of the Holy Spirit. But second, he admitted that many Anglicans who were "outside the Evangelical body, are sound in the main about the five points I have named, if you take them one by one." What was missing, according to Ryle, was the emphasis:

> Propound them separately, as points to be believed, and they would
> admit them every one. But they do not give them the prominence,

14

position, rank, degree, priority, dignity, and precedence which we
do. And this I hold to be a most important difference between us
and them. It is the position which we assign to these points, which
is one of the grand characteristics of Evangelical theology. We say
boldly that they are first, foremost, chief, and principal things in
Christianity, and that want of attention to their position mars and
spoils the teaching of many well-meaning Churchmen.[7]

Especially in times of religious uncertainty, it is emphasis that makes
all the difference. The evangelical laymen who edited *The Fundamentals*
knew this. In the twelfth and final volume of the series, having published eighty-three chapters on important contemporary doctrinal issues
by an all-star team of authors, they published an essay by evangelist
L. W. Munhall, entitled "The Doctrines That Must Be Emphasized in
Successful Evangelism."[8] Munhall's list was not reductionist. It included
the doctrines of sin, redemption, resurrection, justification, regeneration, repentance, conversion, obedience, and assurance. Beyond these
ten points of emphasis, Munhall obviously believed a great many other
things and was prepared to defend them in feisty style against all opponents. But not everything can be said at once, and Munhall, speaking
for those early fundamentalists, knew that the most strategic decision
we ever make is the decision of what to emphasize.

Evangelicalism has always been concerned to underline certain
elements of the Christian message. We have a lot to say about God's
revelation, but we emphasize the business end of it, where God's voice
is heard normatively: the Bible. We know that everything Jesus did has
power for salvation in it, but we emphasize the one event that is literally
crucial: the cross. We know that God is at work on his people through
the full journey of their lives, from the earliest glimmers of awareness
to the ups and downs of the spiritual life, but we emphasize the hinge
of all spiritual experience: conversion. We know there are countless
benefits that flow from being joined to Christ, but we emphasize the
big one: heaven.

Bible, cross, conversion, heaven. These are the right things to
emphasize. But in order to emphasize anything, you must presuppose
a larger body of truth to select from. For example, the cross of Christ

occupies its central role in salvation history precisely because it has Christ's preexistence, incarnation, and earthly ministry on one side and his resurrection and ascension on the other. Without these, Christ's work on the cross would not accomplish our salvation. But flanked by them, it is the cross that needs to be the focus of attention in order to explain the gospel. The same could be said for the Bible within the total field of revelation, for conversion within the realm of religious experience, and for heaven as one of the benefits of being in Christ. Each of these is the right strategic emphasis but only stands out properly when it has something to stand out from.

When evangelicalism wanes into an anemic condition, as it sadly has in recent decades, it happens in this way: the points of emphasis are isolated from the main body of Christian truth and handled as if they are the whole story rather than the key points. Instead of teaching the full counsel of God (incarnation, ministry of healing and teaching, crucifixion, resurrection, ascension, and second coming), anemic evangelicalism simply shouts its one point of emphasis louder and louder (the cross! the cross! the cross!). But in isolation from the total matrix of Christian truth, the cross doesn't make the right kind of sense. A message about nothing but the cross is not emphatic. It is reductionist. The rest of the matrix matters: the death of Jesus is salvation partly because of the life he lived before it, and certainly because of the new life he lived after it, and above all because of the eternal background in which he is the eternal Son of the eternal Father. You do not need to say all of those things at all times, but you need to have a felt sense of their force behind the things you do say. When that felt sense is not present, or is not somehow communicated to the next generation, emphatic evangelicalism becomes reductionist evangelicalism.

Emphatic evangelicalism can be transformed into reductionist evangelicalism in less than a generation and then become self-perpetuating. People who grow up under the influence of reductionist evangelicalism suffer, understandably, from some pretty perplexing disorientation. They are raised on "Bible, cross, conversion, and heaven" as the whole Christian message, and they sense that there must be more than that. They catch a glimpse of this "more" in Scripture but aren't sure where it belongs. They hear it in the hymns, but it is drowned out by the repetition of the familiar. They find extended discussions of it in older authors, but those very authors also reinforce what they've been surrounded by all along: that the most important things in the Christian message are Bible, cross, conversion, and heaven. Inside of reductionist evangelicalism, everything you hear is right, but somehow it comes out all wrong.

That is because when emphatic evangelicalism degenerates into reductionist evangelicalism, it still has the emphasis right but has been reduced to nothing but emphasis. When a message is all emphasis, everything is equally important and you are always shouting. Your powers of attention suffer fatigue from the constant barrage of emphasis. The other problem is that a gospel reduced to four points ceases to make sense unless its broader context can be intuited. "The Bible says Jesus died so you can get saved and go to heaven" is a good start, the right emphasis, and a recognizable statement of the gospel—provided it is securely lodged in the host of other truths that support and explain it. The comprehensive truth of the Christian message needs to be sharpened by having these points of emphasis drawn out, but these points of emphasis need the comprehensive truth of the Christian message to give them context.

Knowing what to emphasize in order to simplify the Christian message is a great skill. It is not the same thing as rejecting nuances or impatiently waving away all details in order to cut to the main point. There is a kind of anti-intellectualism that is only interested in the bottom line, and considers everything else disposable. Certainly that kind of anti-intellectualism can be found in evangelical history, but it is a deviation from the true ideal. Emphatics are not know-nothings. The emphatic approach to Christian witness has a different impulse. It knows that the only way to emphasize anything is precisely to keep everything else in place, not to strip it away. The most proficient communicators always know that they are leaving something out to make their point more clearly and have a residual awareness of what is being left in the background as they direct attention to the foreground. The whole vast network of interconnected ideas left in shadows in the background is what makes the bright object of our focused attention stand out so strikingly, make so much sense of everything else, and point us to the total truth.

The best evangelical communicators have always been skillful emphasizers. John Wesley, for example, pointed to the sufficiency of Scripture by describing his desire to be *homo unius libri*, a man of one book[9]—although as an Oxford graduate, the author of dozens of works, and the editor and publisher of a comprehensive Christian Library, he was conspicuously a man of many books. "Man of one book" was a motto that emphasized Scripture, not a slogan for anti-intellectualism.

The best example of someone who struck the right balance between depth and emphasis is the apostle Paul. When the jailer in Philippi asked him, "What must I do to be saved?" he did not hem or haw, mumble or ramble. He did not stop to search his memory, pondering which passages of Scripture or trajectories of argument might be relevant to this question. He did not correct the jailer by saying, "It would be better if you asked me, 'What has God done to save me?'" He did not take out a piece of chalk and diagram the history of salvation on the walls of the prison, or talk about predestination, or explore the spiritual dynamics of the jailer's quest for meaning. He said, "Believe in the Lord Jesus, and you will be saved" (Acts 16:31). On the other hand, when writing to the Ephesian church, to whom he had declared "the whole counsel of God" (Acts 20:27), he did not just keep repeating "Believe in the Lord Jesus" over and over, as if he had nothing more to say. For them, he described the eternal purposes of God the Father in choosing us to receive redemption through the blood of his beloved Son and to be sealed with the Holy Spirit of promise (Eph. 1:3–14).[10] Paul was hardly a know-nothing, even when he resolved, for strategic reasons, to "know nothing" in Corinth "except Jesus Christ and him crucified" (1 Cor. 2:2). Paul knew how to be emphatic, but he also knew how to lead believers deeper into the mystery which had been made known to him by revelation (Eph. 3:3). He could make the simple point about salvation in a few words, and he could describe the deep background of that emphatic message in all its features. When he turned to the task of exploring that background, he turned to the doctrine of the Trinity: the Father's choosing, the Son's redeeming, and the Spirit's sealing.

The doctrine of the Trinity is the classic statement of the comprehensive truth of the Christian message. It is a summary doctrine, encompassing the full scope of the biblical revelation. When the early church tried to summarize the main point of the Bible in short creeds (such as the Apostles' Creed and the Nicene Creed), they inevitably produced three-point outlines about the Father, the Son, and the Holy Spirit. When emphatic evangelicalism degenerates into reductionist evangelicalism, it is always because it has lost touch with the all-encompassing truth of its Trinitarian theology. What is needed is not a change of emphasis but a restoration of the background, of the big picture from which the emphasized elements have been selected.

A blade is not all cutting edge. In fact, the cutting edge is the smallest part of the knife. The rest of the knife is the heavy heft of the broad, flat sides and the handle. Considered all by itself, the cutting edge is vanishingly small—a geometric concept instead of a useable object. Isolated from the great storehouse of all Christian truth, reductionist evangelicalism is a vanishingly small thing. It came from emphatic evangelicalism, and it must return to being emphatic evangelicalism or vanish to nothing.

Does the doctrine of the Trinity belong to the cutting edge of emphatic evangelicalism? No, it does not. It constitutes the hefty, solid steel behind the cutting edge. We do not need to use the T-word in evangelism or proclaim everything about the threeness and oneness of God as Father, Son, and Holy Spirit in every sermon. But the Trinity belongs to the necessary presuppositions of the gospel. In this book, we will emphasize the doctrine of the Trinity constantly. It will be the continual focus and the explicit subject of our study as we examine how the Trinity changes everything. We will triple underline it. The reason for doing this lies in our current plight of Trinity forgetfulness. Because current evangelicals have ceased to be aware of the deep Trinitarian background that previous generations of evangelicals presupposed, an extended exercise in calling the Trinity back to remembrance is necessary. But if the exercise is successful, the doctrine of the Trinity can and should subsequently recede from the foreground of our attention, back into the background. When evangelical Christianity is functioning properly, and its Trinitarian roots are nourishing its life, the evangelicals are busy telling the gospel, not talking constantly about the doctrine of the Trinity. May that time come! But it is not now; for the foreseeable future, we have a lot of remembering to do if we are to strengthen the bruised reed, or rekindle the smoking flax, of evangelical Trinitarianism.

It would be a false dichotomy to say that we will talk either about the gospel or about the Trinity, but as the genius of evangelicalism instructs us, we know that we can't emphasize everything all at once. We will continue to emphasize Bible, cross, conversion, and heaven. But in the name of the Father, the Son, and the Holy Spirit, we will do it without forgetting the dimension of depth behind it, and without lapsing into reductionism.

GOING FOR GOLD AT THE ECUMENICAL OLYMPICS

Imagine an ecumenical Olympics in which all the branches and denominations of the Christian church came together in friendly, worldwide competition. Some churches would be naturally positioned to take home gold medals in certain categories, leaving other churches to take gold in their own natural strengths. How would the evangelical churches fare? Most of them would probably be well advised not to try for the gold in categories like stately liturgy, historical awareness, or sacramental saturation. It might even be sardonically amusing to watch badly trained and disadvantaged teams do their pitiful best in sports they have no chance of winning, like snowless nations fielding bobsled teams. The literature of contemporary evangelical self-mockery is full of that sort of humor.

But what about the contests in which the evangelical teams would do well? What about the categories in which the evangelicals would, in fact, dominate all other competitors, sweep the field, take home the gold, and show the world what excellence looks like? The list of possibilities is a fun one to make: evangelicals have traditionally excelled in areas like conversion to a personal relationship with Jesus, devotional Bible study, conversational prayer, world missions, biblical literacy, and cooperation across denominational lines for the work of spreading the gospel. This list is neither exhaustive nor uncontroversial. But these six, among others, would be the strong categories for evangelical competitiveness in the imaginary ecumenical Olympics.

In my opinion, Trinitarianism belongs on that list. When evangelicals are being true to the underlying realities that brought the movement into being, they are the advocates of a particularly intense variety of Trinitarian knowledge and experience. When they are not self-forgetful, they know that participation in the life of the triune God is "the distinctive teaching of Evangelical Christianity," as Gerald Bray said. But we cannot simply add Trinitarianism to the list of evangelical strengths as a seventh category, mainly because in the current situation it is not among our conspicuous strengths. Nobody would believe it to be true, least of all most evangelical Protestants with their current self-understandings.

The Trinitarian theology that drives evangelical experience, however, is to be found deep down, underneath each of the half-dozen strengths that are characteristic of evangelical Christianity. In fact, each of the strengths is inherently Trinitarian and can only be explained by reference to the way evangelicals experience the work of the Father, Son, and Holy Spirit. When we read the Bible as if these inspired words carry the living voice of God, or when we pray to the Father in the name of the Son, or when we testify about Jesus in the power of the Spirit, we are always encountering a Trinitarian reality. This book is an excavation into the ground of each of these practices, digging into each until we find the Trinitarian gold buried beneath them. Above all, since the gospel itself is so Trinitarian that the Trinity simply is the gospel, salvation in Christ is an immersion into a Trinitarian reality. When it becomes evident that the factors which most clearly mark evangelicals as evangelicals are also the most elaborately Trinitarian, it will also become evident that the people of the gospel are the people of the Trinity.

CALLING ON EVANGELICAL WITNESSES

Before outlining the chapters of the book, I want to explain something that is unusual about the method I follow here. Whenever possible, I have quoted, appealed to, and engaged authors who are evangelical Protestants. I have gone out of my way to bring in as many evangelical witnesses as I could find, and I have usually avoided interaction with thinkers from other traditions within Christianity. I did not do this because I am unaware of or unimpressed by those other traditions, or because I think that only evangelical voices are worth listening to. No, the reason for giving preferential treatment to these authors rather than others is that I am trying to reintroduce evangelical Protestants to what is best in our own tradition. Here in the Introduction I have asserted that the evangelical tradition is a profoundly Trinitarian tradition within Christianity. The book presents an argument to support that assertion, and along the way, the witnesses that I call will also help build the case, example by example, that evangelicals have historically been not only subliminally Trinitarian but often self-conscious in their passionate commitment to the doctrine of the Trinity and their spiritual experiences with the three persons. The result, I hope, is an extended testimony service in which five centuries of evangelical Protestants stand up and bear witness to the gospel of the Trinity. Every reader can close this book with a long list of great, older evangelical authors on the Trinity that they can go and read.

Throughout the book there are a number of brief case studies of influential evangelical figures, usually entitled "The Trinitarian Theology of . . ." At thematically appropriate places we will explore the Trinitarian theology of C. S. Lewis, Francis Schaeffer, Susannah Wesley, J. I. Packer, Oswald Chambers, contributors to *The Fundamentals*, and so on. Some of these authors have been quite eloquent about the depth of their Trinitarian commitments, and these authors need only to be quoted. J. I. Packer does not need anybody else to write out his Trinitarian theology for him! Billy Graham, on the other hand, has been an active evangelist who was too busy doing his life's work to stop and explain, at a theoretical level, how everything he did in his evangelism and discipleship presupposed the Trinity. He did, in fact, have more to say about the Trinity than most people would expect, and following the lead of what he said on the subject, it is easy enough to connect the dots in his practice. The Trinitarian presupposition is there to be seen just below the surface. Graham is a perfect example of an evangelical who is focused so much on being Trinitarian in practice that he somewhat under-explains the theological presuppositions of what he is doing.

The evangelical heritage, in other words, already has all it needs in order to be robustly Trinitarian. Speaking for myself, what I am teaching here is a doctrine of the Trinity that I first learned in a variety of evangelical settings: a Foursquare Gospel church, then a Methodist youth revival, followed by a Community church, nondenominational charismatic retreats, and parachurch groups like Campus Crusade for Christ. I have honed, deepened, and enriched that theology quite a bit, through graduate studies and broader reading, but the thing itself did not come to me from academic study of theology. It was given to me at an early age by my evangelical church culture. I do not want to cover those first tracks, lest I throw today's young evangelicals off the scent of the Trinity at the point where they are most likely to pick up that trail. That is why quotations from evangelical authors dominate this book. Consistently pointing out these "local" saints is another way of showing evangelicals that they are already surrounded by the Trinitarian reality. The books we already have on our shelves are sufficient to teach us this Trinitarian way of being Christian, and they always have been. The word of the Father, the Son, and the Holy Spirit is not far from you; if you are an evangelical Christian reading this book, you are soaking in it.

The term *evangelical* is, everybody knows, a disputed one historically and sociologically. Whatever else it may mean, and whatever extended meanings it may accommodate, one of the things I mean by it is "Protestant." As a result, the decision to interact primarily with evangelical witnesses means that few of my sources are older than the Reformation of the sixteenth century. The limitation to evangelical sources, remember, is only to make a point. But even to make my point about the depth and richness of evangelicalism, the restriction to the past five hundred years was a little too restrictive. So here and there in the book I have cited some older sources that predate the Reformation. It would be shortsighted to limit ourselves to the most recent one-fourth of the great Christian tradition, even if this is where we are most at home. My principle of selection is clear enough, but "a foolish consistency is the hobgoblin of little minds," and the doctrine of the Trinity is no place for small-mindedness. There are 1,500 more years of great Christian thought and life stretching off behind these recent centuries (as the Reformers themselves, those great interpreters of the patristic and medieval heritage, were quick to point out).

Even to make a point, there is no avoiding Irenaeus (second century), no getting around the great Athanasius (fourth century), and no skipping Augustine (fifth century). Thomas Aquinas (thirteenth century) is so illuminating that it would be obstinate and sectarian to refuse his help in our contemporary project. These classic theologians are important as background for evangelical Trinitarianism, but I have left them mostly in the background, unquoted. Even in more recent centuries, I have occasionally accepted help from nonevangelical authors whose contributions are irreplaceable. The better grasp we have of the Trinity, the more at home we will be in the great Christian tradition, and the more all those Christians from all those centuries will belong to us.

Because the word *evangelical* is disputed, it has become customary to say it can hardly mean anything. Certainly the poor word has been abused and stretched. It has been pressed into service to maintain social boundaries. It has been deconstructed, and its redefinitions have been redefined; it has been co-opted for political uses in the stylebooks of the secular media. It continues to be used as a badge, a thought stopper, a sneer, a weasel word, a self-congratulation, a marketing gimmick, and a billy club. Is the poor word dead, then? No, it is no more dead than usual. In fact, it is not even especially sick. We can take some comfort in knowing that B. B. Warfield declared it "moribund, if not already dead" from "lack of care" as long ago as 1916. "Nobody any longer seems to know what it means."[11] Yet Warfield himself left a legacy of great evangelical writing, and however we may draw the confessional boundaries, we recognize evangelicalism when we see it.

For the purposes of this book, I have no intention to fight about what an evangelical is or even to define the term very closely, except to alert the reader here that I am indulging in an expansive use of it within certain boundaries. I include in my cast of characters all sorts of pietists, revivalists, charismatics, Pentecostals, Baptists, and holiness preachers, right alongside the magisterial Reformers, the high Reformed, and the evangelical Anglicans. It may be hard to imagine a conversation between the Princetonian B. B. Warfield and Amanda Smith the holiness preacher, but here it is, and it's a conversation about the Trinity. The Calvinists and the Arminians are in league here, along with the strict old Fundamentalists and their neo-evangelical descendants who would prefer not to be seen with them in public. Some readers may wish to exclude some of these witnesses from the category of evangelical, and that is their right. But we will cast the net as wide as possible first, with less interest in defining evangelicalism than in carrying out a public performance of it, especially in its Trinitarian character.

OUTLINE OF THE BOOK

The Deep Things of God explains how the Trinity changes everything, and it does this by explaining how the Trinity and the gospel are connected. After some introductory matters (chapters 1–2), the book has two major sections. The first major section is a three-chapter study (chapters 3–5) of the Trinity and salvation, showing salvation's size, the gospel's shape, and our point of access into it. Chapter 3, "So Great Salvation," shows how the Trinity expands our ideas about the sheer size of salvation by exploring the biblical idea of God's self-giving love. Chapter 4, "The Shape of the Gospel," traces the Christian experience of salvation back from our own lives into the life of God as the Father who begets the eternal Son and breathes the eternal Spirit. The Trinitarian shape of the gospel comes from the fact that God, by grace, gives himself to us by opening that eternal triune life to us. Chapter 5, "Into the Saving Life of Christ," shows how the emphasis of this Trinitarian view of salvation rightly falls on Jesus Christ, in whose life and death we find salvation. This three-chapter core of the book is the most important section because it is devoted to the "things of the gospel," which, Thomas Goodwin has reminded us, are "the deep things of God."

The last two chapters take up, from among the many practices that characterize evangelical churches, the two that are most marked and most profoundly Trinitarian: Bible reading and prayer. Because this part of the book is about Christian practices, both these chapters begin with a verbal form: hearing and praying. Chapter 6, "Hearing the Voice of God in Scripture," begins with the practice of reading Scripture as the word of God and argues that whenever believers handle the Bible as a means of grace, the Spirit is carrying the word of the Father to them. Chapter 7, "Praying with the Grain," is a meditation on what is actually going on in Christian prayer and an encouragement to pray intentionally in a way that lines up with that underlying reality. These two chapters, on hearing from God and speaking to him, belong together as an essay on communion with the Trinity. Each of these evangelical practices could be engaged in without any attention to the presence of the Trinity in them, and, in fact, this is how too many evangelical churches currently engage in them. Each is inherently Trinitarian, though, and to direct our attention to this fact is to see what is really going on. Attending to the work of the Trinity restores the dimension of depth to these practices. That is how the Trinity changes everything.

Before the section on the gospel (chapters 3–5) and the section on evangelical practices (chapters 6–7), there are two preliminary matters that demand our attention. For one thing, in a book about how eminently practical the doctrine of the Trinity is for Christian experience, it is important to take a step back and remind ourselves that God is first and foremost Father, Son, and Holy Spirit for himself, not for us. So chapter 2, "Within the Happy Land of the Trinity," is a meditation on what triunity means for God before it makes any difference to us.

And even before beginning that meditation, we can take one further step back and remind ourselves what we are doing when we take up the task of thinking about the Trinity. So chapter 1, "Compassed About by Father, Son, and Holy Spirit," is an opening reflection on the methodology of doing Trinitarian theology. Like all methodological discussions, it is either the most important part of the book (because it lays out the entire subject in the most general and abstract way), or the best part to skip over (because it is not the main subject, but the approach to the main subject) and perhaps come back to. Whether you read it in order or not, the first chapter reminds us that Christians are never starting from scratch when they begin doing Trinitarian theology. A Christian, and especially an evangelical Christian, is somebody who is already immersed in the reality of the Trinity, long before beginning to reflect on the idea of the Trinity.

1

COMPASSED ABOUT BY FATHER, SON, AND HOLY SPIRIT

---

*(Or, How Evangelicals Are Profoundly Trinitarian
Whether They Know It or Not)*

The grace of the Lord Jesus Christ and the love of God and the
fellowship of the Holy Spirit be with you all.
2 CORINTHIANS 13:14

You know me better than you think you know, and you shall come
to know me better yet.
ASLAN TO FRANK THE CABBIE,
THE MAGICIAN'S NEPHEW

Reality comes first, and understanding follows it. If you want to cultivate the ability to think well about the Trinity, the first step is to realize that there is more to Trinitarianism than just thinking well. Specifically, the starting point for a durable Trinitarian theology is not primarily a matter of carrying out a successful thought project. Christians are never in the beggarly position of gathering up a few concepts about God and then constructing a grand Trinitarian synthesis out of them. Christians are also not in the position of pulling together a few passages of Scripture, here a verse and there a verse, and cobbling them together into a brilliant doctrine that improves on Scripture's messiness. Instead, Christians should recognize that when we start thinking about the

27

Trinity, we do so because we find ourselves already deeply involved in the reality of God's triune life as he has opened it up to us for our salvation and revealed it in the Bible. In order to start doing good Trinitarian theology, we need only to reflect on that present reality and unpack it. The more we realize that we are already compassed about by the reality of the gospel Trinity, the more our Trinitarianism will matter to us. Evangelicals in particular should recognize that we have everything we need to think about the Trinity in a way that changes everything.

THE TRINITARIAN THEOLOGY OF NICKY CRUZ

Nicky Cruz is not famous for his Trinitarian theology. He is famous for having been the "warlord" of a violent street gang called the Mau-Maus in New York City in the 1950s and for the dramatic story of his 1958 conversion to Christianity. At the center of his conversion story was a confrontation between this hard-hearted, knife-wielding teenage gang leader and a young preacher who brought the simple message that Jesus loved him. It was a confrontation, that is, between *The Cross and the Switchblade*, as that young preacher David Wilkerson would put it in a book about his Times Square ministry.[1] Nicky Cruz would retell the story from his own point of view in his 1968 biography, *Run Baby Run*.[2] Against the dark background of his young life as a victim and a victimizer, Cruz tells about forgiveness, the power of Jesus Christ, and how he was set free from soul-crushing loneliness. That dramatic turnaround is the story Nicky Cruz is famous for. There is not a word about the Trinity in it. Looking back, Cruz would say, "I came to Jesus because I knew He loved me, and still didn't know anything about God."

But in 1976 Cruz wrote another book to describe what he called "the single most important fact of my Christian growth." The book was *The Magnificent Three*, and the fact that had become central to Cruz's Christian life by that time was the fact of the Trinity:

> Something has emerged in my walk with God that has become the most important element of my discipleship. It has become the thing that sustains me, that feeds me, that keeps me steady when I am shaky. I have come to see God, to know Him, to relate to Him

as Three-in-One, God as Trinity, God as Father, Saviour, and Holy Spirit. God has given to me over the years a vision of Himself as Three-in-One, and the ability to relate to God in that way is the single most important fact of my Christian growth.[3]

The Magnificent Three is Nicky Cruz's personal testimony to the power of the Trinity in his life. It never sold like *Run Baby Run*, but it is vintage Nicky Cruz, from the chapter about the salvation of a drug addict named Chico, to the healing of a nameless prostitute, to the chapter about Cruz being ambushed by rival gang members a few weeks after his conversion. As a theologian whose specialty is Trinitarian theology, I have several hundred books about the Trinity on my shelves, but only one of them includes a knife fight: the one by Nicky Cruz. "Dynamite! A real turn-on!" say the publishers in a prefatory note. "Nicky lays it on you with his hard-hitting straight talk. You are there with him—in the tenement, in the jail."[4]

Cruz's testimony to his experience with the Trinity is indeed powerful. He praises the three persons in turn, beginning with several chapters about Jesus as his "magnificent saviour." He especially emphasizes Christ's presence, reality, and power to save. Cruz has already told us, "When I first became a Christian, I knew nothing about anything. So far as the things of God were concerned, I was a totally ignorant man. I knew nothing. But Jesus reached me despite my ignorance of Him."[5] In these chapters he tries to look back and describe that strange knowledge he gained in his first encounter with Jesus, before he had learned any details. In prose that turns to prayer, Cruz says:

I remember when I saw the real Jesus for the first time. Suddenly I saw You as You really were. I saw that You were human, just like me. . . . I saw that You had courage, You had guts. You had something I couldn't describe, something I had never seen before, something incredibly strong and tender all at the same time. I saw that You had the power to squash me like a bug, and instead You poured out Your blood to save me, to love me, to heal my aching heart.[6]

This is the heart of Cruz's message, and he moves effortlessly from the language of prayer to the language of invitation, directing his readers to the presence of Christ: "He wants to forgive you of your sin. He wants to heal you of your sickness. He wants to keep you from anxiety and fear and guilt. He wants to free you from every kind of bondage. And He is there with you now to do it. He is a wonderful, magnificent Saviour!"[7]

But this intense focus on Jesus does not keep Cruz from celebrating "the Magnificent Father," whose fatherhood "is not simply a figure of speech." God is not our father merely in a "universal and impersonal" sense of having created us but "also in a new, personal, special kind of fatherhood that is reserved for born-again Christians only. He is my Father not just because He created me but now also because He adopted me as His child! I am His creature, but more than that I am His adopted son!"[8] Cruz is no less eloquent and impassioned about God the Father—his fatherly intimacy, his protection, his generosity, and his discipline—than he is about Jesus.

Nicky Cruz does not say very much about how his experience of Jesus and his experience of the Father are related to each other. But when he turns to the third person, "the Magnificent Holy Spirit," he begins tying the three together in one unified view of salvation. He accomplishes this by pointing out the absolute necessity of the Spirit's work in bringing us into contact with the Father and the Son:

> God is a magnificent Father. God is a magnificent Saviour, Jesus Christ. But if it were not for the magnificent Holy Spirit, I would still be a wretched, hateful sinner! It is not enough to have a Father-God who loves and provides for me. It is not enough even to have a Saviour who died for my sins. For any of those blessings to make a difference in our lives, there must also be present in this world that Third Person of God, the Holy Spirit.[9]

In what sense is the ministry of the third person necessary? The Spirit's work is necessary because he is the one who actually brings us into contact with the Son and the Father. It does not take away from the Father and the Son to say that their work depends on the work of the Spirit. As Cruz argues, though Jesus died for us and the Father forgives us, we need to ask ourselves, "But why did you come to Jesus in the first place?" and answer, "Because you were drawn by God the Holy Spirit."

Jesus saved me; the Father forgave me. But the Holy Spirit con-
victed me, brought me to my knees, and showed me God. . . . He
showed me Jesus Christ, and I was gripped by His strong, sweet
love. And then He shoved me toward God, and I gladly fell into the
arms of my loving Father.[10]

In the work of the Spirit, the purposes of God are fulfilled, and all the
salvation, forgiveness, and fellowship are realized.

Nicky Cruz is famous for preaching a simple gospel message in a
way that is relevant to street-hardened young people. He is not famous
for his Trinitarian theology, and it might even seem incongruous to
highlight him early in a book about the doctrine of the Trinity. He goes
out of his way to make sure nobody confuses him for a theology professor: "I don't know everything there is to know about theology. I am not
a Greek scholar. I am just a Puerto Rican street kid whom God picked
up from the slums in New York and made into a disciple and a minister.
But there is one thing I know . . . I know that God is my Father."[11] He
also makes sure nobody can mistake his book for systematic theology:
"This is not a doctrinal treatise on the Trinity. It is not a theological
statement. I am not capable of that. It is a personal statement, a testimony, a simple sharing of how God the Magnificent Three lives in
my life every day."[12] And even though Cruz brings his own voice and
his own life experience to his Trinitarian testimony, he is not trying to
teach anything novel. His Trinitarian theology is not "his" in the sense
of originating with him; it is his personal discovery of something that
has been the common faith and experience of Christians since the time
of the apostles.

There is nothing in Nicky Cruz's book on the Trinity that was not
already implicit in his previous books. His understanding of salvation
and the Christian life did not change between *Run Baby Run* and *The
Magnificent Three*. From the moment of his dramatic conversion, he
had known that Jesus saves and the Father forgives. In his earliest days
of Bible study he came to understand how it had been the sovereign
"shove" of the Holy Spirit that had been at work behind the scenes.
None of this was new information when he began to describe the Trinity
as "the most important element" of his discipleship. In fact, Cruz had

even affirmed the doctrine of the Trinity from the beginning. It seems as if nothing had changed, yet he began writing about his relationship with the Father, Son, and Spirit with the excitement of having made a life-changing discovery. He called it "the thing that sustains me, that feeds me, that keeps me steady when I am shaky." Though Cruz had gained no new information, he wrote as if his new grasp of the Trinity had changed everything about his Christian life.

The difference is that he had gotten on the inside of the doctrine. He had moved from accepting it on the authority of Scripture and his trusted elders to understanding it from within. "I didn't understand it. I believed it was true, though at first only because I had such great confidence in those who taught it to me. Then later I believed it was true because I saw it to be true in the Bible." This was an important transition in itself, maturing from a necessarily immature trust in human authority, to direct reliance on divine authority. But it was still only authority, and only worked on Cruz from outside. "So I believed it, but I still didn't understand it." What Cruz experienced in his Trinitarian awakening was a kind of shift in how he perceived the same idea: first, he saw the Trinity as a difficult doctrine that had to be accepted but could hardly be explained, then he went on to see it as an illuminating doctrine that explained what he read in the Bible and what he experienced in his actual Christian life. Whereas he first encountered the doctrine as a problem, he came to understand it as a solution.

Cruz recalls his early exasperation with the doctrine in a way that probably rings true for many Christians who wouldn't express it so bluntly: "Why have three persons, I thought, when it confuses me so much? It seemed to me such a totally unnecessary complication. Why couldn't God just be God? Then I could understand Him. This 'Trinity' business I accepted by faith, but I could not relate to it at all."[13] The transformation in his life took place when he realized that the things described in the doctrine were things he was already in contact with. He knew Jesus, the Father, and the Spirit through their work in his life. The doctrine of the Trinity was the key to understanding that those three experiences belonged together because the God behind them was the one God, making himself known as Father, Son, and Holy Spirit precisely because he eternally exists as Father, Son, and Holy Spirit. "I understand that God is so much more to me as Three-in-One than He could ever be in a way," Cruz wrote. "I know now how much easier it is for me to relate to Him in that day-to-day way because He is three."[14] He goes on:

> I am not talking about theology. What I am describing is something different from merely believing in the doctrine of the Trinity. I have always believed in the doctrine of the Trinity but I had never experienced God personally as Three-in-One. It was at first merely a doctrine in which I believed, but now it has become a truth of everyday life. God has developed in me a sense of the separate relationships which I can have with Father, Saviour, and Holy Spirit. He has shown me the strength that comes from those separate relationships, the power for living that comes from the three faces of God. He has taught me to feed off the Trinity for my daily sustenance, rather than just having some vague feeling that the Trinity is somehow true.[15]

People can become Christians after learning a very small amount of doctrine and information. As they grow in discipleship, they read more of the Bible and come to understand more than they had understood before. But what Nicky Cruz's Trinitarian testimony highlights is that the decisive factor is not a transfer of information. There was no brand-new data put into his thought process, and he did not have to change his mind about any of his beliefs. He had already been believing in the Trinity for some time when he woke up to the difference the Trinity makes for every aspect of his Christian life. His radical Trinitarianism did not come from an advanced theology lesson; it came from the gospel and then led him to an advanced theology lesson. He was like a man who found a treasure hid in a field that he didn't have to buy, because he already owned it. He heard God calling him to dig into the depths, and what he found there changed everything for him.

SOMETHING MORE THAN WORDS

The kind of Trinitarianism that we need is not simply the acceptance of a doctrine. The doctrine of the Trinity is not, in the first instance, something to be constructed by argument from texts. At best, that method will lead to mental acknowledgment that "the Trinitarian theory" best accounts for the evidence marshaled. The first step on the way to the heart of the Trinitarian mystery is to recognize that as Christians we find ourselves already deeply involved in the triune life and need only to reflect rightly on that present reality. Most evangelical Christians don't need to be talked into the Trinitarian theory; they need to be shown that they are immersed in the Trinitarian reality. We need to see and feel that we are surrounded by the Trinity, compassed about on all sides by the presence and the work of the Father, the Son, and the Holy Spirit. From that starting point, truly productive teaching can begin.

There is certainly a time and place for introducing the words, concepts, propositions, and truth claims of Trinitarian theology. But too often in contemporary teaching about the Trinity, those words not only come first; they come first, last, and exclusively. The Trinity seems to most evangelicals like a doctrinal formula to be received and believed by a mental act of understanding. In short, it is at best a true fact about God that we hold in our minds in the form of words. Teaching about it is then a matter of using words to lead learners to more words. "Words, words, words," was Prince Hamlet's reply when he was asked what he was reading, but that was hardly a sign of a balanced mind or a generous spirit. A Christian who is reading about the Trinity ought to be able to say he is reading more than "words, words, words." Evangelical commitment to the Trinity should not stay confined to the realm of verbal exercises; it ought to dive deeper and rise higher than the power of words. It ought to begin from the experienced reality of the Trinitarian grace of God and lead us to a deeper encounter with the Father, the Son, and the Holy Spirit.

A merely verbal approach to the Trinity is doomed to be shallow, weak, and brittle, because it will be no stronger than our own ability to understand and articulate what we are thinking about. This is in fact the plight that much evangelical Trinitarianism finds itself in at the popular level. As I have taught in various churches about the doctrine of the Trinity in the past twelve years, I have tried to answer the top three questions that evangelicals bring with them: Is it biblical? Does it make sense? And does it matter? These are all good questions and deserve the most helpful answers a theologian can bring to a congregation.[16] But I have learned that if the first two questions are answered only at the

COMPASSED ABOUT BY FATHER, SON, AND HOLY SPIRIT

level of verbal maneuvers, the third question has a tendency to loom impossibly large.

The question, Is it biblical? can be answered by a congeries of Bible verses proving various elements of the doctrine. First we provide biblical proofs of the deity of the Son, then the deity of the Spirit, then the personhood of the Spirit, then the distinction between the Father and the Son, then the distinction between the Son and the Spirit, and so on, either beginning or ending with biblical proof of the unity of God. It is possible to catch a glimpse of the deeper Trinitarian logic of the Bible's total message through this approach, but when time is short, the biblical proof of the Trinity is reduced to a verse-by-verse affair.

That leads to the second question, Does it make sense? There are a few satisfying, logical distinctions to make here, especially in pointing out that God is not one something and also somehow three of the same somethings (which would be a strict, logical contradiction), but one being in three persons (which still requires further explanation, but is not simply a contradiction). But the apparently inevitable next step in pursuing the question, Does it makes sense? is the sub-question, What is the best analogy for the Trinity? This sub-question is usually the death-knell for Trinitarianism's relevance. Analogies can play a useful role in thinking about God, but when the hankering for an analogy arises right here, on the border between "Does it make sense" and "Does it matter," it is usually a sign that Trinitarian thinking has devolved into a verbal project for its own sake. It has become a matter of getting the right words, so they can lead us to more of the right words. Serial proof-texting gives way to broken analogies, confronting us with an unanswerable "so what" question. How do we fall so quickly from three perfectly good questions (Is it biblical? Does it make sense? And does it matter?) to a form of discourse as hollow as an echo chamber? What is the difference between a belief in the Trinity that simply doesn't matter and one that changes everything?

What is needed is an approach to the doctrine of the Trinity that takes its stand on the experienced reality of the Trinity, and only then moves forward to the task of verbal and conceptual clarification. The principle is, first the reality, then the explanation. What goes wrong in so much popular discussion of the Trinity is that Christians approach the doctrine as if it were their job to construct it from bits and pieces of verses, arguments, and analogies. The doctrine itself seems to lie on the far side of a mental project. If the project is successful, they will achieve the doctrine of the Trinity and be able to answer questions like Why have three persons? and What is the Trinity like? But the right method would begin with an immersion in the reality of the triune God and only then turn to the task of explaining. The words and concepts would then find their proper places in the context of a life that is marked by the recognized presence of the Father, the Son, and the Holy Spirit. This kind of teaching about the Trinity would not be a project of constructing a complex idea but of unpacking a comprehensive reality that we would already find ourselves in the midst of as Christians.

What can be done to make the doctrine of the Trinity flourish in evangelical theology as if this were its own native soil? What would it take to inculturate Trinitarianism in the culture of evangelicalism? I am arguing that we need to start with the resources at hand, right where we are. We know more than we can say about the Trinity, and we should not let ourselves be trapped into thinking that everything depends on our ability to articulate the mystery of the triune God. But we do need to be reminded that we are immersed in a Trinitarian reality. It is possible to be radically Trinitarian without knowing it or to have amnesia about one's real status. We may be formed and schooled by a movement that came into being as the most consistently Trinitarian force in the history of Christianity, but we can live in a way that is alienated from those Trinitarian riches.

However impoverished its articulation may be, the Trinitarian reality itself is there in the lives of evangelical churches. Evangelicalism as a movement is unthinkable without a certain underlying Trinitarian logic of experience. Robust Trinitarian theology never occurs in a vacuum; it always flourishes in the context of a rich experiential and cultural setting that provides the background against which the doctrinal formulations register as meaningful. Robert Louis Wilken has celebrated the way the doctrinal theology of Christianity's formative period reasoned "from history, from ritual, and from text," so that "concepts and abstractions were always put at the service of a deeper immersion in the *res*, the thing itself, the mystery of Christ and the practice of the

Christian life."[17] It is common (as we will see below) to argue that a self-consciously high-church setting, well stocked with tradition, liturgy, and sacramental realism, is the proper soil in which Trinitarianism can be best cultivated.

Without denigrating those resources or denying that they can fund a vigorous Trinitarian theology (also among some high-church evangelicals), I want to argue that there is other soil in which the doctrine of the Trinity can thrive. The kind of low-church evangelicalism that is spreading so rapidly around the world in our era contains deep resources for effective Trinitarian theology. Evangelicalism may be the sleeping giant of renewed Trinitarian theology in the life of the church, if it comes to understand itself aright. The "if" is important, and it also figures prominently in the recent assessment by Mark Noll, speaking not of Trinitarian theology but of the life of the mind in general: "For evangelicals (as for other Christians) the greatest hope for learning in any age . . . lies in the Christian faith itself, which in the end means in Jesus Christ. Thus, if evangelicals are the people of the gospel we claim to be, our intellectual rescue is close at hand."[18]

The doctrine of the Trinity flourishes, not when it is merely stated accurately, but when it is affirmed in the context of a pre-discursive, nonthematic background awareness of the reality of the Trinity. This noncognitive background (or tacit dimension) is necessary to fund productive, thematic, theological reflection on the doctrine. There are in fact gospel resources for robust Trinitarianism that have yet to be articulated in a recognizably evangelical idiom. We need to beware the danger of evangelical self-misunderstanding and highlight instead the properly evangelical resources which are in danger of being overlooked. The evangelical saints are already living out the primary Trinitarianism, this communion with the Holy Trinity. But evangelicalism's theorists have often failed to give voice to the things their people are experiencing. There is already something deeply Trinitarian going on in evangelical churches, and when that something begins to fund theological reflection, we can expect a significant contribution from these churches. "If evangelicals are the people of the gospel we claim to be," to extend the implications of Noll's conditional, then all that is required is for evangelical theologians to grasp the way gospel and Trinity mutually presuppose each other, in order for them to become manifestly what they are tacitly: people of the Trinity.

HOW A DOCTRINE STOPPED WORKING

It is now a commonplace to note how poorly the doctrine of the Trinity fared when the world turned modern. The regime of rationalism and this-worldliness that took hold of intellectual culture sometime around the late seventeenth century was not kind to this central Christian doctrine. That story, along with the tale of the doctrine's supposed rescue by theologians like Karl Barth and Karl Rahner, is frequently told in histories of the doctrine.[19] But there is a distinctively evangelical version of the quiescence and ineffectiveness that took hold of Trinitarianism for so long. In this community, the doctrine has been hung on the horns of a dilemma: one horn is subjective religious experience and the other is reduction to mere propositional formula. The tiresome oscillation between pietism and rationalism, not especially healthy for any aspect of Christian life, has been especially hard on the doctrine of the Trinity. From neither place, head nor heart, can the doctrine be articulated as it must be, with an inherent connection to the gospel. A quick survey of how the evangelical tradition has handled the doctrine of the Trinity will show that evangelical Trinitarian theology has an unfinished task: to describe how the Trinity is connected to the gospel and avoid the extremes of subjective religious experience and mere propositionalism.

Friedrich Schleiermacher (1768–1834) grappled seriously with the problem of how to show a connection between gospel and Trinity. Perverse though it may be to start an enquiry into evangelical theology with a glance at the father of Protestant liberalism, it is necessary. His way of handling the doctrine of the Trinity is the right point of departure for the evangelical story, and his major decisions about this doctrine were driven by the evangelical instincts he inherited from his family. He came from an evangelical background in the pietist theology of Herrnhut, Moravia. But he resolutely developed that pietistic evangelicalism into a thoroughly modern system of thought.

In standard accounts of how the Trinity came to be neglected in modern thought, Schleiermacher typically receives much of the blame.

He famously placed the doctrine in the last few pages of his influential work *The Christian Faith*, making it something of an appendix to the main work.[20] One could make too much of a doctrine's location in a book, but in the case of a thinker so consummately systematic as Schleiermacher, location does signify a great deal. Since Christianity is "essentially distinguished from other faiths by the fact that in it everything is related to the redemption accomplished by Jesus of Nazareth,"[21] Schleiermacher's theology is entirely centered on that redemption, or rather on the knowledge of that redemption, the contents of the self-consciousness of the redeemed. "We shall exhaust the whole compass of Christian doctrine if we consider the facts of the religious self-consciousness, first, as they are presupposed by the antithesis expressed in the concept of redemption, and secondly, as they are determined by that antithesis."[22]

To "exhaust the whole compass of Christian doctrine" by analyzing redemption may seem to run the risk of reducing theology to a study of salvation, but Schleiermacher's method is expansive enough to include much besides salvation. The Christian consciousness of redemption presupposes concepts such as God's holiness, righteousness, love, and wisdom; the opposing negative states of evil and sin; and the transition between them by way of Christ and the church through rebirth and sanctification. These concepts, further, presuppose others: creation and preservation, an original state of human perfection, and the divine attributes of eternity, omnipresence, omnipotence, and omniscience. Even angels and devils can be given a place within the redemption-centered project of *The Christian Faith*, although only a bit tentatively, since their alleged operations are so far at the periphery of the Christian consciousness of redemption that angelology "never enters into the sphere of Christian doctrine proper."[23]

The Trinity, however, could not be admitted to the doctrinal system proper, because it could not be related to the gospel, or, in Schleiermacher's terms, it is not directly implicated in redemption: "It is not an immediate utterance concerning the Christian self-consciousness but only a combination of several such utterances." Piecing together doctrines to construct more elaborate doctrines was something Schleiermacher regarded with horror, because it led out from the living center of the faith to the arid regions of *theologoumena* (words about words!), where dogmaticians do their deadening work. Schleiermacher had long since rejected that approach in his early speeches *On Religion*: "Among those systematizers there is less than anywhere, a devout watching and listening to discover in their own hearts what they are to describe. They would rather reckon with symbols."[24]

The young Romantic may have grown up to write a big book of doctrine, but he continued his "devout watching and listening" and never betrayed his basic insight or became one of "those systematizers" content to "reckon with symbols." Because the Trinity could not be directly connected to redemption, Schleiermacher placed it well outside the life-giving core of *The Christian Faith*. In the heading of the section where he finally treated it, Schleiermacher pointed out that the doctrine of the Trinity could not be considered an issue that was "finally settled," because after all it "did not receive any fresh treatment when the [Protestant] Church was set up; and so there must still be in store for it a transformation which will go back to its very beginnings."[25] Schleiermacher considered it obvious that if the Trinity were implicated in the *evangel*, the *evangelisch* (that is, Protestant) awakening of the sixteenth century would have transformed and deepened it as it had everything central to Christian redemption.

The whole point of our book is to insist that gospel and Trinity are internally linked, so we obviously dissent from Schleiermacher's judgments about Trinitarianism. However, we are tracing the story of what goes wrong that makes this doctrine stop mattering to evangelicals. And Schleiermacher's assessment that there is nothing Trinitarian to be discerned in the Christian consciousness of redemption has had its forecasts and echoes throughout the evangelical tradition. The characteristic evangelical response, however, has not been to deny the doctrine, or even to move it to an appendix of the systematic theology texts, as Schleiermacher did. The evangelical tradition at large has not usually been as phobic about propositional revelation as Schleiermacher was nor as allergic to the clear doctrinal statements that propositional revelation makes possible. Indeed, connecting discrete propositions found in Scripture, and believing them on the basis of the authority of Scripture as the word of God, has been a crucial method in evangelical theology all along. Our path has been different from Schleiermacher's, though we started from the same blind spot. When a theologian has to function under the salutary pressure of authoritatively revealed sentences, but in the debilitating absence of a lively sense of the connection between gospel and Trinity, Trinitarian commitments take on a particular pathos. This tension is pervasive in evangelical history, but its workings can be seen instructively in three examples from three centuries: John Bunyan, Isaac Watts, and Amanda Smith.

John Bunyan (1628–1688) devoted only one extended meditation to this doctrine, a piece entitled "Of the Trinity and a Christian," whose title suggests an interest in something practical and perhaps edifying. The descriptive subtitle specifies that it is about "How a young or shaken Christian should demean himself under the weighty thoughts of the Doctrin of the Trinity." The problem Bunyan wants to solve for the "young or shaken Christian" is that the Trinity is a difficult doctrine, seeming to contradict reason by proposing that one is three or vice versa. This intellectual conflict could lead the believer to question what is clearly revealed in Scripture, which is tantamount to questioning God himself. But Bunyan warns: "It is great lewdness, and also insufferable arrogancy to come to the Word of God, as conceiting already that whatever thou readest must either by thee be understood, or of it self fall to the ground as a senseless error." The proper response to this hard doctrine is to submit one's human judgment to God's greater wisdom: "But God is wiser than Man, wherefore fear thou him and tremble at his Word, saying still, with godly suspicion of thine own infirmity, what I see not teach thou me, and thou art God only wise; but as for me, I was as a beast before thee."[26]

Surely Bunyan strikes the appropriate human posture in the face of God's wisdom, but we might ask why it is the doctrine of the Trinity in particular that spurs his reflection on humility of mind. Why is it precisely here that we are invited to yield our understanding before the incomprehensibility of God and his secret counsels? The answer, sadly, seems to be that when Bunyan thought about the doctrine of the Trinity, he thought of something remote from the business of salvation, but authoritatively revealed and necessary to be believed. The doctrine seems to have turned from a mystery of salvation to a problem of intellectual coherence.[27]

Isaac Watts (1674–1748) felt the same tension, but by his era there had been considerable debate about whether this hard doctrine was in fact scriptural.[28] The debates took their toll on Watts, and although most of his hymns and sermons are a glorious legacy of Trinitarian worship, he became much less confident about the traditional form of the doctrine later in his life. Watts was as submissive to scriptural revelation as Bunyan but was deeply troubled about what doctrine he was being asked to submit his understanding to: "Dear and blessed God, hadst thou been pleased, in any one plain scripture, to have informed me which of the different opinions about holy Trinity, among the contending parties of christians, had been true, thou knowest with how much real satisfaction and joy, my unbiased heart would have opened itself to receive and embrace the divine discovery."

If only God had shown "plainly, in any single text, that the Father, Son, and Holy Spirit, are three real distinct Persons" in one divine nature, Watts says, "I had never suffered myself to be bewildered in so many doubts, nor embarrassed with so many strong fears of assenting to the mere inventions of men, instead of divine doctrine; but I should have humbly and immediately accepted thy words, so far as it was possible for me to understand them, as the only rule of my faith." Nowhere in his impassioned prayer does Watts give the impression that he is grappling with a mystery of salvation; his angst all stems from the situation of being faced with a doctrine lacking the kind of direct biblical support that would bind it on his conscience as an article of faith, and its sheer intellectual difficulty. "How can such weak creatures ever take in so strange, so difficult, and so abstruse a doctrine as this?"[29]

The way this tension has come to expression in the devotional life of evangelicals is startlingly expressed by the Holiness evangelist Amanda Smith (1837–1915) in her autobiography *The Story of the Lord's Dealings with Mrs. Amanda Smith, the Colored Evangelist*.[30] Without explaining what provoked her, Smith records that she "became greatly exercised about the Trinity. . . . I could not seem to understand just how there could exist three distinct persons, and yet one. I thought every day and prayed for light, but didn't seem to get help. I read the

Bible, but no help came." Smith records the two weeks during which her anxiety mounted and she felt guided toward a definite experience of personal revelation, a kind of intellectual counterpart to the experience of entire sanctification expected by Holiness people in America. Encouraged that "every blessing you get from God is by faith," Smith asked herself, "If by faith, why not now?"

> I turned around and knelt down by an old trunk that stood in the corner of the room, and I told the Lord that I wanted to understand the Trinity, and that I was afraid of fanaticism, and I wanted Him to make it clear to me for His own sake. I don't know how long I prayed, but O, how my soul was filled with light under the great baptism that came upon me. I came near falling prostrate, but bore up when God revealed Himself so clearly to me, and I have understood it ever since. I can't just explain it to others, but God made me understand it so I have had no question since. Praise the Lord! Then He showed me three other things.[31]

Smith undeniably had a powerful spiritual experience centered on the doctrine of the Trinity, but it is equally undeniable that the problem her experience solved for her is the problem of how the doctrine itself can make sense. In a single ineffable moment, a "great baptism," she leapt the divide between doctrine and life. Perhaps if she had been able to "explain it to others," her explanation would have laid bare the evangelical substructure of Trinitarian commitment; perhaps this is what God made her understand to her own intellectual satisfaction. As it stands, however, the implicit advice from Smith's experience seems to be that troubled believers should likewise "pray through" to an ineffable moment of inward clarity and peace over this teaching.

For evangelicals, then, from Bunyan to Smith and down to the present, the doctrine has shrunk to a set of propositions that are to be held in the mind as verbalisms, remote from any possible direct experience or relevance. Because we believe in God's power to reveal truth, we believe that this is a revealed truth: God is triune. There seems to be no intrinsic reason God could not have revealed some other proposition to us, for instance, that God is quadrune, quintune, or blue. Karl Rahner famously lamented the parallel situation in Roman Catholic theology,

in which it seemed as if "this mystery has been revealed for its own sake
. . . we make statements about it, but as a reality it has nothing to do
with us at all."[32] Although the doctrine may still be dutifully taught and
just as dutifully learned, it has long been viewed as an abstract series
of propositions, an undigested lump of tradition or of revealed ideas.
Like anything that should be living but is dead, it stays in its place and
decays.

THE TACIT DIMENSION OF TRINITARIANISM

As these case studies show, when we lose our ability to see the Trinity
as directly connected to the gospel, we tend to reduce it to an issue of
authority and mental obedience. No wonder, then, that the doctrine of
the Trinity has been treated as something of a burden by many evangelicals. But this dysfunction of the doctrine is only one side of the story
of evangelical Trinitarianism. The other side of the story is that the life
of every healthy church and every true Christian is a manifestation of
the work of the Trinity. Evangelicalism, even when it is handling the
doctrine of the Trinity as a foreign artifact difficult to deal with, is nevertheless always already immersed in the rich, Trinitarian reality of the
gospel. We are often in the strange position of being Trinitarian without
knowing it, or of living in an encounter with the Father, Son, and Holy
Spirit that we then give very weak and inadequate explanations of. We
have the thing itself but act as if we do not know we have it.

The way forward for evangelical Trinitarianism is to get in touch
with the deep, Trinitarian roots of our own history as evangelicals. The
main way this will happen is by cultivating a deeper understanding of
the gospel of salvation in all its Trinitarian contours. What we need is
an advance in our theological understanding that does not take us anywhere new but directs us to the depth and richness right in the gospel
resources at the heart of evangelicalism. Evangelicals especially need to
learn to see the big picture of biblical Trinitarianism as one coherent
whole rather than as a series of isolated parts.

It is worth asking why we should bother going on to clearer understanding of what is Trinitarian about the gospel. If it's possible to be
subliminally Trinitarian as a Christian, what benefit is there to taking

the next step of being explicit about it? The advantages are too numerous and comprehensive to list, but all of them flow directly from making that cognitive jump from unawareness to awareness. When we bring an idea this important out from the backs of our minds into the spotlight of our conscious attention, we change everything in our theological understanding. Furthermore, we move out of the preposterous situation of being Trinitarian without knowing we're Trinitarian.

Anybody who has encountered God in Christ through the Holy Spirit has come to know the Trinity. But not everybody in this position knows that they know the Trinity. When they move to that next level of knowing that they know the Trinity, a bright light shines on everything they knew before. The situation is like a vivid learning experience I had as a child. I was standing on the front lawn of my great-grandmother's farm watching clouds pass in front of the moon. It was early evening, the sun had just gone down, the moon was already very bright, and the clouds were blowing quickly across the face of the moon. It was very beautiful, and I was standing on the front lawn, just looking at it. My Uncle Dan came out and asked, "What are you looking at?"

I said, "I'm watching the clouds go by the moon."

He asked, "What does that make you think about?"

I replied, "Well, really I'm waiting to see if any of the clouds will go behind the moon. So far they've all gone in front of it."

Uncle Dan stood there with me watching clouds, and after a while he asked, "Where is the moon?"

"It's in outer space."

Some more time went by. "And where are clouds?"

"They're in our upper atmosphere," I said.

More silence.

"Oh . . . right," it dawned on me. "I'm going to stand here a long time before I see a cloud going behind the moon. In fact, it's not going to happen."

What I always come back to when I think about that story is the question, Did I know that clouds are closer than the moon, or did I not know that? I had in my mind all the information I needed to draw the right conclusion, but I had never put it together. It was a situation in which I knew something but didn't know that I knew it. And that put me in an awkward position, made it very likely that I would say foolish things and even waste my time waiting for something that was never going to happen.

If you trust Jesus to be your salvation, you already know the Trinity. But it's a great benefit to know that you know the Trinity. It's a great benefit to know that you're a Christian because you've received a Spirit of adoption from the Father, a Spirit that lets you call God "Abba, Father." The Trinity is lurking in the gospel, just as it is lurking in the life of every believer. This Trinitarian reality is going on in our Christian lives whether we know that we know it or not.

Vital Trinitarianism, the kind that matters and changes everything, does not occur in a vacuum. The doctrine of the Trinity, although it can be stated as a series of propositions embodying truth claims about God ("God is one being in three persons"), involves much more than that. Trinitarianism is the encompassing framework within which all Christian thought takes place and within which Christian confession finds its grounding presuppositions. It is the deep grammar of all the central Christian affirmations. Therefore, when the theologians of the patristic age finally stated it explicitly as an article of faith (beginning with the Council of Nicaea in 325, though with obvious precursors), they were not simply adding an item to a list of beliefs but performing an act of intellectual foregrounding, bringing a background element from the periphery to the center of Christian attention. By doing so, they were equipping later theologians to think coherently about the entire structure of our saving knowledge of God in a single act of focused inquiry. In the passage from implicit awareness of God's triunity and an inarticulate experience of salvation, to explicit confession of faith in the Father, Son, and Holy Spirit, Christian theology came of age epistemologically. Having always known the Trinity, Christian thinkers now knew that they knew the Trinity.

Because Michael Polanyi (1891–1976) wrote extensively about epistemological moves of this type, his analysis has been recognized as a help in coming to terms with the doctrine of the Trinity. Polanyi began his scholarly career as a research chemist, but over the course of his long career he turned his interests gradually to the philosophy of science and from there to epistemology. His work is part of a larger mid-century trend toward the demotion of science from its role as absolute arbiter of all truth claims. Polanyi's work fits, for instance, somewhere between Thomas Kuhn's "historicist turn" in the philosophy of science,[33] and Stephen Toulmin's critique of the abstraction introduced into theories of knowledge by the Enlightenment.[34]

Polanyi's most famous work is 1958's magisterial *Personal Knowledge: Toward a Post-Critical Philosophy*, which was primarily devoted to exposing the fiduciary and participatory character of all knowledge, not least scientific knowledge. "I start by rejecting the ideal of scientific detachment," he begins, but moves on to confess frankly: "I want to establish an alternative ideal of knowledge, quite generally."[35]

This research project set him on a trail which resulted in him turning his attention to epistemology proper, and to describe knowing as a skill comparable to focusing one's eyes on a particular object in a complex field of visual stimuli:

> I regard knowing as an active comprehension of the things known, an action that requires skill. Skilful knowing and doing is performed by subordinating a set of particulars, as clues or tools, to the shaping of a skilful achievement, whether practical or theoretical. We may then be said to become "subsidiarily aware" of these particulars within our "focal awareness" of the coherent entity that we achieve.[36]

This skill cannot be gained by lone practitioners determining for themselves what they should focus their attention on. Knowing what data to ignore and what data should be sought out as meaningful evidence presupposes an established framework within which knowledge is assembled: "We must now recognize belief once more as the source of all knowledge. Tacit assent and intellectual passions, the sharing of an idiom and of a cultural heritage, affiliation to a like minded community: such are the impulses which shape our vision of the nature of things on which we rely for our mastery of things. No intelligence, however critical or original, can operate outside such a fiduciary framework."[37] Polanyi developed these ideas about knowledge most elaborately in his book *The Tacit Dimension* (1966).

In reflecting on the process of scientific discovery, Polanyi became aware of the crucial importance of elements normally disregarded as imponderable factors and left unexamined in the background of standard accounts of how scientific knowledge comes about. There is real creativity involved when research scientists engage in their characteristic tasks of following hunches, discerning meaningful patterns, and framing the right experimental situations. Beginning from this insight into the process of theory formation, Polanyi explored gestalt psychology, the mechanics of visual perception, and the experiential training process by which young doctors learn to recognize meaningful patterns of symptoms and pronounce with some confidence a diagnosis on the basis of evidence which to the uninitiated is a mere haze of insignificant, incoherent observations. These skills and insights cannot be accounted for by merely heaping up greater quantities of clear and distinct ideas or by honing propositions to greater precision. They require the knowing agent to acquire a framework of understanding and a practiced skill of forming judgments. These skills are generally inculcated by a community committed to maintaining a convivial relationship centered on values agreed upon and presupposed by all who participate. This enveloping culture forms a precognitive, nonthematic awareness of where to direct one's attention and what bits of information are worth considering explicitly. Lest this seem like a preparation for sheer subjectivity, it should be noted that Polanyi was a firm believer in the value of objective knowledge, and he repeatedly took pains to show how personal beliefs are to be held honestly, with "universal intent" as beliefs about how things really are.

Polanyi thus drew attention to the all-important, not-yet-cognitive awareness that makes thematic knowledge possible. This tacit dimension is the nonarticulated element in perception and knowledge, an unreflective awareness of things that is quite different from the clear-cut awareness we have when we perform the mental act of focusing our attention directly and thematically on an object. Polanyi's most famous catchphrase was the expression, "We always know more than we can tell."

These Polanyian insights into the nature of knowledge have some helpful implications for theology in general but for Trinitarian theology

in particular. Scottish theologian Thomas F. Torrance offers the following compressed account of tacit knowledge:

> It is on this deep subsidiary awareness that all skills, explicit
> thought, formal reasoning, and articulate knowing and commu-
> nication rely. Even the most completely formalised knowledge
> (e.g. through logic or mathematics) must include informal or
> tacit coefficients, for it is only by relying on them that formal
> systems can operate meaningfully. This is evident in the bear-
> ing of thought and speech upon some reality or the bearing of
> some skill upon an intended end; and also in the way our minds
> spontaneously integrate particulars into significant wholes, as
> in the recognition of a physiognomy, or integrates clues into a
> focal target, as in scientific intuition and discovery. Tacit know-
> ing, Polanyi claims, is the fundamental power of the mind which
> creates explicit knowing and lends meaning to and controls its
> use. Tacit knowledge and explicit knowledge are opposed to one
> another but they are not sharply divided. While tacit knowledge
> can be possessed by itself, explicit knowledge must rely on being
> tacitly understood and applied. Hence all knowledge is either
> tacit or rooted in tacit knowledge. A wholly explicit knowledge is
> unthinkable. This tacit dimension provides the unifying ground
> of all knowledge, rooting it in the concrete situations of life and
> society in the world; and as such provides the continuous epis-
> temological field which integrates the sciences and the arts and
> does away with the age-old dualisms which have led to the frag-
> mentation of human culture.[38]

Explicit knowledge, then, depends on a prior unity richer and fuller
than the propositions gathered around it. This tacit coefficient of all
explicit knowledge is especially important for coming to conscious and
disciplined understanding of very large, subtle, or complex subjects that
bear within themselves implications for a broad range of subsidiary
fields. This brings us back, at last, to Trinitarianism.

The tacit dimension of knowledge is especially relevant in Trinitarian
theology. It is what enables the theology teacher to utter that all-important phrase "You know" and expect realistically to make connections
with the audience. The Christian teacher taking up the subject of the
Trinity should be able to invoke some range of experience or of implicit

understanding and familiarity that can then be explicated in propositional teaching on the subject:

"You know, the Trinity, like we sing about in church";
"You know, the Trinity, like is all over the Bible";
or "You know, the Trinity, like every Christian believes in."

Without this tacit awareness of the Trinity, explicit teaching on the subject will always seem like a foreign body rudely interjected into an otherwise reasonable nexus of beliefs. This is because the doctrine of the Trinity is so large, fundamental, and all-encompassing.

Scottish theologian Thomas F. Torrance, whose summary of Polanyi's categories we just quoted at length, has done more than any other theologian to use Polanyian insights for theology in general and for the Trinity in particular. Here is his masterly account of how vigorous Trinitarianism relies on the tacit dimension:

A child by the age of five has learned, we are told, an astonishing amount about the physical world to which he or she has become spontaneously and intuitively adapted—far more than the child could ever understand if he or she turned out to be the most brilliant of physicists. Likewise, I believe, we learn far more about God as Father, Son and Holy Spirit, into whose Name we have been baptised, within the family and fellowship and living tradition of the Church than we can ever say: it becomes built into the structures of our souls and minds, and we know much more than we can ever tell. This is what happens evangelically and personally to us within the membership of the Church, the Body of Christ in the world, when through the transforming power of his Word and Spirit our minds become inwardly and intuitively adapted to know the living God. We become spiritually and intellectually implicated in patterns of divine order that are beyond our powers fully to articulate in explicit terms, but we are aware of being apprehended by divine Truth as it is in Jesus which steadily presses for increasing realisation in our understanding, articulation and confession of faith. That is how Christian history gains its initial impetus, and is then reinforced through constant reading and study of the Bible within the community of the faithful.[39]

According to Polanyi according to Torrance, we know more about the

Trinity than we can say. Indeed, if we did not have tacit knowledge of the triune God by virtue of our existence as Christians, the theological tradition would never have developed the conceptual tools necessary for explicit understanding of this doctrine, which is at once a particular confession (one doctrine among many) and the pervasive context of all confession (the doctrinal matrix that makes sense of all the rest).

LITURGY, TRADITION, AND SACRAMENTS, OH MY!

There is widespread agreement among many theologians that Trinitarian theology is so expansive that only a sophisticated approach via tacit awareness is likely to produce effective and productive understanding of it. We have seen the logic of this position and have seen some of its promise for reinvigorating Trinitarian theology. However, at this point we can begin to reapproach the question of inculturating the doctrine of the Trinity into evangelical culture. In doing so, we will part ways with the answers normally given to the question, Where do we locate the tacit awareness of Trinitarianism that can fund explicit understanding of the doctrine? The question is a good one, but the standard answers are less helpful for our purposes. The standard answer is as follows: the tacit dimension of Trinitarian thought, the nonthematic awareness of Trinitarian reality that makes productive understanding possible, is located in the richness of the Christian liturgy, in the profound experience of continuity with tradition, and in the real presence of Christ himself in the sacrament of the Lord's Supper. The sources, then, are liturgy, tradition, and sacrament. Let us examine each briefly.

Liturgy in the sense intended here is an order of service and a set of practices attached to regular Christian worship. The best liturgies in use in Christian churches are ancient, well-worn compositions permeated with scriptural language skillfully deployed across a series of pastoral pronouncements, prayers, congregational responses, and songs. These are correlated with a series of symbolic actions arranged with equal artfulness to embody the theological commitments of the church. At crucial junctures, select passages of Scripture are read aloud as the word of the Lord for that day in the church calendar. The synergy of the words and actions constitute a worship experience intended to convey the entirety of the Christian message in symbolic form, and all of this takes place in its own liturgical language, regardless of the content of the actual sermon preached that day. Of course a good liturgical homilist will do his best to preach a message that harmonizes with the particular liturgical setting at hand and thus work with the grain of the overall service rather than against it. However, as Gerald Bray points out, the power of a set liturgy is partly in its independence from any particular sermon:

> If the sermon is good and the spirit of the congregation is right, a fixed liturgy may appear to be an irrelevance, even a constraint on the freedom of the Spirit. . . . But when the times of dryness come, when we reach a plateau in our spiritual growth, then the structure of a liturgy that keeps both the biblical depth and the biblical balance can provide us with fresh inspiration and keep us from falling into the many different errors caused by our natural proclivity toward omission and distortion. A person who is well trained in biblical liturgy will have a feel for what is orthodox because it will be embedded in his consciousness. Furthermore, he will have a sense of the right kind of Trinitarian balance, because whatever the sermon may be like, there will be a doctrinal framework to restore his spiritual equilibrium and keep him from going off the deep end.[40]

Bray goes on to make the connection between this benefit of liturgy and the doctrine of the Trinity:

> Good theological liturgy . . . is not (or should not be) a substitute for preaching, or a way of stifling spiritual fervor, but a framework in which to place biblical teaching and an encouragement to explore areas of it that we might otherwise neglect. Once again, words like structure and framework provide the key. Start disciplining your faith into a structure, and you will inevitably come to the doctrine of the Trinity, which is the most basic and universal structure of all.[41]

Thus liturgy functions as the tacit dimension that provides the basis for explicit Trinitarian doctrine. Indeed, as Bray suggests, on more than one occasion a healthy liturgy has kept a church from sliding into errors it would otherwise have embraced. A Unitarian theologian once lamented the fact that it was nearly impossible to turn Anglican churches against the doctrine of the Trinity as long as they kept using the Prayer Book. "The Prayer Book used by the Unitarian clergymen . . . familiarized the minds of worshippers with addresses and petitions to the three persons of the Trinity. Whatever the parson said or left unsaid from the pulpit could not sink into the mind as did the prayers from the reading desk and the responses from the pews repeated Sunday by Sunday."[42]

Another location of this tacit dimension, according to conventional wisdom, is tradition itself, especially the deep sense of tradition espoused by churches in which the ecclesiology is centered on claims of apostolic succession and institutional continuity. For these churches, tradition is a kind of deposit that we can adhere to and exercise implicit faith in without necessarily specifying the propositional content of that faith, or at least not needing to specify all of it at any given time. "I believe what the church believes" is the guiding principle here. However, there is an even deeper sense of tradition sometimes invoked by high-church theologians. Andrew Louth, in his evocative study *Discerning the Mystery: An Essay on the Nature of Theology,*[43] advocates an approach to Christianity that lays greater stress on liturgical action than on proclaimed words. Claiming to follow Richard Hooker in laying "emphasis on the deeper power and significance of deeds," Louth links "the importance of the Incarnation, and, in dependence on that, the importance of the sacraments, and indeed of liturgical worship—which is a matter not just of words but of actions—in general" and argues that this constellation of concerns points to a very special significance for tradition:

> For the central truth, or mystery, of the Christian faith is primarily not a matter of words, and therefore ultimately of ideas or concepts, but a matter of fact, or reality. The heart of the Christian mystery is the fact of God made man, God with us, in Christ; words, even his words, are secondary to the reality of what he accomplished. To be a Christian is not simply to believe something, to learn something, but to be something, to experience something. The role of the Church, then, is not simply as the contingent vehicle—in history—

of the Christian message, but as the community, through belonging to which we come into touch with the Christian mystery.[44]

In Louth's view, the prioritizing of life over doctrine finds its clearest expression in the epistemological priority of the church as a history-spanning community that provides the tacit dimension on which explicit theological awareness can develop. In this connection he invokes "Polanyi's idea of the importance of a community and of a tradition, within which one learns to perceive and know"[45] and praises it as the inescapable background and framework within which faith is possible. "We come back to the fact that Christianity is not a body of doctrine that can be specified in advance, but a way of life and all that this implies. Tradition is, as it were, the tacit dimension of the life of the Christian: what is proclaimed . . . is only a part of it, and not really the most important part."[46]

Tradition provides, for theologians like Louth, a sense of fullness and presence, and thus it constitutes, in one of his favorite metaphors, the fecund silence in which the Word can be spoken and heard:

> To hear Jesus, and not just his words, we have to stand within the tradition of the Church; we have to put our trust in those to whom our Lord entrusted his mission, his sending. Part of the stillness that is needed for us to hear the words of Jesus is a sense of presence, and it is this that tradition conveys. We become Christians by becoming members of the Church, by trusting our forefathers in the faith. If we cannot trust the Church to have understood Jesus, then we have lost Jesus: and the resources of modern scholarship will not help us to find him.[47]

From this thick account of tradition it is a short step to the third standard answer for where to locate a tacit dimension capable of funding Trinitarian thought. A high view of the sacraments is often invoked in this context. Baptism in the name of the Trinity is not merely a ritual performed as the right formula is spoken (though that is important), but is actually viewed as a mysterious, physical immersion in the life of the triune Godhead via the death and resurrection of Christ, sacramentally mediated to the individual baptized. This experienced reality of the life of the Trinity thus contains in itself the actual content that can later be unpacked or expounded in definite Trinitarian teaching. The sacraments are concrete, while the doctrine is necessarily abstract. This view of the relation between sacrament and doctrine has naturally generated the catechetical practice known as mystagogy, which means teaching that is provided for those who have already been introduced to the mysteries. In a fully sacramental mystagogy, the Christian would receive the thing itself in the sacraments and then learn about it in doctrinal form. Converts make a profession of faith and are admitted to baptism and the Eucharist, which is followed then by teaching and preaching that further explicates in conceptual form the mysteries they have just encountered in experiential form.

EVANGELICAL RESOURCES ALREADY AT HAND

What are we to say to these proposals for cultivating the tacit dimension of Trinitarian theology? For some varieties of evangelicals, these relatively high-church resources have been, and continue to be, nourishing sources of Christian life that underwrite the church's ability to think well about the Trinity. Furthermore, we do not need to enter the interminable debate about the essence of evangelicalism, or its true center, by asserting that evangelicalism by definition must be nonliturgical, nontraditional, and nonsacramental. Millions of evangelicals are, of course, and this includes a wide swath from Southern Baptists to Pentecostals in the global south. Nevertheless, the movement as a whole, or certain ecclesial strands within the movement, could certainly grow in the three areas discussed above without losing compromising evangelical identity. A more formal and elaborate use of liturgy, a firmer grasp of the great tradition, and a higher view of the sacraments are all possibilities within some of the churches that make up the evangelical movement. Insofar as they actually help provide a tacit awareness of the reality of the Trinity, they can even be recommended as strategically valuable directions in which the movement could develop. Gerald Bray's remarks about liturgy cited above, for example, are clearly that: a recommendation that evangelicalism could become more Trinitarian by becoming more liturgical.

However, if such advice were to be taken programmatically and urged as necessary, it seems to lead to the conclusion that some evangelicals will become more Trinitarian only if they become less evangelical. Minimally, such a program for Trinitarian renewal would require that those segments of the evangelical world which are nonliturgical, nontraditional, and nonsacramental would be involved in Trinitarian renewal only to the extent that they change their practices enough to accommodate the tacit resources of their high-church brethren. But this would be an unhelpful recommendation for many reasons. The primary reason is that these churches have theological convictions in place about this whole range of issues. There may be churches that are nonliturgical, nonsacramental, and nontraditional by accident, ignorance, or default, but most of them adopt these stances because they have biblical reasons for doing so. It's no good telling members of a credobaptist church that if they became paedobaptist they would feel the Trinity working in their lives more deeply. They have made decisions about infant baptism on other grounds and will hold to those decisions. To approach them as if they simply hadn't thought about the sacraments yet is by turns naïve and insulting.

The other reason to dissent from the conventional wisdom about the tacit dimension of Trinitarianism is that our task is to present the Trinity so that it will take deeper root in the soil of evangelicalism. That may require tilling the soil quite a bit, but it should not mean selling the farm. Suggesting that a nonliturgical, nonsacramental, nontraditional church should change all these practices is tantamount to declaring that their evangelical culture (and the constellation of doctrinal and practical characteristics connected to that culture) should be altered. What we are undertaking, however, is to inculturate the doctrine of the Trinity into evangelicalism, and we are therefore more interested in finding elements in that culture which are consonant with the tacit framework required for robust Trinitarianism. Evangelicalism certainly would profit from becoming more thoroughly Trinitarian by whatever means necessary. However, rather than pushing evangelicalism to shift its resource base, I am recommending that evangelicals should work harder with the resources already available in plenty.

What are the resources at hand? When teaching evangelical

Christians about the doctrine of the Trinity, what are the powerful but unstated realities that the theologian can invoke in order to make connections with experience? What tacit awareness is lying latently ready in the minds of these believers from which to generate conceptual tools for this theological feat of conscious reflection? Evangelicals who demur from deep tradition, elaborate liturgy, and realist sacramentalism still have plentiful resources for deep Trinitarianism. Everything they do is grounded in Trinitarian commitments, and every evangelical practice repays further reflection: proclamation of the gospel, personal appropriation of salvation, assurance of salvation, submission to biblical authority, knowledge of the Bible, authoritative preaching, affective worship, conversational prayer, world missions, and many of the other standard features of evangelical church life are rich resources for Trinitarian exploration. Dig anywhere and you will hit Trinitarian gold.

The evangelical emphasis on the conscious experience of salvation is an obvious characteristic of the movement. It has come to be associated with the phrase "born again" and is described in more sociological language as "convertive piety." This experience of conversion is the concrete, experiential reality that the abstract, conceptual terminology of Trinitarian doctrine can appeal to in order to find a connection with existing knowledge. Because God saves us by opening himself to us and making the divine life available for our restoration and rescue, salvation occurs according to a Trinitarian order. The sentence of salvation is coherent and correct because it operates according to an underlying Trinitarian grammar, whether the speaker can codify those grammatical rules or not. All who are born again are born again by the power of the Trinity, as the Father sends the Spirit of his Son into their hearts. When the rules of this grammar of salvation are made explicit, what emerges into understanding is the doctrine of the Trinity. The thing itself is there, making possible rational reflection on it which explicates the rules of its own being.

Evangelicalism is characterized by an awareness of the personal character of knowing God and an experience of the actual presence of another Someone in intimate contact over the course of a shared history. The evangelistic shorthand for this has to do with inviting Jesus to take up residence in your heart as your personal Savior or with the theme of friendship with God. "Person" is a key term in Trinitarian theology, and it is no accident that the personal emphasis of evangelicalism coheres well with this element of Trinitarianism. This pervasive personalism also gives a particular tone to evangelical prayer, one which emphasizes a freedom of speech and a direct, even informal manner of talking to God.

From Wesley's hymns to contemporary choruses, affective worship experience is a recurring mark of evangelical church life. This emotional depth, while not adequate to support theological reflection on its own, provides a rich and engaging context for Trinitarian theology. Above all, it provides the kind of incentive and communal sanction necessary to encourage anybody to undertake the kind of challenging thinking required to bring Trinitarian theology into sharper focus. This stirring up of the depths of the heart and mind is crucial to the Polanyian strategy: "Since tacit knowing depends on where your attention is focussed, it won't work without caring. . . . There is no discovery without a desire to know and a belief that there is something to know."[48] Emotionally engaging worship is a communal effusion of that caring without which the attention will not be focused and without which there will be no confidence that there is something worth expending cognitive energy toward investigating. Communal praise of God is itself already a focusing of the mental apparatus of attentiveness in the right direction.

One of the most important resources evangelicalism has for developing the tacit dimension of Trinitarianism is its distinctive posture toward Scripture. Evangelicals are a variety of biblicists (if the term has not grown too pejorative), and they believe that the Scriptures are the medium of God's personal address to them; the Bible is God's word. Accordingly, evangelicals have developed a host of spiritual disciplines focused on the Word of God that provide perfect examples of the Polanyian motif of indwelling a subject in order to understand it better.[49]

I believe that the above resources show enough promise for developing a rich fund of tacit Trinitarianism that it is fair to assert that evangelicalism has within its own particular genius all that it takes to be more robustly Trinitarian. If I am right about resources like these as sources for Trinitarian understanding, then the evangelical malady is

Chart 1.1: Tacit Trinitarianism of Evangelical Practices

The Evangelical Practice	Its Tacitly Trinitarian Dimension
Getting saved	Being adopted as sons by encountering the gospel Trinity
Knowing Jesus personally	The Spirit joining believers to the life of Jesus
Devotional Bible reading	Hearing the Father's word in the Spirit
Conversational prayer	The logic of mediation; prayer in the name of Jesus

actually more mysterious than ever because we have everything necessary for health and yet we remain ill. It would be good if evangelical theology would lay hold of its tacit resources for Trinitarian theology and fulfill its potential. At this point, even a bit of amicable competitive spirit would be beneficial on all sides: if a nonliturgical, nontraditional, and nonsacramental family of Christians would undertake to prove itself more solidly and productively Trinitarian than its liturgical, traditional, and sacramental cousins, both parties would benefit from the competition, to the benefit of the ecumenical church. Everybody could be a winner in the "more Trinitarian than thou" fight that might break out if evangelicals rise to their potential and develop the genius of their own movement in the direction of reinvigorating Trinitarianism as a force in Christian life and thought.

This chapter has necessarily been more abstract and methodological than the others in this book. I hope it has also been more suggestive of future possibilities in the broad field of evangelical Trinitarianism. In the following chapters we will not be following up every one of those possibilities. Instead, we will focus on the main things: the gospel and its application to individuals, Bible study, prayer, and the church as a community on a mission.

2

WITHIN THE HAPPY LAND
OF THE TRINITY

(Or, God in Himself)

I glorified you on earth, having accomplished the work that you
gave me to do. And now, Father, glorify me in your own presence
with the glory that I had with you before the world existed.
JOHN 17:4-5

(H)e is being itself, and as such must necessarily be infinitely happy in the glorious perfections of his nature from everlasting to
everlasting; and as he did not create, so neither did he redeem
because he needed us; but he loved us because he loved us.
SUSANNA WESLEY (1738)

In the following chapters, we will see that the Trinity makes all the
difference in the world for practical things such as salvation, spirituality, prayer, Bible study, and church life. The doctrine of the Trinity is a
practical doctrine, and has immediate implications for Christian life. In
some ways, we will be answering the question that Nicky Cruz asked,
"Why have three persons . . . when it confuses me so much? Why
couldn't God just be God?" It is a question that has occurred to many
Christians: What is the Trinity for?

But the first and clearest answer has to be that the Trinity isn't ultimately for anything, any more than God is for the purpose of anything.
Just as you wouldn't ask what purpose God serves or what function
he fulfills, it makes no sense to ask what the point of the Trinity is or

what purpose the Trinity serves. The Trinity isn't for anything beyond itself, because the Trinity is God. God is God in this way: God's way of being God is to be Father, Son, and Holy Spirit simultaneously from all eternity, perfectly complete in a triune fellowship of love. If we don't take this as our starting point, everything we say about the practical relevance of the Trinity could lead us to one colossal misunderstanding: thinking of God the Trinity as a means to some other end, as if God were the Trinity in order to make himself useful. But God the Trinity is the end, the goal, the telos, the omega. In himself and without any reference to a created world or the plan of salvation, God is that being who exists as the triune love of the Father for the Son in the unity of the Spirit. The boundless life that God lives in himself, at home, within the happy land of the Trinity above all worlds, is perfect. It is complete, inexhaustibly full, and infinitely blessed.

IMAGINE THERE'S NO HEAVEN . . . OR EARTH

There is something even better than the good news, and that something is God. The good news of the gospel is that God has opened up the dynamics of his triune life and given us a share in that fellowship. But all of that good news only makes sense against the background of something even better than the good news: the goodness that is the perfection of God himself. The doctrine of the Trinity is first and foremost a teaching about who God is, and God the Trinity would have been God the Trinity whether he had revealed himself to us or not, whether he had redeemed us or not, whether he had created us or not.

Obviously, these "whether or not" statements are counterfactual: they are about situations that are not the case. God has in fact made himself known, has redeemed his people, and, to say the most obvious thing, has created us. That being the case, what is the good of asking hypothetical questions about what would have been the case if God had not done these things he has done? Indeed, isn't it even ungrateful to forget, or to pretend to forget, God's mighty acts? No, in this case, far from being ungrateful, it is an opportunity to become more grateful. Hypothetical questions are useful tools for understanding how things really are by imagining how they might have been otherwise.[1] They can be used as mental cures for sick patterns of thought. If you are tempted to think that God's triunity is something he puts on in order to reach some further goal, or to interact with the world, you can cure yourself of that tendency by thinking away the world and asking yourself: If there had been no world, would God have been Father, Son, and Spirit? If you are tempted to think of Christmas as the time when the Son of God first began to exist, you can cure yourself by asking: If the Son of God had not taken on human nature, would he still have been the Son of God?

The answer to these hypothetical questions is yes, God would have been Trinity with no world, and the Son of God did in fact preexist his incarnation. God minus the world is still God the Holy Trinity. In the words of the hymn by Frederick W. Faber:

When Heaven and Earth were yet unmade
When time was yet unknown,
Thou, in Thy bliss and majesty,
Didst live, and love, alone.[2]

The emphasis in these excellent lines is on God's self-sufficient "bliss and majesty." Faber would be quick to point out that the final word, "alone," is very different from "lonely." Otherwise God could not "love, alone." Indeed, God is the only one who can love alone, for Trinitarian reasons: God the Father loves God the Son in the love of God the Holy Spirit.

Is it too bold of us to declare what God was like, or what he was doing, before creation? It requires boldness, to be sure, but only the boldness of the New Testament. One of the characteristic differences between the Old Testament and the New Testament is that the New Testament is bold to make such statements. Look, for instance, at the way the New Testament takes a step further back with its declaration of salvation: where God declares in the old covenant, "I have chosen you," the new covenant announces that "he chose us in Christ before the foundation of the world." The prophets do not make declarations about what happened "before the foundation of the world," but the apostles do. The main reason for this is that the coming of Christ forced the apostles to think farther back, farther down, into the ultimate foundation of God's ways and works.

When Christ brought salvation, the apostles had to decide whether the life of Jesus Christ was one more event in the series of God's actions or whether, in meeting the Son of God, they had come into contact with something that was absolutely primal about God himself. Christ did not leave them the option of considering him just another prophet or servant of God. They even had to decide where to start in telling the story of Jesus: With his birth? With ancient prophecies about his coming (as in Mark)? With a genealogy connecting him to Abraham (as in Matthew) or all the way back to Adam (as in Luke)? Ultimately, they knew that the best way to acknowledge Jesus as the eternal Son of God was to go back further than the foundation of the world and confess that he had been there previous even to that. That backward step behind the foundation of the world is a step into the eternal nature of God. So the Old Testament starts with the foundation of the world: "In the beginning, God created the heavens and the earth" (Gen. 1:1). But the story of Jesus starts before that, because the Son of God was already present by the time of the beginning: "In the beginning was the Word, and the Word was with God, and the Word was God" (John 1:1).

As a result, we are speaking from solid New Testament ground when we say that God was the Trinity from all eternity, or that God is Father, Son, and Spirit without reference to the creation of the world. Scottish bishop Robert Leighton (1611–1684) elaborated on this fact when his commentary on 1 Peter brought him to the phrase "before the foundation of the world" (1 Pet. 1:20):

> Before there was time, or place, or any creature, GOD, the blessed Trinity was in Himself, and as the Prophet speaks, inhabiting Eternity, completely happy in Himself: but intending to manifest and communicate His goodness, He gave being to the world, and to time with it; made all to set forth His goodness, and the most excellent of His creatures to contemplate and enjoy it.[3]

Imagining God without the world is one way to highlight the freedom of God in creating. Thinking away the world makes it obvious that God didn't have to make a world. Creation was not required, not mandatory, not exacted from God, neither by any necessity imposed from outside nor by any deficit lurking within the life of God. The Bible does not directly answer the question, Why did God create anything at all?[4] but it does let us know what some of the most glaringly wrong answers to that question would be. It would be wrong to say that God created because he was lonely, unfulfilled, or bored. God is free from that kind of dependence.

Such divine freedom is one of the things meant by grace. Notice how deeply imprinted this aspect of grace is, even into our language: When something is gratuitous (from *gratia*, grace) and given to us gratis (for free), the appropriate response is gratitude (responding to *gratia*) or gratefulness. Sometimes when a person gets a surprise gift, he blurts out, "You didn't have to do that!" Well, of course. That sentiment, too obvious to need saying, is a tiny meditation on the nature of the freedom that lies behind a true gift. So is the redundancy of describing something as a "free gift," as if there were any other kind of gift. Grace calls forth gratitude, and we answer with "thank you." This is also, by the way, why we say the word *please* when we ask for something. It is a shortened form of the expression, "If it pleases you," which is a way of recognizing that the person you are asking a favor from is not your servant but a free person who isn't required to do your bidding. Good manners are good theology.

The same logic of freedom and gratitude applies to redemption: once man had fallen, God was not strictly required to redeem. We can rest our thoughts for a moment between creation and redemption, and ask, What if God had not redeemed his fallen creatures? If thinking away creation is an uncomfortable thing to do, thinking away redemption is terrifying: God did not have to save us. There was no external necessity imposed on him, nor did he have any internal need. The perfect blessedness of God would not have been compromised by the final failure of humanity. God did not save us to rescue himself from sadness over our plight. He saved us freely, out of an astonishing abundance of generosity. There is an ancient prayer that praises God that he "didst wondrously create, and yet more wondrously renew the dignity of human nature."[5] That prayer expresses the doctrine of "double gratuity," a term that means God created freely and also redeemed freely.[6] Both are wonderful, or amazing grace. Even more than we depend on God's free act of creation, we hang on his mercy for salvation, approaching him "without one plea" and answering his grace with gratitude.

But back behind even that double grace of creation and redemption is the sheer fact of God's being as Father, Son, and Holy Spirit. The doctrine of the Trinity calls us to recognize, and ponder, and rejoice in the sheer reality of who God essentially is, at home in the happy land of the Trinity above all worlds. To recognize this is to come face-to-face with the final foundation of all God's ways and works. And when we have carried out the thought experiment of thinking away everything we can (both redemption and creation), leaving nothing but God, we are not left with a formless and solitary divine blur. Instead we confess that God exists essentially and eternally as Father, Son, and Holy Spirit. Christians have much to say about grace. But the ground of grace is God's absolute triune self-sufficiency.

THE TRINITARIAN THEOLOGY OF SUSANNA WESLEY

Christians through the ages have always grasped the connection between the self-sufficiency of God as Trinity and the graciousness of grace, but there is one evangelical who understood it especially deeply and expressed it exceptionally well. For Susanna Wesley (1669–1742), mother of John and Charles, the first thing that came to mind whenever she thought about the Trinity was this absolute self-sufficiency of God, with the accompanying sense of his graciousness in reaching out to us in total freedom. "Consider the infinite boundless goodness of the ever blessed Trinity," she exhorted herself in her private devotional journal . . .

> adore the stupendous mystery of divine love! That God the Father, Son and Holy Ghost should all concur in the work of man's redemption! What but pure goodness could move or excite God, who is perfect essential blessedness! That cannot possibly receive any accession of perfection or happiness from his creatures. What, I say, but love, but goodness, but infinite incomprehensible love and goodness could move him to provide such a remedy for the fatal lapse of his sinful unworthy creatures?[7]

Because her starting point was the idea of the fullness of the life of God as Father, Son, and Holy Spirit, which is "perfect essential blessedness," Susanna recognized that the love of the "ever-blessed Trinity" is a "stupendous mystery." When one is suitably impressed with the absolute completeness of God's life, one recognizes that it is impossible to increase the perfection and happiness of it. As a result, the graciousness, the "infinite incomprehensible love and goodness," of God stands out more conspicuously against this vast background of Trinitarian self-sufficiency. For Susanna Wesley, the doctrine of the blessed Trinity is what makes grace so perpetually amazing.

"We know there is but one living and true God," she wrote in a letter to a friend in 1737, "though revealed to us under three characters—that of Father, Son, and Holy Spirit." Susanna wrote a few more lines about the distinct roles of the three persons in the Christian life, and then, with her thoughts elevated by these ideas of the Trinity, she broke out in praise: "Let me beseech you to join with me," she wrote, "in adoring the infinite and incomprehensible love of God." And:

> He is the great God, "the God of the spirits of all flesh," "the high and lofty One that inhabiteth eternity," and created not angels and men because he wanted them, for he is being itself, and as such must necessarily be infinitely happy in the glorious perfections of his nature from everlasting to everlasting; and as he did not create, so neither did he redeem because he needed us; but he loved us because he loved us, he would have mercy because he would have mercy, he would show compassion because he would show compassion.[8]

In this model piece of theological reflection, Susanna Wesley begins with recognition of God's infinite happiness in being God, affirms the double gratuity of divine freedom in creation and redemption, and ends with an allusion to God's self-description (Ex. 33:19) of the only basis of his mercy: "He would have mercy because he would have mercy." Finally, she sums up her doctrine of the graciousness of grace with the simple paraphrase: "He loved us because he loved us."

Susanna Wesley may have been a warmhearted pietist with a burning experience of God's grace in her own life, but she was not just expressing a heartfelt religious sentiment when she wrote this. She was also writing from a well-formed Trinitarian theology that she had thought out to the end. Her journal from about 1710 includes an impressive entry that shows how seriously she took the doctrine. She began by accusing the great Aristotle of falling into error when he taught that the world eternally existed along with God, "streamed by connatural result and emanation" from all eternity. She mused that "this error seems grounded on a true notion of the goodness of God," which Aristotle "truly supposes must eternally be communicating good to something or other." It is true that the Supreme Being is infinitely good and that his goodness is of a kind to be always inclined to give itself away to others. Without any further information, this speculation would demand an eternal world as the eternal recipient of God's self-giving goodness. An eternally, essentially self-giving God would require an eternal world. But that sort of eternal world would make God dependent on the world for his own satisfaction. Without the world, God would be a frustrated giver.

The conclusion, which Susanna Wesley found utterly unacceptable, would be that God depended on something outside himself to make possible his full self-expression. Pondering this mistake in the great Aristotle's philosophy, Susanna mused, "It was his want of the knowledge of revealed religion that probably led him into it." Aristotle's problem came from the fact that he had no access to the revealed doctrine of the Trinity.

> For had he ever heard of that great article of our Christian faith concerning the Holy Trinity, he had then perceived the almighty Goodness eternally communicating being and all the fullness of the Godhead to the divine Logos, his uncreated Word, between whose existence and that of the Father there is not one moment assignable.[9]

In Susanna's Trinitarian worldview, the eternal Son has eternally existed alongside the eternal Father, always receiving the full goodness of divinity from him. The world, therefore, does not have to bear the burden of being God's eternal recipient of self-giving goodness. To put it another way, unless the Son were the eternal recipient of the Father's self-giving, the world would be metaphysically necessary to the being of God. The point Susanna made here has also been seen by numerous thinkers. The Baptist theologian Augustus H. Strong (1836–1921) put it this way: "Neither God's independence nor God's blessedness can be maintained upon grounds of absolute unity. Anti-Trinitarianism almost necessarily makes creation indispensable to God's perfection, tends to a belief in the eternity of matter, and ultimately, leads . . . to pantheism."[10]

Susanna Wesley's skirmish with Aristotle is a pretty tidy speculative engagement with the philosopher, and it is worth remembering that Susanna was not a theology professor but a full-time homeschooling mother when she wrote it. Little John Wesley was probably about seven years old at the time Susanna recorded these thoughts in her personal devotional journal. She obviously had a lively intellect and a mind for what mattered. What mattered, in her well-formed evangelical Trinitarianism, was that the deep Trinitarian background of the gospel stayed firmly in place so the astonishing graciousness of God's free grace could be seen for what it is.

WHO GOD IS AND WHAT HE DOES

Susanna Wesley is a perfect case study in well-balanced evangelical Trinitarianism because she maintained a healthy sense of proportion between who God is and what God does. She was certainly passionate about what God has done to save his people, but she knew that the gospel derives its power from the infinite background of who God is. That infinite background of God's "perfect essential blessedness" formed the ultimate horizon against which she could "adore the stupendous mystery of God's love." Balanced evangelical Trinitarianism does not just throw itself into the river of good news and swim away downstream; it also acknowledges the fountain from which that river flows. Like Susanna Wesley, it keeps one foot in the happy land of the Trinity and one foot on the ground of the gospel. When evangelicals lose their sense of proportion, they begin to talk as if they no longer care about the character of God unless they get something from it. The best defense against this has always been the doctrine of the eternal Trinity in itself.

Pondering the eternal, essential Trinity is the most concrete and biblical way of acknowledging the distinction between who God is and what he does. God is eternally Trinity, because triunity belongs to his very nature. Things like creation and redemption are things God does, and he would still be God if he had not done them. But Trinity is who God is, and without being the Trinity, he would not be God. God minus creation would still be God, but God minus Father, Son, and Holy Spirit would not be God. So when we praise God for being our creator and redeemer, we are praising him for what he does. But behind what God does is the greater glory of who he is: behind his act is his being. In the sentence "God saves," the subject, "God," is the foundation of the predicate.

As is the case with so many of the deep things of God, it is possible to consider the depth of God's being behind his acts at two levels: in a preliminary way, without yet invoking the doctrine of the Trinity, or in a more concrete way, with explicit reference to the Father, Son, and Holy Spirit. The Old Testament often shows, in a striking way, the truths that will be unpacked and intensified in a more Trinitarian fashion in the New Testament. So in this case. The distinction between who God is and what he does is an important element of the Old Testament's way of offering praise to God. In Psalm 86:10, for example, the psalmist declares both: "For you are great and do wondrous things; you alone are God." Even more strikingly, Psalm 119:68 has the brief sentence, "You are good and do good," or, in the King James Version with its now-antiquated verbs, "Thou art good, and doest good." We will see the New Testament intensification of this motif when the internally triune God behaves in an externally Trinitarian way; that is, when God, who is Father, Son, and Holy Spirit, saves us by being Father, Son, and Holy Spirit for us. We could paraphrase the psalm's "Thou art good, and doest good," with the extension, "Thou art triune, and doest Trinitarian works." But we should never rush to new covenant clarity if it means leaving behind old covenant profundity.

In this case, the Old Testament itself gives us more than enough to meditate on: God's being is the ground of his actions for us. When God does great and mighty things, his behavior, or performance, is in accordance with his own character. His behavior flows from his character; it is good because he is good. But his character is greater than his behavior, because it is essential to him. He could have withheld any particular behavior; he will go on to carry out more behavior; but he is who he is. There will be further divine performances grounded in his character, but his character itself is immutable. "I the LORD do not change" (Mal. 3:6).

The Puritan Thomas Manton (1620–1677), commenting on "Thou art good, and doest good," called it a "compellation and confession of God's goodness, both in his nature and actions." "God is good of himself, and doth good to us," Manton paraphrased the verse. First he dwelt on the goodness of God's nature:

> He is good of himself, good in himself; yea, good itself. There is none good above him, or besides him, or beyond him; it is all from him, and in him, if it be good. He is primitively and originally good, *autagathos*, good of himself, which nothing else is; for all creatures are good only by participation and communication from God. [11]

Indeed, "all candles are lighted at his torch," said Manton. The second half of the verse, "and doeth good," does not have the same infinite depth to it, because it is an event within the story of God's life with the world he freely created. "When God made the world, then was it verified, He is good, and doeth good." [12] We are always prone to ingratitude, but Manton was especially concerned that we should cultivate gratitude toward God for who he is. The only way to do that is to dwell on the subject:

> It is the fruit of deep and ponderous meditation. Glances never warm the heart, it is our serious and deliberate thoughts which affect us. . . . To be ravished with love, affected with love, always thinking of love, speaking of love, expressing their sense of love, that is a work behoving saints. [13]

The contemporary praise song "Good to Me" strikes the right proportion when it directs us to sing the three lines to God, "For you are good / for you are good / for you are good to me." [14] Two-thirds of our attention on the goodness of God, followed by one-third on how he has directed that goodness toward us—that is just about the right ratio for the Christian affections if they are to correspond to God's being and act. On the other hand, it is possible to sing that song as if everything before the words "to me" is just a way of triple-underlining what God has done on your behalf: good, good, good to me. But a better way of underlining what God has done on our behalf is to keep it securely anchored in his own inherent goodness.

TRINITARIAN THEOLOGY TO THE RESCUE

The priority of who God is over what he does may seem too obvious a point to spend much time on, and it may also seem like something nobody disagrees with. But, in fact, people routinely make a host of objections against this prioritizing. They say that while it is a fine, spiritual thought to focus on who God is in himself, it is too abstract and formless a task. All we know of God is what he does, specifically what he does for us. While it may be logically true that God's being is greater than his acts, it is irrelevant to us once we have acknowledged it intellectually, since it is always God's acts that we are dealing with.

Then there is the practical problem: even if we consent that it is some sort of spiritual duty to acknowledge the greatness of God's inherent character over and above his external actions, how are we supposed to keep our attention focused on something like the being of God? If we turn our attention from the recitation of God's actions for us (creation, election, the incarnation, the sending of the Spirit, daily mercies), we have nothing specific to think about and will be reduced to saying "you are good" over and over. Finally, objectors say that God himself is adequately glorified when we are grateful for his actions toward us; we do not need to try to go beyond that to some higher level of adoring God in himself. We have an interest in what God has done for us, they say, and it would be a kind of false humility to try to rise above gratitude for the benefits we get from God.

These are all sensible objections, but it is precisely here that the doctrine of the Trinity can be spiritually helpful. Consider for a moment how the doctrine of the Trinity enters the consciousness of a Christian. A person hears the gospel and accepts it. That person is conscious of being a sinner, and of being saved from the penalty and power of sin by Jesus Christ. But as soon as he begins reflecting on that salvation, he has to ask, how did Jesus bring about this salvation? The answer is: through his death and resurrection, Jesus paid for my sin by making atonement to God. That is how the Bible portrays the predicament we are in and the deliverance that Jesus brings. As soon as this answer is given, though, it raises another question: Who must Jesus Christ be, if he is capable of saving people in this way? The answer is that he must be fully human and fully divine. See how the logic of salvation works its way out into ever wider circles of understanding. Beginning with the awareness of salvation, the Christian is driven to understand what salvation is (atonement) and who the savior must be (the Son of God incarnate).

But there is a further question to be asked as the logic of salvation unfolds. If Jesus is divine, then who must God be? If we are serious when we add "God" to the description of Jesus, we must be equally serious that, in some way, "Jesus" is to be added to the description of God. The eternal Son, who in the fullness of time became incarnate for us and our salvation, belongs essentially to the definition of the true God. As soon as a person is converted to Christian faith, and that faith begins seeking understanding, the logic of salvation leads inevitably through these steps: from the experience of salvation, to the nature of salvation, to the nature of the savior, to the nature of God. You can see the ripple effect of faith seeking understanding, radiating outward from its first thought in Diagram 2.1.

Diagram 2.1: The Logic of Salvation

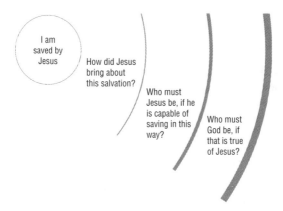

As we see in Diagram 2.1, with each outward step we turn our attention from what is most immediately available to us and try to discern what larger realities are presupposed. We have to look away; we couldn't understand our experience of salvation fully if we just kept analyzing that experience more and more deeply or minutely. We have to turn our attention to the reality outside of our experience, which gives our experience its character: the work that Jesus did for us. The same logic applies at the next circle, where we can only get so far in contemplating the work of Christ before we have to look to what it is founded on: the person of Christ. And finally, the confession that Jesus is God requires us not just to concentrate on Jesus but to turn our attention to our very idea of God.

You may have noticed that each of those concentric circles is in fact another level of theology. We can redescribe these circles in systematic theological terms. At the center, the point of impact on our experience, is soteriology, or the doctrine of salvation. Soteriology is a doctrinal field that includes things like justification, regeneration, conversion, and sanctification. Soteriology is grounded in the atonement, the objective work of Christ. Christ's work is grounded in his person, meaning the doctrine of the incarnation. And finally, the doctrine of the incarnation presupposes the doctrine of the Trinity. Scottish theologian James Denney called the doctrine of the Trinity "the change in the conception of God which followed, as it was necessitated by, the New Testament conception of Christ and His work."[15] So faith seeking understanding moves directly to the biggest doctrines of Christian theology: soteriology, atonement, the incarnation, and the Trinity (see Diagram 2.2)

If you notice, in Diagram 2.2, how much bigger the outer circle is, you can begin to see how Trinitarian theology can help us maintain a proper sense of proportion. The Trinity is bigger than you and your salvation and has other things going on in the parts of the circle that don't overlap with your circle. Those other parts of the Trinity circle are the rest of the fullness of God's own life, the happy land of the Trinity. It is not possible to draw it to scale, because it is infinite, boundless, and finally inconceivable. There are parts of that happy land that you don't go to, and you never will. I cannot describe to you what happens there and neither can anybody else, for God has remained silent about those regions. Trinitarian theology should never be an attempt to transgress the boundary marked by God's Word in Deuteronomy 29:29: "The secret things belong to the LORD our God, but the things that are revealed belong to us and to our children forever, that we may do all the words of this law."

Diagram 2.2: The Logic of Theology

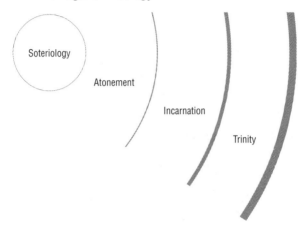

That sense of proportion is something that Trinitarian theology can bring to the Christian life. A concentric diagram like this can help us gain that perspective, see how the most important doctrines flow into each other, and unpack the implications of what God has done for us. But in the process, it nevertheless obscures something else. It takes for granted the fact that all our thinking starts where we are, and then works outward from that center point. That is true enough, since in the process of learning we begin with what is closest and clearest. But the resulting diagram is not so much an objective map of the theological territory as it is a chart of How Everything Looks from Where I Am Standing. If you mistake it for a map, you will suffer from the optical illusion of parallax error and draw the conclusion that you are the center of all God's works and ways, as if the incarnation of the Son, and the eternal being of the triune God, are centered on you. Even if this approach is not self-centered in the sinful sense, it is intentionally salvation-centered and thus unreliable in establishing the big picture of doctrines as huge as Trinity, incarnation, and atonement. There must be some larger map on which we can more helpfully locate our "You Are Here" marker.

A more objective map of the theological territory can be produced by switching from the order of knowing, which traces how we become aware of truths, to the order of being, which traces how those truths are related to each other, without reference to our learning about them. That map would be something like Diagram 2.3.

Diagram 2.3: Relation of the Doctrines

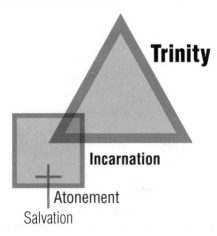

Of course, the scale of Diagram 2.3 is still not proportional, since it includes the infinite God. If we started with a shape representing who God is and then drew a proportionally sized shape representing what God does, the second shape would be invisibly tiny. On this diagram, which is meant to show the right perspective rather than the actual proportion, the relative size of the big triangle can suggest only that we should recognize the infinitude of the triune God over against the more focused nature of his works: the incarnation, the atonement, and your own little salvation, down there at the foot of the cross.

Though the relationships mapped out on the more objective diagram are a great step forward in theological understanding, the concentric circles diagram is still superior in two ways. First, being centered on our experience, it is a better guide to which part of the Christian message ought to be emphasized for all practical purposes. It would be preposterously hyper-intellectual to begin a description of the Christian faith with the Trinity and the incarnation before ever approaching the human situation. Second, and closely related, is the fact that the New Testament is mostly devoted to the things in those inner circles of the concentric diagram: sin, forgiveness, and the utter competence of Jesus to save those who trust him. The Trinitarian presuppositions of these central truths get only a few pages of exposition in the Bible. But they bear the same kind of weight that is borne by God's testimony to Job, that he is the kind of majestic creator who has lots of interesting things going on that are far beyond Job's understanding. Most of the Bible is not about that, but only a fool would fail to take it into account in dealing with God. As the horizon and background of everything that happens in the Bible, Trinitarian and incarnational theology are crucially important if we are to understand the foreground properly. But even when we have done our important work of elucidating and commenting, we should never imagine that we have made an improvement on the New Testament's way of delivering the truth.

GOD LIFE IS LIVELIER THAN ALL OTHER LIFE

The clear categories of systematic theology can be helpful in the task of setting our affections in order. But nobody gets saved by getting the diagrams right. What's at stake here is ultimately a spiritual issue. We ought to take God so seriously that we consider him more interesting than ourselves. In fact, if we had a proper sense of proportion, we would think of the life of God as the liveliest of all lives. In his classic work *The Religious Affections*, Jonathan Edwards proposed that one of the best ways to tell if a person is genuinely converted is to see if he has a sense of how good the things of God are as things in themselves. When a person is saved, he is able to perceive the goodness of God as something delightful in its own right; there is "a change made in the views of his mind, and relish of his heart, whereby he apprehends a beauty, glory, and supreme good, in God's nature as it is in itself."[16] Of course the saints are boundlessly grateful to God for what he does on their behalf, but that gratitude alone is easily explained on purely human grounds. What sets the redeemed mind apart from the natural mind is that, beyond and behind the benefits of what God does, it can distinguish who God is in himself. This is what they delight in the most:

> They do not first see that God loves them, and then see that He is lovely, but they first see that God is lovely, and that Christ is excellent and glorious, and their hearts are first captivated with this view, and the exercises of their love are wont from time to time to begin here, and to arise primarily from these views; and then, consequentially, they see God's love, and great favor to them.[17]

Edwards makes a persuasive case, but many readers of *The Religious Affections* are left with the questions: Is this too high a standard? Is it really possible to be so theocentric in our thoughts of God? Can we learn to "first rejoice in God as glorious and excellent in Himself, and then secondarily rejoice in the fact that so glorious a God" is our God? Is there a way for our thoughts to become so God-centered?

Anglican churchman Robert Hawker (1753–1827) was convinced that there was a way and that the spiritual benefits of learning to think theocentrically would be immense: "Were it possible to divest ourselves of that selfishness which inseparably cleaveth to our present fallen nature," he wrote, "our apprehensions of the Son of God, in his own personal glory, would rise to a standard far above any ideas we can now form, and open a contemplation at once most blessed and delightful."[18] Again, Hawker made that crucial distinction between what the Son of God has done for us, and who he is:

> For although all that the Son of God hath done, and wrought, and sustained, and suffered, for his church and people is great, yea, incalculably great and precious in her esteem, yet his person far exceeds all.[19]

Hawker found a uniquely powerful way to help his readers adopt this God-centered point of view. In a short doctrinal tract defending the divine sonship of Christ, Hawker set aside all other lines of biblical evidence and argued his case solely from the express statements in which God the Father tells us what he thinks of his Son. Especially in those places where the voice of the Father speaks from heaven (Matt.

WITHIN THE HAPPY LAND OF THE TRINITY

3:17; 17:5 and parallels), God the Father declares that he is already "well pleased" with his "beloved Son," without reference to his works. "And I pray the reader . . . to observe with me," said Hawker, "that it is the person of God's dear Son which is above every other consideration in the esteem and affection of God the Father." The Father loves the Son for the incarnation, for the redemption, for "the whole of what he hath done, is now doing, and will to all eternity do, for his body the church." But these acts are secondary to the thing that the Father finds most precious and delightful in the Son: "It is the Son of God, as Son of God; his person, and not his works, which fills the heart of the Father with delight."[20]

The main point of Hawker's book is to demonstrate from Scripture that Jesus Christ is the eternal Son of God. But when he chose to focus on the Father's testimony about the identity of the Son, he opened up a realm of biblical interpretation that is altogether remarkable, because it is the realm of conversation within the Trinity. In attempting to find out how we should think about Jesus, the biblical evidence leads us further up and further in, to the relationship between the Father and the Son.

There is somewhat very delightful even in the bare contemplation of it. For the consideration of the person of the Son of God, as he is in himself, and independent of his relationship to his people, opens to a subject at once both sublime and blessed. . . . And as God the Father is more glorious in what he is in himself, than in all his ways and works towards his creatures, so God the Son is more glorious in himself, and his own personal glory, in common with the Father and the Holy Ghost, in the essence of the GODHEAD, than in all the grace and love he hath manifested to his people. His love to us is indeed precious; yea, very precious; and as the apostle saith, "we love him because he first loved us." (1 John 4:19.) Nevertheless, had he never loved us, had he never taken our nature, nor done and suffered for us, what that love prompted him to do and suffer; yea, had we never been, the Son of God, as Son of God, would have been what he is in himself, in his divine nature, from all eternity and to all eternity, being "One with the Father, over all, God blessed for ever. Amen."[21]

Amen, indeed. Pondering what God the Father thinks of his own Son introduces us to the "sublime and blessed" subject of the eternal conversation that is the fellowship within the Holy Trinity.

G. K. Chesterton, in a few enigmatic lines, evoked how hauntingly this eternal conversation lurks at the back of the biblical revelation:

> The meanest man in grey fields gone
> Behind the set of sun,
> Heareth between star and other star,
> Through the door of the darkness fallen ajar,
> The council, eldest of things that are,
> The talk of the Three in One.[22]

Someone has said that the doctrine of the Trinity is not so much heard in the New Testament as it is overheard. The negative part of that statement probably denies too much,[23] but the positive part is important to notice. One of the most powerful features of the Trinitarianism of the New Testament is that it is revealed to us largely in the conversation between the Father and the Son. The hearers of the New Testament get to listen in on the prayers of Jesus the Son to his God and Father. All through his ministry he converses with the Father in a way that prompts his disciples to ask him for instruction in prayer. Even in the darkness of the cross itself, the Son keeps up an intimate running dialogue with his Father. Jesus is confident that his prayers are heard and that the Father is with him, and in a few spectacular instances of a voice speaking from heaven we get to hear the Father declaring his attitude toward his beloved Son. All this inner-Trinitarian conversation is intentionally held in public, for our instruction. What must have passed in private between Father and Son in the unity of the Holy Spirit is more than we can safely guess. But what they said to and about one another for us to overhear is not only a solid foundation for the doctrine of the Trinity, but it is also a marvelous invitation to us to be included in that conversation.

One of the things we want from the doctrine of the Trinity is a proper spiritual orientation. We want some cognitive assistance in learning to think from a center outside ourselves, and in laying aside for a moment the ways we benefit from what God has done for us. Since all of us are indebted to God's mercy, and approach the majesty of the person of the Son only through what he has done for us, where could we turn for a disinterested testimony to the infinite value of the Son's person? The answer, as obvious as it is fascinating, is that we can turn to the Father's testimony about the Son. When the Father expresses his love for the Son, he cannot possibly be doing it out of self-interest or because he has something to gain. Where could we ever find a more objective point of view about who Jesus is? And of course the Son's testimony about the Father is just as valuable for us. We hear all this through the words of Scripture brought home to us by the Holy Spirit, who inspired them. When we hear Father, Son, and Holy Spirit bear witness to each other in this manner, we are overhearing the doctrine of the Trinity from three privileged insiders, and learning about nothing less than the inner life of God. As Gerald Bray has said, in receiving this New Testament revelation "Christians have been admitted into the inner life of God."[24]

This inner life that God lives, in the happy land of the Trinity above all worlds, is a livelier life than any other life. We know about it because we have overheard Father, Son, and Holy Spirit talking amongst themselves with the intent that we overhear them and be brought into the conversation. Simply knowing that the life of God in itself is the liveliest of all lives is a medicinal correction to our sick, self-centered thinking. But while we are thinking about the eternal, internal Trinity, there are three mistakes we should avoid making: (1) we should not settle for a kind of grudging acknowledgment of the fact; (2) we should not build up our knowledge of it by mere negatives; and (3) we should not fill out our knowledge of it with lush mythological imaginings.

First, we should not settle for a grudging acceptance of the fact that the life of the eternally triune God is a great and lively thing in itself. The crucial thing here is not that we examine some arguments and conclude that God would be God without us, or that God's eternal life is a life in Trinity, on the basis of some scriptural passages and the force of argument. The crucial thing is that we should rejoice in it. The knowledge that God enjoys perfect blessedness is a great thing. Even if it stays a kind of secret at the back of our minds, as something that we cannot say much about, it nevertheless exerts a tremendous gravitational pull on the rest of our thoughts and affections. Thomas Traherne said, "I have found that things unknown have a secret influence on the soul, and like the centre of the earth unseen violently attract it."[25]

Second, we should not build up our knowledge of the eternal Trinity by mere negatives, taking our own experience of life as the standard and then subtracting from it anything that would not characterize God's life. This negative approach to the knowledge of God may have its place, but that place is not here in the doctrine of the Trinity. In this doctrine we know only what God has positively revealed, so argument by negation has a limited place. We have already seen how counterfactuals can be helpful, when we imagined away everything but God and concluded that he would still be the Trinity. But the problem with overusing this negative mode of thinking is that when you have subtracted everything you can imagine from the internal life of God, you are left with nothing in your mind to think about, and it becomes impossible to conceive of that blankness as being more lively and interesting than what you have subtracted.

The life of God, considered in itself, is not still, or uneventful, or boring. If you think away the green grass and the course of history and the sidereal time of geological movement and all the music you have ever heard, what you have left is God. What you have to do with what is left is somehow acknowledge that he is more than what you have thought away. If you start with the baptism of Christ as an inner-Trinitarian conversation in which the Father and the Son are talking about our salvation, and take away the Jordan River, the incarnation, and the office of Messiah, you are left with no movement, shape, or color to focus on. But you still have to insist that the eternal divine conversation is bigger, livelier, and more wonderful than the things you have subtracted. It is impossible to get, by subtraction, to the absolute fullness of God's eternal life. That life is so full that everything else comes from it, as a small trickle from an infinite plenty.

Third, we should not fill out our knowledge of the life of the eternally triune God with elaborate, mythological imaginings. This is the perfect place for some realism and restraint in the use of the imagination in theological thinking. We know that God's life as Father, Son, and Spirit is eternally rich and full, but we do not know its details, and we should not manufacture them. We cannot describe the geography of the happy land of the Trinity. We do not know what kind of music the persons of the Trinity listen to, or what they cook for each other, or who does the dishes, or if they carpool. We do not know if they hold hands and do some kind of liturgical round-dance, as has often been suggested in some of the more purple theological literature. The perfect life of the blessed Trinity is lived above all worlds, including all worlds that we can fill out with imagined furnishings.

The main practical reason for learning how to think well about the eternal life of the Trinity is that it is the background for the gospel. The blessedness of God's inner life is the only thing that is even better than the good news. The life of God in itself is the source of all the riches that fund the economy of salvation. It is also the guarantee that God's grace is based on his character rather than on anything outside himself. Recall Susanna Wesley's statement: "He loved us because he loved us." This is why Paul calls the Christian message "the gospel of the glory of the blessed God" (1 Tim. 1:11). William Burkitt (1650–1703) explained why Paul used this phrase:

> He styles God the giver of that gospel, the blessed God; to signify thereby unto us, his transcendent mercy and excelling goodness, in that being infinitely happy in the enjoyment of himself and his divine perfections, and incapable of any profit from, or advantage by, his creatures, he was yet pleased to give us his Son, his gospel, his Holy Spirit, to qualify us for, and bring us to, the enjoyment of himself: According to the glorious gospel of the blessed God.[26]

The glory of the gospel is grounded in the blessedness of God, the eternal Trinity.

ETERNAL FATHER, ETERNAL SON, ETERNAL SPIRIT

We have seen that God is triune at the deepest level, at the level of who he essentially is rather than merely at the level of what he does. We have described how we ought to think about the fact that God is not just the Trinity when he chooses to go out to do things, but that he is Trinity "at home," as it were, in the happy land of the Trinity. God is Trinity primarily for himself and only secondarily for us. One of the consequences of this is that the Father has always been the Father, the Son has always been the Son, and the Holy Spirit has always been the Holy Spirit.

We meet the triune God as he gives himself to us in the history of salvation, as the Father, the Son, and the Holy Spirit. Specifically, we meet the Trinity as the incarnate Son, his heavenly Father who loves the world and elects a people, and the Holy Spirit of Pentecost, whom Jesus and the Father poured out on all flesh after the ascension of Christ. We meet them, that is, in the middle of their missions for us and our salvation. We might say that we meet a salvation-history Trinity, in the Bible and in our Christian experience. But the persons of the Trinity have a depth of life behind those missions, and that infinite depth is precisely what the actual doctrine of the Trinity points to.

Each of the three persons is unique in the way they reveal to us this dimension of infinite depth behind their presence, so we ought to attend to them in different ways. Perhaps the easiest one to understand is the Son. When Jesus Christ was conceived in the womb of the Virgin Mary and born in Bethlehem, he began his incarnate existence. He became fully and truly human, without ceasing to be fully and truly divine. But he, the person who became incarnate, had already existed before his human birth. He preexisted, in the absolute sense of the term. This is not true of any other human beginning, and it is the chief difference between Jesus and the rest of the human family (more foundational than his virgin birth or his sinlessness). All other humans come into existence from a state of nonexistence, and can only be said to preexist in the improper sense that in the hearts of their parents, or in the providence of God, plans and provisions have been made for them. But when it comes to the Son of God, we have a case of actual preexistence. It is not a paradox, for we do not say that Jesus preexists his own existence; we only say that the Son preexists his incarnation. The *pre-* in the doctrine of the preexistence of Christ points backward from his taking on human nature; that is the event which this person exists *pre-*.

Previous to the Word becoming flesh (John 1:14) by taking on human nature, the person who is Jesus Christ already existed. Admittedly, it is odd to call this person "Jesus Christ" before his birth in Bethlehem and his receiving a human name (Jesus) and title (Christ). You could say, if you wanted to be very precise, that he may have existed, but he wasn't

Jesus Christ yet. That is a distinction worth making. But there are several reasons not to enforce such scrupulosity in the way we talk about him. First, we know this person, and we have to call him something. "Unincarnate Word" is just not warm enough to call to mind all that we know about him based on his time among us. Second, there is biblical warrant. On those rare occasions when the Bible explicitly points back to the eternal depth behind the incarnation, it usually anchors its statements in the concrete name of Jesus. When Paul, for example, talks about the eternal Son and calls him Christ Jesus ("have this mind among yourselves, which is yours in Christ Jesus, who, though he was in the form of God . . ." Phil. 2:5–6), we should not rush to correct him: "Oh Paul, the pre-incarnate one was not yet Jesus nor Christ." Paul may be using the kind of shorthand we use when we say, "The sixteenth president of the United States was born in this cabin." At the time he was born, of course, he wasn't the sixteenth president of the U.S. and he may not yet have been named Abraham; he was an unnamed, mewling infant. And before Abe Lincoln was conceived, he was nothing, unless you want to count as preexistence such things as a twinkle in his father's eye, or the plan for Lincoln in the foreknowing mind of God. But unlike Abe Lincoln and everybody else, Jesus Christ was already somebody before he was the newborn infant of the first Christmas.

We should take note of the reason why all created analogies break down at one crucial point in understanding the doctrine of Christ's preexistence. When we say that Jesus Christ existed "pre" his incarnation, we do not mean he preceded it by any finite amount of time. The Son of God preexisted his incarnation the way the Creator preexisted creation: infinitely. Preexistence may be easy to say, but that one little syllable, *pre-*, is a quantum leap from Here to There, from time to eternity. Before you have finished saying that syllable, you have left behind everything measurable and manageable. Following the biblical argument that leads to this affirmation is one thing, but once you have followed the trail to the place where you confess, with the Christian church of all ages, the preexistence of Christ, you have framed a thought that catapults you into the being of God. Jesus Christ preexisted his incarnation eternally, as God.

But who was this person before he took on the nature of humanity, the name of Jesus, and the title of Christ? He was the Son of God. When the biblical authors say that God sent his Son into the world (John 20:21; Gal. 4:4; 1 John 4:14), gave his Son for the world's salvation (John 3:16; 1 John 4:10), or spoke definitively through his Son (Heb. 1:1), they are presupposing that the Son was already in existence as the Son, a person present with God the Father from eternity. He did not become the Son when he became incarnate; God did not so love the world that he gave somebody who became his Son in the act of being given. God, already having a Son, sent him into the world to become incarnate and to be a propitiation for our sins. So when the apostles encountered Jesus Christ, they were encountering "that which was from the beginning . . . the eternal life, which was with the Father and was made manifest to us." That is why they could claim to have "fellowship . . . with the Father and with his Son Jesus Christ" (1 John 1:1–4).[27]

Jesus Christ, then, is eternally the Son of God; or, he is the eternal Son, the second person of the Trinity. He is God the Son, in the first place, for Trinitarian reasons. He is called Son because he is the Son of the Father from all eternity. When he becomes incarnate, he becomes the son of Mary, the promised son of David, the Messiah. But there was never a time when he became the Son of God; that is who he eternally and essentially is. For us and our salvation, the eternal Son became the incarnate Son.

Having paid close attention to how the eternal Son made himself known, we can also see how, in the same central event of salvation history, the first person of the Trinity revealed the eternal depth behind his personhood. The first person of the Trinity is God the Father. God is called the Father, in the first place, for Trinitarian reasons. He is the Father because he is Father of the Son, from eternity, at home in the happy land of the Trinity. He did not become the Father at Christmas, or at any point in human history, or in any pre-temporal history. He did not undergo any transformation from being not-the-Father to being the Father. There was never a time when he existed as a solitary God without his Son, so he was always God the Father. This is a straightforward implication of confessing the deity of Christ. If Jesus is God the Son, God must always have included Son and Father.

Usually when we think about God the Father, we are tempted to consider his fatherhood as being grounded in something else besides this core Trinitarian basis. We tend to associate his fatherhood with the things he has freely chosen to do in salvation history. For example, God the Father predestined the chosen ones to be adopted as sons (Eph. 1:5), an act in which he determined himself to become the adoptive Father of the elect. But great as this saving, adoptive fatherhood is, it belongs in the sphere of something God does, not something that determines who he is. He would have been God the Father if he had never adopted created sons and daughters, because he would have been God the Father of God the Son. It is understandable that when we think of God the Father, our minds and hearts leap first to this gracious adoptive fatherhood. But there is something behind that adoptive fatherhood, and when we ask about the essential grounding of God's fatherhood, we must look further into the being of God, where we find a foundation of fatherhood that does not presuppose us. It would be a mistake to make the fatherhood of God the Father depend on human sons and daughters: he was the Father before we got here.

An even bigger mistake, however, is the more common one of thinking that the main reason God is "the Father" is that he has created, or "fathered," the world. In the few places where the Bible does talk about God as the parent of all creation, or the Father of all humanity, it tends to use this language in a metaphorical or poetic way (see Job 38:28; Acts 17:28). The main idea in Scripture is not that every creature already is a child of God the Father but that those who receive Jesus are given the right to become sons of God (John 1:12) on the basis of the work of Jesus, the essential Son of God. There was a school of thought in nineteenth-century liberal theology that proclaimed the central idea of Christianity to be "the fatherhood of God and the brotherhood of man."[28] Turned into a system, this idea of universal fatherhood was theologically disastrous. Classic FOGBOM (Fatherhood Of God, Brotherhood Of Man) liberalism made the gospel seem like a description of a general state of affairs rather than an announcement of what God has done in Christ; it was never able to account for sin or recognize the need for a costly redemption; and it quickly lost its grip on the doctrine of the Trinity.

But it is not only nineteenth-century liberals who made the mistake of thinking first of creation when they hear God called "Father." It is an easy mistake to make if we let our minds be guided by a general symbolism of fatherhood instead of by the main lines of biblical teaching. The generalized, cosmic idea of fatherhood is probably one of the reasons many people visualize God as an old, white-haired, bearded man. God the cosmic father is always devolving into God the cosmic grandpa in the popular mind. Scripture, by contrast, points to something very specific and much less sentimental when it calls God "the Father." It points to the fact that within the life of the one God, there is an eternal relationship of fatherhood and sonship. The first person is Father for Trinitarian reasons first of all. He is the Father of the Son by definition. That is who he is. Consequent to that is what he does: he acts to become the Father of those whom he predestined for adoption as sons (Eph. 1:5). Finally, in an extended or poetic sense, it may sometimes be appropriate to depict God's general love and care for all his creatures by using a parenting metaphor. But to start with cosmic fatherhood is exactly backwards. God did not have the world as his son; he so loved the world that he gave his only Son (John 3:16).

The same logic that we have seen with the Father and the Son applies also to the Holy Spirit: he is who he is for Trinitarian reasons, as the eternal third person of the Trinity. Based on that Trinitarian identity in which he exists together with the Father and the Son, he freely steps into the history of salvation and does what he does. The work of the Spirit is closely linked to that of the Son at every point. It is the Spirit who brings about the Son's incarnation by causing his conception in the womb of the virgin. It is the Spirit who anoints and empowers the Son in his messianic mission. And the Spirit is finally, at Pentecost, poured out on all flesh only when the Son's work is completed. The Spirit's work is to indwell believers, applying the work of Christ directly and personally to them. He is who he is as the eternal Spirit, and he does what he does in salvation history as the Spirit of Pentecost.

Because the eternal Son became the incarnate Son, we had much to say about his sonship. Tracing the line back from his appearance in Bethlehem is how we learned anything about the Trinity at all, for this is the central event in which God revealed that he had a Son. We had relatively less to say about the Father, and most of it was directly connected with the Son: the Father is the person of the Trinity who is obviously at the other end of the relationship that makes the Son the Son. But we have least of all to say about the eternal divine person who is the Holy Spirit, not because he is any less God, or any less a person, or any less related to the other persons of the Trinity. He is all those things, just as fully as the Father and the Son are. But his self-revelation is less direct than the Son's, and his relationship to the other persons is not as immediately evident as the Son's and Father's, whose mutual relationship is built into their very names. We should avoid the urge to fabricate more concrete things than have actually been revealed about the Spirit or to pretend that our knowledge of the Spirit's corner of the Trinitarian triangle is as intricately detailed and elaborated as the Son's.

The New Testament obviously features these three characters, the Father, the Son, and the Holy Spirit. Classically, Christian theology has traced these persons back to an eternal Trinity of God in himself. Since this threefoldness belongs to what God actually is rather than being only something he freely does, it has been called the ontological Trinity, the essential Trinity, or the Trinity of being. Theologians have also called it the immanent Trinity, because *immanent* means "internal to" itself.

Diagram 2.4: The Immanent Trinity

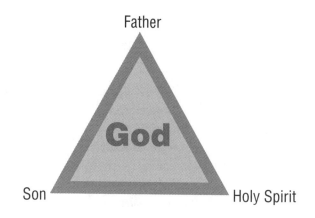

THE DEEP THINGS OF GOD

There are not many alternatives to taking this mental step back into the eternal Trinity. One alternative would be to say that God in himself is really unipersonal but that when he reveals himself to us, he reveals himself in different aspects as Father, Son, and Spirit. But that would mean that a unipersonal God shows himself as tri-personal, which is not properly showing himself at all, but showing precisely what he is not. Another alternative would be to say that a merely unipersonal God was first the Father, then the Son, and then the Spirit. But that kind of serial monotheism cannot do justice to the biblical episodes in which the Father and the Son address each other in interpersonal communication. A one-personed God who puts on different masks for different tasks, or goes into different modes when he is in different moods, or plays different roles with different rules, is not the Trinity of the Christian faith.

Another alternative to the classical position would be to admit that there are three persons in the one being of God but to refuse to apply the names "Father," "Son," and "Holy Spirit" to those three, except in their outward actions. That is, we could say that the three persons we encounter in salvation history do actually reveal that the one God is eternally and internally three persons but restrict the names "Father" and "Son" and "Holy Spirit" to the level of what God does for us and shows us in salvation history. We would then remain agnostic about what the three persons might be in themselves, at home in the happy land of the Trinity. Here, for us, they might be Father, Son, and Spirit. But if we took this third alternative, we would have to say nearly nothing about who they are in themselves. Perhaps they would be indistinguishable if it were not for the incarnation, or perhaps only they could tell each other apart by some unrevealed, secret distinctions. As far as we would know, however, there would be no Father, Son, or Spirit in heaven: only The Anonymous Three.

To settle for such limited knowledge of the Trinity would be a theological tragedy, not as bad as the heretical modalisms of the other alternatives but still quite debilitating for Christian faith. We know much more than that there are three somebodys in God. When the Word became flesh and dwelt among us, the glory that he showed the apostles was "glory as of the only Son from the Father" (John 1:14). We have met the Son and the Holy Spirit, in person, as the Father has sent them into human history. The Christian experience of salvation is an encounter with the true God as he truly exists: as Father, Son, and Holy Spirit. We certainly do not know everything about the persons of the Trinity, but what we do know extends all the way into who God is, internally, eternally, and essentially.

Once we have confessed that the one God is a Trinity of the eternal Father, the eternal Son, and the eternal Spirit, there is one more conceptual step we should take. It is the step that makes the best sense of the biblical revelation of the Trinity, and it is also the step recommended by the classic tradition of Christian doctrine. The basic idea is that there are relationships of origin in the life of the Trinity. Once again, the best place to see this is in the revelation of who the Son is. The second person of the Trinity is eternally the Son of the Father, but there are certain elements of sonship, as we know it among humans, that could not apply to a son who is eternal and essential. For one thing, he could not be younger than his father. For another thing, he could not be one of many possible sons, because he exhausts the totality of essential sonship in himself. For similar reasons, he could not have a mother. When all these aspects of sonship as we know it are subtracted, what is left? Two things. First, the Son cannot be a different kind of being than his Father. A Father may create a statue or a house out of something besides himself, but a Son comes from his very being. He is not a lower order of being but is on the same level as the Father. Second, the Son stands in that relationship of originating from the Father—he comes from the Father. The classic word for that relation of origin is *begetting*, so we say that the Father begets the Son.

If we wanted to speak as minimally and modestly as possible about it, we could say that the relationship between the Father and the Son is that the Father fathers the Son. But what we want is a more direct way of characterizing the relationship, not just a repetition of the same term. We could say the Father sires the Son, but *sire* is an old-fashioned word that now evokes only thoughts of horse-breeding. What Christian doctrine has classically said is that the Father begets or generates the Son. *Beget* is also an old-fashioned word, but for most hearers it carries with it no connotations beyond sounding like the King James Version of the Bible. If we call it eternal begetting or eternal generation, we are only guarding ourselves against possible misunderstandings. It is not that once upon a time the Father begat the Son, having previously not begotten the Son. No, the eternal Father and the eternal Son have always existed together, the Son always standing in this relationship of from-ness or begottenness from the Father. Once again, the same logic extends to the Holy Spirit, though, once again, with less explicitness or clarity. He is eternally from the Father, but since he is not the Son, we use a different word to secure and specify his eternal relation. Traditionally, since "Spirit" means "breath," the word "breathing" has been applied to the relation of origin of the Spirit.

This is the classic way of describing the eternal life of the triune God in itself. In the happy land of the Trinity above all worlds, God eternally exists as Father, Son, and Holy Spirit. This is who God is, in absolute logical priority over what he freely chooses to do. Without reference to creation or redemption, the perfectly blessed life that God lives is a life as the Father who always has his only begotten Son and his uniquely breathed-out Spirit in fellowship with him. The ontological Trinity (also called the immanent Trinity) includes these eternal relations of origin.

Diagram 2.5: The Immanent Trinity with Relations of Origin

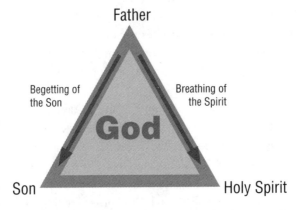

Is it really necessary to affirm these eternal relations of origin? I believe it is. The doctrine of the Trinity is not something we have learned from general logical principles, from natural revelation, or from common sense. It is a truth about God that is only made known by special revelation. As a result, Trinitarian theology needs to handle its knowledge in a particularly careful way. Above all, the doctrine of the Trinity should not be stated in a way that goes one step beyond what God has revealed. The secret things belong to the Lord! Evangelical Protestants are likely to be good guardians of that boundary line. But there is another boundary line marking off the opposite error: we should also take pains to ensure that we make the most of everything that has been revealed. Trinitarian information is a precious theological commodity, and we should never be found falling short of receiving what God has made known. The things revealed belong to us and to our children forever! Eternal divine sonship is revealed, and calling it eternal generation has been the classic Christian way of ensuring that we keep a firm grasp on the meaning of sonship.[29] Trinitarian theology affirms this about God the Trinity: the Son and the Spirit stand in particular relationships to the Father, and those relationships are relationships of origin. The Son and the Spirit come from the Father and always have.

A GOSPEL THAT STARTS OUTSIDE OF YOU

The rest of this book is about how the Trinity is the gospel. The fact that God the Father saved us by sending the Son and the Holy Spirit: this is the good news. This chapter, though, has taken one step back from the incarnate Son and the outpoured Spirit, and we have contemplated the depth of God's triune life in itself. Whereas the Trinity in salvation history just is the gospel, the Trinity in itself is the background of the gospel. It is the presupposition of the good news, since "God for us" makes sense only if there is such a thing as "God in himself." In order to prepare ourselves to understand the good news better, we have tried to peer into the infinite depth out of which that gospel comes to us. The burden of this chapter has not yet been the actual gospel, and we have not yet looked closely at the Father's sending of the Son and the Spirit. In order to contemplate the ontological Trinity, of course, we had to start with the salvation-historical Trinity. We couldn't have started anywhere else, because the Trinity is a revealed doctrine, and it was revealed when Christ and the Holy Spirit showed up. It was the sending of the Son on the mission of incarnation and atonement that gave us the starting-point for discerning his eternal sonship and revealed the proper meaning of the fatherhood of God the Father. We followed a parallel line for the Holy Spirit, from his sending at Pentecost back into his eternal procession from the Father.

But we have also said that the eternal life of God in himself is something "even better than the good news," if it is possible to say so reverently. What we mean by this is that God's eternal life as Father, Son, and Holy Spirit is a thing of infinite blessedness and perfection. There is a blessed God at the core of the glorious gospel. God in himself is perfect, and perfectly happy. Being perfect, he cannot essentially improve. Susannah Wesley told us that God is "perfect essential blessedness," a being "that cannot possibly receive any accession of perfection or happiness from his creatures." He can make happiness and blessedness available to those creatures because he always already has it. This vision of a God with no unmet needs is a glimpse of the depths of the living God and the fund out of which he spends himself so freely in the economy of salvation.

The good news, in other words, starts far outside of us, in the life of the blessed Trinity which is complete in itself and suffers from no lack. This is not a cold abstraction, but a great thing worth praising God for. John Piper has worked hard to remind Christians that "God's glory consists much in the fact that he is happy beyond our wildest imagination." His 1986 book *Desiring God* is mostly devoted to the way "Christian hedonism," or living to enjoy God, works its way out in every area of the Christian life (Scripture, prayer, money, missions, marriage, suffering, etc.). But Piper builds all these practical points, necessarily, on the solid foundation of "the happiness of God" as an eternal Trinitarian event of the Father and the Son rejoicing in each other's presence. While he admits that "we stand at the foothills of mystery in all these things," Piper also affirms that "the Scriptures have given us some glimpses of the heights."[30] Those heights are Trinitarian:

> Within the triune Godhead (Father, Son, and Holy Spirit), God has been uppermost in his own affections for all eternity. This belongs to his very nature, for he has begotten and loved the Son from all eternity. Therefore God has been supremely and eternally happy in the fellowship of the Trinity.[31]

It may seem counterintuitive to start so far back in the divine mystery of God's own being, if the goal is to change lives. The cry in our day always seems to be for a practical doctrine of the Trinity, for relevance, application, and experiential payoff. Indeed, it is true that the doctrine of the Trinity changes everything about Christian life. But the wisest Christian teachers have always known that shortcuts to relevance are self-defeating. In bypassing the deep sources of reality, they not only miss the truth but ultimately deliver less practical benefit. When it comes to the difference that the doctrine of the Trinity can make in our lives, it is crucially important that we begin with a recognition of God in himself before moving on to God for us. What we need to begin with is a profoundly impractical doctrine of the Trinity. With that in place, we can really get something done.

Some of the benefits of taking our stand on the doctrine of the ontological Trinity can be clarified by double negatives. This doctrine expels bad ideas about God. Just think of the many unworthy ideas and attitudes about God that the doctrine of the Trinity can help us name, reject, and even deride. The doctrine of the Trinity expels unworthy ideas about the perfection of God's life. It is unworthy to think that God without us is lonely or bored. God is not looking for something to do in the happy land of the Trinity. God did not create the world in order to fill the drafty mansion of heaven with the pitter-patter of little feet. God is not pining away for companionship in a lonesome heaven. Good theological reflection, taking its lead from the Bible, would always reject the idea of divine loneliness or boredom. But as soon as you entertain the truth of the doctrine of the ontological Trinity, the unworthiness of the idea of a lonely or bored God becomes patently obvious. The triune God is one, but not solitary. Nothing that God does in creation or redemption is done because God lacked employment and occupation. The incarnation of the Son of God was not undertaken as an excellent adventure to provide diversion from the dullness of being the eternal Son. All these ideas are unworthy of God, as the doctrine of the Trinity makes obvious.

The doctrine of the Trinity expels a host of unworthy ideas about God's love. The tri-personal love of God is not a love that needs any completion. Consequently, we should avoid presenting the gospel in a way that suggests God is begging us to come back home so he can

finally be happy again, as if our redemption repairs a breach that rup-
tured the blessedness of God. It is unworthy of the glorious gospel of
the blessed God to give the impression that we are begging for people
to please be reconciled to God so his life won't be ruined by sadness.
It is an alienation of affections to think that the love at the heart of the
universe is a romantic love in which the creature yearns for the Creator
or in which God yearns for the souls of the lost. That kind of love takes
second place to the love we have learned about from Jesus: the love of
the Father for the Son, and the Son for the Father, in the unity of the
Holy Spirit. It is certainly true that God loves you and has a wonderful plan for your life.[32] But behind that famous "spiritual law" is the
eternal love of the Father for the Son in the happy land of the Trinity.
"Nothing shines more radiantly in the New Testament than the eternal
love of the Father for the Son (John 1:18; 5:20; 17:24, etc.)," wrote
Bishop H. C. G. Moule.[33]

The doctrine of the Trinity expels a host of unworthy ideas and
attitudes about God's glory. God displays his glory to creatures, chiefly
through redemption. But it is unworthy to think that God without us
would have nobody to show his glory to. The Father is always delighting in the beloved Son, and the Son is always adoring his holy Father
in the unity of the Holy Spirit. Robert Leighton said, "It is most true of
that Blessed Trinity, *Satis amplum alter alteri theatrum sumus*"; that is,
each is to the other a theater large enough.[34] Furthermore, God arranges
all things to the end that they promote and proclaim his own glory, but
the doctrine of the Trinity shows one of the ways that this divine self-
glorification is unselfish. In it, the persons of the Trinity bring about the
more conspicuous display of each other's glory.

In this glance at the way the doctrine of the Trinity expels unworthy ideas, we have taken a very negative approach to what the doctrine
shows about God. It shows that God is not lonely, or bored, or selfish.
But if we turned it around and said it in a positive way, we would simply
say that God is love. Not by coincidence, this is also how the Bible puts
it. This is what the doctrine of the Trinity helps us learn with greater
precision: that God is love. The triune God is a love that is infinitely
high above you, eternally preceding you, and welcoming you in.

3

SO GREAT SALVATION

(Or, The Depth of the Gospel)

The things of the gospel are depths. The things of the gospel . . .
are the deep things of God.

THOMAS GOODWIN

How shall we escape, if we neglect so great salvation?

HEBREWS 2:3 (KJV)

Usually evangelicals get only a few steps down the road of theological reflection before they begin asking for reassurances that the trip is going to be worthwhile. They often express this in the curt question, Is this necessary for salvation? Bad motives may lurk behind such a question: shortsighted pragmatism, intellectual laziness, a desire to reduce everything in Christianity to the bare minimum of experiential, and preferably emotional, accessibility. There's no use denying that these traits do exist in evangelical churches, and formally the question itself is dismayingly similar to the questions, Will this be on the test? and Can I get to heaven without thinking about this?

But the question also gives voice to a deep-seated evangelical instinct that is surely right. Everything in the Christian faith should be connected, clearly and directly, to the one central thing, the gospel of salvation in Christ. If there is not the closest possible connection between Trinity and gospel, then arguments about Trinitarian patterns latent in Bible study (chap. 6) and prayer (chap. 7) are relatively insignificant. These church practices would point to interesting social phenomena in a certain subculture but would not touch the heart of evangelical existence, the central point that gives life to all the rest—salvation.

Anybody who wants to win the hearts of evangelicals will have to talk about salvation, because that's where evangelical hearts are. They are gospel people or they are nothing. When they are confronted with a complex doctrine, as the doctrine of the Trinity undeniably is, they quickly become restless and demand some proof that the intellectual journey they're being invited to undertake is actually going to pay off in terms of understanding the gospel. The central claim of this book is that the Trinity is the gospel. Seeing how closely these two go together depends on seeing both Trinity and gospel as clearly as possible, in a large enough perspective to discern their overall forms. When the outlines of both are clear, we should experience the shock of recognition: Trinity and gospel have the same shape! This is because the good news of salvation is ultimately that God opens his Trinitarian life to us. Every other blessing is either a preparation for that or a result of it, but the thing itself is God's graciously taking us into the fellowship of Father, Son, and Holy Spirit, to be our salvation. It will take the next three chapters to develop the entire argument, examining the size of the gospel, the shape of the gospel, and the crucial point of access by which we are brought into the gospel. This chapter takes up only the first of those tasks.

THE SIZE OF THE GOSPEL

To discern the size of anything, you have to be able to locate its edges. Where are the edges of the gospel, and what is its size? J. B. Phillips once wrote a book with such a great title that people feel enlightened simply by hearing it, whether they go on to read the book or not. The book is good, but it can hardly measure up to its own name, which is *Your God Is Too Small*. Those five syllables jar the mind with the suggestion of something inconceivably vast and free and at the same time the danger of settling for a pale imitation of it. I have often thought about writing a book with the title *Your Gospel Is Too Small*, and as G. K. Chesterton once said, "Like every book I never wrote, it is by far the best book I have ever written."[1] This nonexistent book is filled with thrilling accounts of the rediscovery of the riches of the gospel and of believers' reawakening to the fullness of what belongs to them in Christ after desperate years of trying to eke out a Christian existence in self-imposed scarcity of spiritual resources. And the surprise ending of this best-seller is that their gospel was too small precisely because their God was too small. Thinking inadequate thoughts about the holiness and love of God, they could not help having inadequate conceptions of the salvation he has provided. The gospel so outstrips our created measurements that it can be measured only against something as immense as God himself. Since the only thing as immense as God himself is God himself, we must look to him to get our bearings on the magnitude of the gospel.

There is one place in Scripture where this sheer greatness of the gospel is most profusely described: the blessing with which Paul opens the epistle to the Ephesians. Paul begins by praising God for the gift of the gospel: "Blessed be the God and Father of our Lord Jesus Christ, who has blessed us in Christ with every spiritual blessing in the heavenly places," and then he takes a deep breath and starts counting out those blessings, one after another, in a 202-word avalanche of praise without pause or punctuation in verses 3 through14.[2] Paul speaks here from the fullness of his heart as well as the keenness of his insight. The theme of "blessing" overwhelms him and pushes him to compose a correspondingly overwhelming sentence. It runs from heaven to earth, taking sudden turns and detours as it doubles and triples back on itself, oscillating between God and man and circling its subject to view it from every angle. For all this wildness, the blessing has also a stateliness and coherence which reflects the wisdom which it praises. No translation or paraphrase can capture it all definitively, but here is one of the possibilities:

God chose us in Christ
before the ground of the world was laid
to be holy and blameless before him;
In his love he determined us in advance
for adoption into sonship through Jesus Christ
through the good pleasure of his will
to the praise of his glorious grace —

Grace which God graced us with in the Beloved
through whose blood we have redemption,
the forgiveness of sins,
according to the riches of his grace
which he poured out on us in abundance;
In all wisdom and insight
he made us know the mystery of his will
according to his own counsel,
which he had settled beforehand in Christ:
through an economy in which, when the times were fulfilled,
he would sum up everything, things in heaven and things on earth,
under one heading: Christ!
In him we too have been given an inheritance
as we were predestined according to the purpose
of the one who works out everything
in accord with the counsel of his will
So that we would be a praise of his glory;

We who were the first to hope in Christ, who you also,
—you who have heard the word of truth,
the gospel of your salvation—
when you believed, you were sealed in Christ
with the promised Holy Spirit,
who is the down payment on what we will inherit
when God redeems his own possession
to the praise of his glory.

Every line, and nearly every word, of the great blessing could prof-
itably be unpacked at length. However, in order to clarify the way it
shows the size and shape of the gospel, we can stay out of the details and
notice instead only two things about the passage as a whole: first, that it
is unmanageably large and complex, and second, that it has a decidedly
Trinitarian contour.[3] The blessing of the gospel, in other words, is big
and God-shaped.

First let us attend to its size and complexity, leaving its shape until
the next chapter. In this translation I intentionally divided the blessing
into three sections to highlight its Trinitarian logic, from the electing
and adopting Father, through the redeeming and revealing Son, to the
promised and sealing Spirit. But if the sentence is, as some commenta-

tors have said, "a monster," I hope I have done nothing to domesticate it.[4] The wildness of the blessing is an important aspect of it, and the reader who does not feel some degree of vertigo from its outrageous breadth of thought is not reading it properly. It contains more ideas, pointing in more directions, than anyone could reasonably be expected to take in. On the basis of Ephesians 1:3–14, nobody can accuse Paul of having a gospel that is too small. There is an abundance here bordering on excessiveness. And Paul's sentence has that character precisely because, as Scripture breathed out by God, it faithfully corresponds to the character of the reality it points us to: a gospel of salvation that is the work of the untamable holy Trinity. Like all Scripture, this passage is the word of God and has within itself the life, activity, and incisiveness we would expect in an almighty speech-act through which God does his work (Heb. 4:12). It is an effective word, and one of its effects here is to snatch its listeners out of their own lives and drop them into Christ. It immediately takes the reader to the heavenlies, to the world of the Spirit, and from that vantage point invites us to join in blessing God for the blessing he blessed us with.

The reason Paul starts the letter with such a disorienting blast is that he is summoning us to praise God, and in order to praise God rightly the thing we need most is a good dose of disorientation. All of us think from our own point of view, starting from a center in ourselves and how things look to us. This is unavoidable, since everyone has to start from where they are. It is simply how finite minds work and is not even related to the kind of self-centeredness that is sinful. However, when finite minds come to encounter the infinite God, we run the risk of adding God to the catalog of items we are interested in studying, or acquiring, or reaping some benefits from. Especially when the issue is the blessing of salvation, the danger is great that the finite mind will treat God and his blessings as enhancements to be added to our lives. The only way to escape this tendency is to be drawn out of ourselves into the bewilderingly large and complex gospel of God. The excessiveness of Paul's sentence seeks to disorient our existing categories in order to reorient us by drawing us in to the divine orientation. What we need is the miracle of being able to see our own situation from an infinitely higher point of view. We need to start our thinking from a center in God, not in ourselves. If it is not too much of a pun, Paul invites us to an ecstatic gospel: the good news of standing outside (*ek-stasis*) of ourselves.

Paul doesn't expect to pound his readers rhetorically into adopting the right point of view. He may have composed a stunning sentence to start his letter, but he knows that nobody has the resources for that cognitive leap to thinking from a center in God. No writer can express that point of view effectively, and no reader can learn it directly. A miracle has to happen.[5] That is why Paul's argumentation and description are linked with invocation throughout the letter. Immediately after the blessing he prays for a divine gift of spiritual revelation and illumination:

> [I pray] . . . that the God of our Lord Jesus Christ, the Father of glory, may give you a spirit of wisdom and of revelation in the knowledge of him, having the eyes of your heart enlightened, that you may know . . . (Eph. 1:17–18)[6]

And in the third chapter Paul prays for his readers to comprehend all the dimensions of this truth, and to "know the love of Christ that surpasses knowledge" (v. 19). Fully aware that he is asking for what is humanly impossible, Paul plays "knowing" and "unknowable" off of each other oxymoronically. He is not being absurd; rather he "makes a seemingly absurd combination of opposites in order to emphasize a particular point."[7] To underline our need for this direct revelation even more, Paul urges his readers to give glory to God, who "is able to do far more abundantly than all that we ask or think" (v. 20), or, in an overly literal translation as awkward as the original Greek, "who is superabundantly able beyond everything we can ask or think."

The strategy of Ephesians is to give us a bird's-eye view of the gospel, which is only available from a vantage point far above all created powers. When by the grace of God that miracle of reorientation happens, we are not just ready to read Ephesians, but we are already taken in to the spiritual blessing of God in Christ. After all, the only "standing outside of ourselves" that really results in salvation is standing "in Christ," a phrase which Paul hammers home at least once in each verse of the sentence.[8]

Because of the singular power with which Ephesians focuses on this message, the epistle has always had its special devotees throughout church history. The greatest of all theological commentators on Ephesians is the Puritan Thomas Goodwin (1600–1679), whose massive commentary on the book is at once a detailed verse-by-verse exposition and a masterful synthesis of all that is best in the Puritan Reformed vision. In the first few verses, Goodwin spots the character of God's blessing as being ultimately coterminous with God himself. Before expounding the great blessing of Ephesians 1:3–14 word by word, Goodwin establishes the larger picture: "Not only God doth bless with all other good things, but above all by communicating himself and his own blessedness unto them."[9] The blessing of the gospel is essentially God declaring, "'Thou shalt have all my blessedness to make thee blessed,' which the Apostle fitly renders, Eph. 3, 'being filled with all the fulness of God;' and indeed all things else without God or besides God could never make us blessed."[10]

HAVE EVANGELICALS BELIEVED THIS?

What we have been calling, metaphorically, the "size of the gospel" surveyed in Ephesians is something with which the evangelical tradition is quite familiar. I am not trying to be shocking or innovative when I say the gospel is God-sized; I am only reiterating what evangelicalism has long known and confessed. I call here a handful of evangelical witnesses to testify to the fact. These voices do not prove that the gospel is as comprehensive as I assert; they only demonstrate that evangelicals have a heritage of saying so.

It was, for example, a constant theme of A. B. Simpson (1843–1919), founder of the Christian and Missionary Alliance. His classic book *A Larger Christian Life* shows this preoccupation with abundance and excess in its title and in most of its chapter titles: "More than Conquerors," "Grace Abounding," "From Strength to Strength," "God's Measureless Measures," "Spiritual Growth, Enlarged Work." Speaking specifically about the way Ephesians articulates the message, he says,

If we would rise to the full measure of God's standard for us, let us realize the magnitude of God as well as of our own being, for it is with nothing less than Himself that He means to fill us. Let us take in the full dimensions of His resources of grace, their length, their breadth, their depth, their height; and then let us measure, if we can, the magnitude of God who is the living substance and personal source of all this grace, and we shall have some approximation at least to what the apostle means when he exclaims, "Now unto Him that is able to do exceeding abundantly above all that we ask or think, according to the power that worketh in us, unto Him be glory in the church by Christ Jesus, throughout all ages, world without end. Amen."[11]

So fluent was Simpson in the rhetoric of gospel abundance that he wrote hymns saturated in the theme:

The mercy of God is an ocean divine,
A boundless and fathomless flood.
Launch out in the deep, cut away the shore line,
And be lost in the fullness of God.[12]

Admittedly, "lost in the fullness of God" may sound a bit overly mystical, and language like that may bring to mind the anti-mystical remark, "I'd rather be found in Christ than lost in God."[13] If we are going to discuss subjects like the fullness of the gospel, however, we will have to come to terms with the mystic. There are some subjects that impel us to use such language, whether we are temperamentally prone to it or not. Adolph Saphir (1831–1891) thought it wise to open his greatest book on the Christian life with the sentence, "Not every mystic is a Christian, but every Christian is a mystic."[14] When Paul reflects on his work as a preacher of the gospel to Gentile and Jew without distinction, he describes himself as "a steward of the mysteries of God." We will devote more space to this in the final chapter.

Without running right up to the brink of the mystical, however, we can see that evangelical history is full of reforms, revivals, and awakenings that left believers astonished with the sudden reappearance of the sheer scope and reach of the gospel. Every time a group names itself "the full gospel" something or another, it implies that somebody somewhere was living with only a partial gospel. What they are saying, in their own idiom, is that they have discovered that the gospel is a great thing, and that it includes whole regions of insight and experience that beg to be explored. R. A. Torrey (1856–1928) reports that he was counseling with a man whose life as a Christian was so dominated by sin that he was forced to question whether he was saved. Listening to the man's testimony, Torrey mused, "That sounds like an evangelical conversion." But as he pressed for further insight, Torrey suddenly grasped the problem and told the man: "You only believed half of the Gospel, that Christ died for our sins according to the Scriptures, and was buried. Will you now believe the other half of the Gospel? Will you believe that He rose again?" The man heartily agreed, and Torrey summarized the fullness of truth he had been led into:

> Christ not only died, but He rose again, and is a living Saviour to-night. He has all power in Heaven and on earth, and the devil is no match for Him; the risen Christ has power to snap the fetters of strong drink, to snap the fetters of opium, to snap the fetters of lust, and of every sin; and if you will trust Him to do it for you, He will do it.[15]

The catalog of sins ("strong drink . . . opium") is Victorian, but the instinct is perennial: evangelicals are constantly daring themselves, each other, and the world to embrace the entire gospel rather than a fragment of it. They have a vision of the scale and scope of salvation, because they understand that salvation must be measured against the competence and capacity of the one doing the saving.

The Savior, as we are told in Hebrews 7:25, is "able to save to the uttermost them that come unto God by him." I quote this in the King James Version because (like the title of this chapter) it was that particular combination of words which stuck in the minds of English-speaking evangelicals and became a motto for embracing the full scope of the gospel. Two of evangelicalism's greatest preachers, John Wesley (1703–1791) and C. H. Spurgeon (1834–1892), were drawn to these words repeatedly. Wesley cited them often, and in his *Notes on the New Testament* explained the "uttermost" of Hebrews 7:25 as "all the guilt, power, root, and consequence of sin."[16] Wesley preached a version of full salvation that struck many as outrageously optimistic about how far salvation could go in personal transformation. Defending the message of the early Methodists, Wesley wrote that "what most surprised us, was, that we were said to 'dishonour Christ,' by asserting that he 'saveth to the uttermost;' by maintaining he will reign in our hearts alone, and subdue all things to himself."[17]

Spurgeon too was warm to the words "saved to the uttermost" and asked his audiences, "How far can salvation go? What are its limits and its boundaries? Christ is a Saviour: how far is he able to save?"[18] For Spurgeon, the outrageous scope of this salvation extended to the eternal security and perseverance of the saved: "Wherever I go, I hope always to bear my hearty protest against the most accursed doctrine of a saint's falling away and perishing." Spurgeon saw the character of the gospel as total, final, and comprehensive, and articulated it especially in terms of its permanence.

Never mind that each of these preachers tended to elaborate on the same text by appealing to their own characteristic theological emphases. Spurgeon, who drew power from his Calvinist convictions, preached "the uttermost" as an unshakeable assurance of salvation grounded in the perseverance of the saints. Wesley, with a vision of perfect holiness, pictured "the uttermost" as entire sanctification. It would be all too easy to dwell on their differences (which I have not attempted to conceal), and it would conveniently allow us to evade the challenge which, with one united voice, they present to any age that diminishes the gospel. The fact that Spurgeon had a Calvinist uttermost and Wesley had a holiness uttermost is insignificant compared to the more basic fact that both of them had big thoughts about the gospel and pushed hard to communicate them. They perceived the scope of salvation and struggled to frame thoughts big enough to accommodate it. Neither of them could be reproached with "your gospel is too small."

A gospel which is only about the moment of conversion but does not extend to every moment of life in Christ is too small. A gospel that gets your sins forgiven but offers no power for transformation is too small. A gospel that isolates one of the benefits of union with Christ and ignores all the others is too small. A gospel that must be measured by your own moral conduct, social conscience, or religious experience is too small. A gospel that rearranges the components of your life but does not put you personally in the presence of God is too small.

DECADENTLY NEGLECTING SO GREAT SALVATION

Early in the book of Hebrews, the author asks an alarming question: "How shall we escape, if we neglect so great salvation?" (Heb. 2:3 KJV). The old covenant was glorious: administered by angels, shining with glory, bringing knowledge of the true God. But the new covenant, the gospel, is incomprehensibly greater. It was not spoken through angels (v. 2), but spoken by God the Father through the Lord Jesus himself in person (v. 3, echoing 1:1, where God has spoken in his Son), and authenticated by the Holy Spirit (v. 4). "Neglecting" it means undervaluing it or failing to acknowledge how great it is. What is this "great salvation" we should pay heed to? How great is it? As Spurgeon asked, "How far does salvation go?"

A besetting problem in recent evangelicalism, in contrast to the older evangelical tradition, is the tendency we have been describing of treating salvation as less than it is. Some people think of salvation as nothing but forgiveness, perhaps a do-over or a clean slate to try not messing up again. Others have bigger ideas about forgiveness, thinking of salvation as forgiveness-in-advance for all future sins. If that's all salvation is, it could easily lead to antinomianism. In reaction to this, some people view salvation as an opportunity for moral reform: you can tell who is a Christian by seeing who is moral, or at least who is making moral progress. It is possible to pick and choose from the elements of the faith, to produce your own lethal mixture of the elements.

There are Christians whose three cardinal doctrines are (1) once saved always saved; (2) perfection on earth is impossible; (3) my future sins are already forgiven. These are less of a doctrinal system and more of a plan for excusing carnality. This kind of Christianity is matched by its evil opposite, which holds three truths to be scripturally evident above all else: (1) faith without works is dead; (2) nobody goes to heaven without true holiness; (3) we have free will. These are less of a doctrinal system and more of a declaration of intent to pursue righteousness by works. Any of these propositions might underwrite a healthy life of faith if placed in their proper contexts. But taken by them-

THE DEEP THINGS OF GOD

selves, or combined with other emphases that reinforce their dangers without balancing them out, they are disastrous.

For some evangelicals, salvation is an experience of conversion, a moment of religious encounter in which you decide to believe the gospel, to accept Jesus, and to identify yourself from now on as Christian. For others, salvation is a better attitude made possible by God's changing his mind about you: he used to scowl, but now he smiles. Some people think of it as missing hell and hitting heaven.

There are "gospels of sin management,"[19] gospels of prosperity,[20] and gospels of self-esteem. In these last three examples, the "gospels" on offer are obviously not good news at all but very bad news indeed: not *evangel*, but *dysangel*. J. C. Ryle (1816–1900) noted that the gospel is "a most curiously and delicately compounded medicine, and a medicine that is very easily spoiled." It can be spoiled, he said, by substitution, addition, interposition, or disproportion.[21] That's why Paul warned the Galatians that "another gospel" is not really a gospel at all, and its preachers are not evangelists but anathema.

But the earlier examples sound at least partly right: doesn't salvation include forgiveness, assurance, an experience of conversion, straightening out your life, and heaven when you die? Certainly it does. But it is not reducible to any of these things, and it can't be cobbled together just by making a long enough list of elements like these, even if they are biblically warranted elements. Underneath all these is the thing itself, the gospel. The gospel is the underlying reality that gives rise to all these benefits. The salvation that we are in danger of undervaluing is in itself a great thing, which radiates blessings and benefits in every direction, at all levels. "Don't neglect so great salvation" implies both a gift and a task: to have experienced salvation is to have received an incomparably great gift, but to esteem it as it deserves is a dauntingly great task. God put his own Spirit into us not only to give us something but to make us understand what it is that we've been given: "Now we have received not the spirit of the world, but the Spirit who is from God, that we might understand the things freely given us by God" (1 Cor. 2:12).

Every one who is saved is by definition in possession of this great thing. But think how poorly some Christians articulate what they have. Faced with this enormous blessing in its staggering scope and its manifold complexity, we do what we can to get it under control. We've learned a useful label that we can use to signify it for purposes of communication: we say we're saved. If we have to explain what saved means, we add the next most comfortable term: "born again." Pushed past that, we may supply words like "forgiven," or "redeemed" (though that sounds a bit fancy), or specify that we are Christians, or go on to explain that we have a personal relationship with Jesus, or have accepted him into our hearts. Any of these, or all of them together, may get the job of communication done. They work especially well if we're talking to somebody who shares the experience and only needs to be shown a flash card in order to identify the thing itself. But taken by themselves, these words we use can come to seem abstract. I often encounter believers who wonder why the language "personal relationship with Jesus" isn't in the Bible, and if they should quit using it, and what it means.

In these cases, our problem is not so much that we've distorted the gospel by adding to it or taking away from it. The problem is that we have taken one true element of it and characterized the whole by that part. Our situation is like the legend of the six blind men who encountered the elephant: one leaned against its side and said "elephants are like walls." Another felt its leg and said "elephants are like trees" and so on until each of them had described the elephant as like a snake (the trunk), a spear (the tusk), a fan (the ear), and a rope (the tail). Each of them had grasped something real, but because of their blindness none of them could produce overall descriptions that did justice to the reality. Even combining the six descriptions would not solve the problem, because no matter how you arrange a wall, a tree, a snake, a spear, a fan, and a rope, you will not assemble anything worthy of the name "elephant."

All cultures and subcultures move through stages, and evangelicalism is, among other things, a distinct subculture of Christianity. In cultural terms, a classical period is a time when all the parts of a community's life seem to hang together, mutually reinforce each other, and make intuitive sense. By contrast, a decadent period is marked by dissolution of all the most important unities, a sense that whatever initial force gave impetus and meaningful form to the culture has pretty much spent its power. Decadence is a falling off, a falling apart from a previous unity.

Inhabitants of a decadent culture feel themselves to be living among the scraps and fragments of something that must have made sense to a previous generation but which now seem more like a pile of unrelated items. Decadent cultures feel unable to articulate the reasons for connecting things to each other. They spend a lot of time staring at isolated fragments, unable to combine them into meaningful wholes. They start all their important speeches by quoting Yeats's overused line, "Things fall apart, the center cannot hold. Mere anarchy is loosed upon the world." Decadents either fetishize their tribal and party distinctions or mix absolutely everything together in one sloppy combination. Not everybody in a decadent culture even feels a need to work toward articulating unities, but those who do make the attempt face a baffling challenge. At best, the experience is somewhat like working a jigsaw puzzle without the guidance of the finished image from the box top; at worst, it is like undertaking that task while fighting back the slow horror of realization that what you have in front of you are pieces that come from several different puzzles, none of them complete or related. Evangelicalism in our lifetime seems to be in a decadent period. In some sectors of the evangelical subculture, there is not even a living cultural memory of a classical period or golden age; what we experience is decadence all the way back.

Under conditions of decadence, two types of reaction typically occur. Conservative temperaments tend to grab up all the fragments and insist on keeping them as they were found. They may be totally inert lumps that nobody knows how to make use of, but the conservative will faithfully preserve them as museum pieces. Liberal temperaments, on the other hand, tend to toss the fragments aside as rapidly as they stop proving useful. Imagine a conservative and a liberal in some future dark age, pondering an antique internal combustion engine that either can operate but neither could build. Bolted to the side of the engine is an inscrutable gadget that is not clearly adding anything to the function of the vehicle. The liberal would reason that since it cannot be shown to do anything for the motor's function, it should be removed and discarded. The conservative would reason that since it cannot be shown to do anything, it must remain precisely where it is forever. Perhaps if we knew what it did, it could be removed, but as long as we do not understand it, it stays. Whatever the merits of their temperaments (and neither can be right in this case), under the condition of decadence liberals become streamliners and conservatives become pack rats. Evangelicals have long tended toward the pack rat temperament, even though there are some signs that we may currently be exchanging that temperament for its relatively less happy alternative. What it leaves us with is an impressive stock of soteriological bric-a-brac that we don't know what to do with or how it originally went together.

The inability to grasp the wholeness of salvation is actually one of the primary manifestations of our decadent theological culture. Is Christian salvation forgiveness, a personal relationship with Jesus, power for moral transformation, or going to heaven? It is all of those and more, but a true account of the thing itself will have to start with the living whole if we ever hope to make sense of the parts. Just think how tricky it is to combine free forgiveness and moral transformation in an organic way if what you are starting with is the individual parts. A dreary back-and-forth between cheap grace and works-righteousness is one of the bedeviling distractions of evangelical experience under the conditions of decadence.

Taking up the materials at hand, is it possible to assemble a coherent doctrine of salvation that takes all the particulars into account? An instructive exercise is to take the main ways that evangelical Christians articulate salvation, and try to order them logically. Are we born again because we are forgiven, or forgiven because we are born again? Does "saved" refer to deliverance from condemnation now, or to deliverance from hell later? Does Jesus live in your heart because God has chosen to consider you as if you were righteous, or does God look at you and see righteousness because he sees Jesus in your heart? Most of us can make some progress on these questions and start assembling a logical *ordo salutis*, a structured (though not necessarily chronological) order of salvation. But when you start with the parts, it is hard to escape the sense that there is too much guesswork involved in combining them into a whole. The solution is to start from the whole and then descend to the parts. But where is the whole to be found? And how do we get to wholeness if we are forced to start from our current situation among the fragments?

THERE MUST BE MORE

A first step along the route from disintegration to integration is to clarify the false hopes that currently suggest themselves to us as the true core of Christian life. If we have learned from Ephesians, and from the older evangelical tradition, to think large thoughts about salvation, then we may already be in a position to keep ourselves from falling into certain traps. When Christians undertake to describe the central reality of their existence as Christians, what possibilities typically come to mind? The three most serious candidates are perennially the same: doctrine, behavior, and emotions.

Henry Scougal (1650–1678), a Scottish theologian who lived only to the age of twenty-seven, wrote a classic book that addressed this subject directly. His book, *The Life of God in the Soul of Man*,[22] is not widely read anymore, but it has exerted a tremendous formative influence on the evangelical tradition, especially through its impact on the leaders of the eighteenth-century awakenings. Susannah Wesley (1669–1742) seems to have loved the book and recommended it to her sons John and Charles. Charles (1703–1788) in turn gave a copy to George Whitefield (1714–1770), who later testified that he "never knew what true religion was" until he read Scougal. In saying this, Whitefield was testifying to the book's role in his conversion and also putting his finger on the main thing Scougal sets out to address: the nature of true religion. "Religion" in our era is often a pejorative term, even among evangelicals who are so obviously religious. The term is used to indicate a formal or artificial mode of behaving and is usually put in contrast to something with more reality or immediacy. There are two groups who are especially likely to start their self-descriptions with "I'm not religious:" evangelical Christians and self-consciously secular people. The evangelical will finish the sentence (or T-shirt or bumper sticker) with ". . . I just love the Lord," while the secular person will finish with the now ubiquitous canard, ". . . but I'm very spiritual."

If a modern paraphrase of Henry Scougal's book were put on the market, the best translation of "true religion" for our ears would probably be "authentic spirituality." But let us at least attempt to hear him in his own voice first: "I cannot speak of religion, but I must lament that, among so many pretenders to it, so few understand what it means." He then anatomizes the three most common mis-locations of true religion:

> Some [place] it in the understanding, in orthodox notions and opinions; and all the account they can give of their religion is, that they are of this or the other persuasion, and have joined themselves to one of those many sects whereinto Christendom is most unhappily divided.

These are the "head" Christians, who not only take care to have correct doctrine—which we should all do—but who mistakenly believe that being "theologically correct" is the sum and substance of the Christian life. As Scougal points out, they also tend to be unduly divisive, though of course they insist that it's all in defense of truth. Their problem is not that they care about being orthodox but that they care about nothing else, to the point for all their wisdom they can't quite conceive of what it is you think might be missing from their lives. Of the three kinds of inadequate Christians Scougal indicts, I consider these "orthodox notions" believers to be nearest to the real thing, but for that reason they are probably the most thoroughly trapped. If you tell one of these top-heavy believers that they are missing out on the reality of salvation, they will immediately make room in their intellectual system for a doctrine about "the reality of salvation." They earnestly seek to embrace all God's truth, but if you tell them they are missing the power of godliness, they will buy (or write) a book about it, do a Bible study about it, or in some other way try to put together a proper doctrine about it.

> Others place it in the outward man, in a constant course of external duties, and a model of performances: if they live peaceably with their neighbors, keep a temperate diet, observe the returns of worship, frequenting the church and their closet, and sometimes extend their hands to the relief of the poor, they think they have sufficiently acquitted themselves.

This "outward man" religion practiced by the "hand" Christians is the moralistic reduction Christianity. At its worst, this mind-set can be a practical atheism that treats Christianity as a useful mythology to underwrite a decent life. It's hard to shake the feeling that these believers are just naturally good people and that if they were adherents of any of the world's religions, they would be just as generous, peaceful, devout, and prudent in their conduct. You want these people for neighbors and you don't care what they believe, because the proof is in their good behavior. At its best, this version of true religion is in harmony with the demands of God's law, animated by a holy zeal, and especially sensitive to social justice and the physical needs of the poor. Again, there is nothing wrong with this mentality except that it leaves out the main thing. The problem is not that they pursue good works—which we should all do—but that they see these manifestations as the essence of Christianity.

> Others again put all religion in the affections, in rapturous heats and ecstatic devotion; and all they aim at, is, to pray with passion, and think of heaven with pleasure, and to be affected with those kind and melting expressions wherewith they court their Saviour, till they persuade themselves that they are mightily in love with him; and from thence assume a great confidence of their salvation, which they esteem the chief of Christian graces.[23]

Of the three types that Scougal describes, these "heart" Christians are the most easily recognizable. In fact, they have apparently not changed very much since the seventeenth century, and Scougal's language probably calls to mind contemporary examples: "rapturous heats and ecstatic devotions," "kind and melting expressions," "mightily in love." Heart Christianity is so good and so powerful that it is a constant temptation to the head and hand Christians. If you can once awaken the other believers out of their intellectual and moral reductionism, they are very likely to run straight to heart Christianity and spend the rest of their lives testifying to how they once were cold but now are hot and how they have been delivered from abstraction and brought into contact with reality. But they have only transferred their allegiance from one reductionism to another.

An American author writing in 1947 similarly started a book with the Scougalesque[24] task "to disabuse certain minds of the erroneous idea that is so widespread, that the Christian Life consists in accepting certain articles of belief and conforming to a certain code of conduct."[25] This is a warning that must be sounded repeatedly because the temptation is constant. The problem of heart Christianity is not that it cultivates and rejoices in a warm emotional apprehension of God in Christ—which we should all do—but that it confuses this for salvation and true Christian experience.

Head, hand, and heart Christianity each testifies to an element of the truth, but none of them is the thing itself. You cannot come into contact with the nature of salvation, or see the gospel in its full scope and magnitude, by staying in any of these three reductionisms. You may be able to expand and enrich your Christian experience by learning to move from one to another in turn. Emotional Christians, for instance, can and should profit from attending to doctrine; and, conversely, it is a wonderful thing to behold a coldly rational Christian suddenly discover the existence of an affective domain previously unimagined. But looking for true religion under these three headings is a shell game, because the thing itself is not under any of them. Nor is it to be found in the transcendent unity of the three, by simply drawing a bigger circle around them. After all, these three factors are all elements in what we would traditionally call the soul:

Diagram 3.1: Elements of the Soul

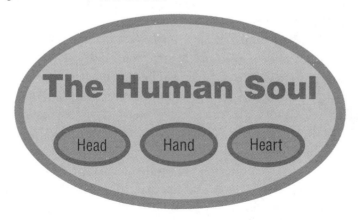

It may be clearer that we are talking about the human soul if we refer to the domains with the longer Latinate terms *intellect, volition,* and *emotion*. But whatever language we choose for these human faculties that give rise to our doctrine, behavior, and emotions, the point is that what is under discussion is a set of phenomena immanent to human nature. When we behave, we behave from head, hand, or heart.

These things, Scougal says, each have a "resemblance of piety" but "at the best are but means of obtaining it, or particular exercises of it," and they are "frequently mistaken for the whole of religion," but they are not.

> Certainly religion is quite another thing; and they who are acquainted with it, will entertain far different thoughts, and disdain all those shadows and false imitations of it. They know by experience, that true religion is an union of the soul with God, a real participation of the divine nature, the very image of God drawn upon the soul; or, in the Apostle's phrase, it is Christ formed within us.

Beyond the notional, social, and emotional-devotional reductions of the gospel, Scougal points to "union of the soul with God" and then mobilizes scriptural and traditional language about partaking of the divine nature, being conformed to the image of God, and having Christ formed within us. Finally, he sums up his message with the line that gave his book its title and forms the outline of the rest of the book: "Briefly, I know not how the nature of religion can be more fully expressed, than by calling it a divine life." Christianity is nothing less than the life of God in the soul of man.

Here Scougal breaks through to the fact that the gospel can be accounted for only by reference to something above and beyond the immanent realities of head, hand, and heart. True religion is a divine life, and by definition divine life is something found in the living God. Our salvation and our existence as Christians come from and consist in the union of that divine life with what we are in ourselves. Salvation comes from it: this is the point of contact that brings about salvation. Christian existence consists in it: this is the state in which we have our ongoing being. True religion, says Scougal, consists in the life of God in the soul of man.

Diagram 3.2: The Life of God in the Soul of Man

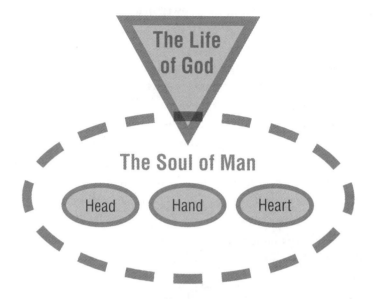

Scougal helps put the various manifestations (the "particular exercises" of piety, in his language) into their proper places and distinguishes them from the source and essence that alone can give rise to them. That source is the living God. With this analysis we have come back to the original thesis of the present chapter, that when we ask about the magnitude of the gospel, the only appropriate thing to measure it against is God. The gospel is God-sized, because God puts himself into it. The living God binds himself to us and becomes our salvation, the life of God in the soul of man. We are saved by the gospel of God to worship the God of the gospel.

GRACE AS GOD'S SELF-GIVING

Salvation, according to the Christian idea, is a thing given to us by grace. But just as we have traced a variety of reductions and constrictions in soteriology, so there are reductions and constrictions of grace itself. Briefly, there are two concepts of grace currently on the market, which are each inadequate and which are impossible to reconcile with each other. On the one hand, grace is often considered "God being nice to us," especially in not holding sins against us. Alternatively, grace is thought of as God-given power, power that enables us to transform our lives. Stated this baldly, they are debased versions of Protestant and Roman Catholic teaching, respectively. It might be possible to start from one of these points of departure, stating them more fairly, and building out from them to establish a more comprehensive teaching on grace. If we were trying to do justice to these two poles of the fight over grace, we could engage great minds like Luther and Aquinas, respectively, to feel the force of their presentation. But a cartoonish caricature, for all its grotesqueness, does capture enough of a resemblance to make a point. I am intentionally stating them in drastically abbreviated form in order to emphasize their real limitations. On the popular level, we often operate with such truncated ideas about grace: on the one hand, God winking at sin, on the other hand God boosting us into holiness. Neither of these is adequate to the biblical reality of God's grace. Neither the wink nor the boost is amazing.

But grace, as evangelicals well know and have taught the world to sing, is amazing. When John Newton put the adjective "Amazing" in front of the noun "Grace," he hit on a sound so sweet that we now recognize "amazing" as part of the definition of grace. Anyone who teaches a grace that is not amazing is teaching something that is not grace. We must cast the net wider in order to take in enough of the full biblical witness to grace. The Methodist theologian Thomas Oden, attempting to summarize the doctrine of grace from the first several centuries of the church, tried to put it all into a few sentences:

> Grace is an overarching term for all of God's gifts to humanity, all the blessings of salvation, all events through which are manifested God's own self-giving. Grace is a divine attribute revealing the heart of the one God, the premise of all spiritual blessing.[26]

Oden's account still doesn't manage to say everything, but he at least attempts to be broad enough to take in the various dimensions required in a description of grace. It reaches out widely to the far ends of the history of salvation and extends up into the being of God himself as "a divine attribute revealing the heart of the one God." His description surely reaches the heights here but does not descend to the depths of sin.[27] And it should be no surprise that as he reaches out to "the height, the breadth, the length and depth" of this grace, Oden is driven to speak the language of Ephesians, echoing Ephesians 1:3 in calling grace "the premise of all spiritual blessing."

Furthermore, by describing grace as "God's own self-giving," Oden makes contact with the hidden center of the great blessing of Ephesians 1:3–14, the fact that God gives us "every spiritual blessing in the heavenly places" by giving us first and foremost himself. We have already seen Thomas Goodwin expound Ephesians in these terms: "Not only God doth bless with all other good things, but above all by communicating himself and his own blessedness unto them . . ."[28] The thousand pages Goodwin wrote on Ephesians are crammed with further extrapolations of the same insight, that God blesses by putting himself forward in person as the blessing. Goodwin was especially concerned to underline the way this self-giving reveals the depth of God's love and concern for us:

> And surely if God communicates himself to whom he blesseth, his blessing of them must proceed from the deepest good-will; and indeed is the reason why he giveth himself, as in marriage they bestow themselves and all, to whom they bear their special good-will.[29]

God's self-giving for human salvation is a motif that pervades not just Ephesians but the whole Bible and is particularly prominent in parts of the Old Testament. Goodwin refers to God's pledge to Abraham, "I am thy shield, and thy exceeding great reward" (Gen. 15:1 KJV).[30] God does not promise to give Abraham a reward but personally to be his reward, which certainly illuminates why the reward is "exceeding great." The song Israel sings when delivered from Egypt praises God that "the LORD is my strength and my song, and has become my salvation" (Ex. 15:2), similarly eschewing weaker formulations like "he has made my salvation" or "he has carried out my salvation" in favor of a formulation that puts God himself forward as salvation.

This characteristic Old Testament language saturates the Psalms, of course, which praise God as "my rock and my fortress and my deliverer, my God, my rock, in whom I take refuge, my shield, and the horn of my salvation, my stronghold" (Ps. 18:2). The messianic intensification of the theme is present on every page of the New Testament, being, as it is, the core of what is New in the New Testament. This new-covenant intensification is especially striking in the Gospel of John, where Jesus in the famous series of "I am" statements puts himself forward as being, in person, the vine, the bread of life, the way, and the truth. There is much more to be said about this, but since almost none of it can be said without an explicitly Trinitarian vocabulary, it must wait for the next chapter.

The good news that Jesus brings is that God has chosen to accomplish our salvation by being himself for us, by opening up his own life and bringing us into fellowship. It is worth underlining that God has chosen to accomplish our salvation this way, that he has freely and graciously elected this particular option as the way he wants to exercise mercy. For all we know (and we should admit that it isn't much), human salvation could have been secured with considerably less cost and effort. God has all power and infinite creativity at his disposal, and no obstacle can stand before him. If we were bound by chains, he could break them. If we owed a debt, he could remit it by issuing a proclamation. If our lineage was infected, he could annihilate the substance of which we are made and speak us back into existence uninfected. If the Devil had bought us, God could have opened the storehouse of heaven and bought us back with whatever currency is fungible in the heavenlies, at whatever the going exchange rate is. If an enemy oppressed us, the Lord is a warrior whom no foe can stand against.

For all we know, God could have done a lot less than he did, but it is worse than silly to speculate about roads not taken by the Almighty. The one thing we know is that what God in fact chose to do was to give himself to us personally to be our salvation. Apparently that self-giving is what counts for God as the kind of salvation he wants to extend to fallen humanity. There may be deep reasons for that, reasons that extend back into God's purposes for creation irrespective of sin and the fall. Perhaps the soteriology of divine self-giving gives us a glimpse of what unfallen humanity is for in the first place. But that too is a road not taken, indeed the most epochal road ever not taken, but nevertheless one about which we can only speculate. Speculation of that sort can only take our eyes off the actual economy of salvation, which is clear and evident: God has given himself to us to be our salvation and has done so at great cost, with amazing grace, in a way that outstrips anything we could have asked, expected, or imagined.

THE GOSPEL AND THE DEEP THINGS OF GOD

Here for certain we have a truth that evangelicalism has always grasped firmly. It is the central idea of that beloved text John 3:16 in which we can see the extent of the Father's love for the world by attending to the greatness of the gift that he gave for our salvation: his Son. And it is at this point, where God's self-giving is most conspicuous, that we are forced to break through to explicitly Trinitarian confession if we want to go any further. For in the case of God, *himself* is not a word that points to an isolated individual existing alone with his aloneness. When God finally fulfills all his promises by giving himself to be our salvation and our shield, this takes place as the Father gives the Son.

The index of how much God loves us is how much he gave to accomplish our salvation. Paul drives this point home as the climax of his far-ranging argument in Romans 8, grounding Christian hope and assurance in the fact that since God has already given his own Son, it obviously follows that nothing is too great for God to give. Dwight L. Moody, sometimes called "Mr. Evangelical," preached frequently on this theme, and one of his last sermons was on the text of Romans 8:

> Now Paul puts some questions. "Who can be against us? He that spared not His own Son, but delivered Him up for us all, how shall He not with Him also give us freely all things?" (verse 32). When God the Father gave Christ, the Son of His bosom, He literally gave up all that heaven had. He gave the richest jewel that heaven possessed. And if He has given us His Son, is there anything too great for us to ask? If a man should give me a diamond worth one hundred thousand dollars, I think I would make bold to ask him for a little piece of brown paper to carry it away in. If the Lord has given me the Son of His bosom, I can ask for anything. How shall He not freely give us all things?[31]

One of the typical ways evangelicals introduce the gospel is with the statement "Jesus loves you." But when the time comes to take the full measure of that love, we have to look further than mere human sympathies. F. B. Meyer, preaching on John 15:9 ("As the Father has loved me, so have I loved you"), said:

> Do you want to know how much Jesus loves you? Ah! soul, before thou canst master that arithmetic thou must learn another mode of computation. Tell me first the love of God the Father to His Son, and I will tell thee the love of the Son to thee.[32]

When we consider the gospel of salvation in Christ, we are not dealing with the outer fringes of God's ways but with the very core and center of who God is. God is not trifling with us in the gospel but opening up in the most intimate way his very heart. Of course, God remains incomprehensible, mysterious, and far above all created things in a way that is not at all diminished by the way he makes himself lavishly available to fallen humanity in the economy of salvation. But his infinite transcendence over all created things cannot be construed as any kind of reserve or standoffishness. The Father's giving of the Son renders that interpretation impossible. Having sent servants already, God takes the ultimate step and reaches out to his people by sending an agent more dear and intimate to himself: "What shall I do? I will send my beloved son; perhaps they will respect him" (Luke 20:13).

Thomas Goodwin brought all these insights together tersely when he said that "the things of the gospel are depths—the things of the gospel . . . are the deep things of God."[33] Goodwin loved to ponder the many ways in which the gospel was a mystery. He noted that this gospel was the thing into which prophets "inquired and searched diligently," and that angels "desire to look into" its content (1 Pet. 1:10–12 KJV). But beyond this, Goodwin said, it was a mystery in the sense that God himself considered it uniquely precious, because it "lay (as I may so speak) at the bottom of his heart, the great secrets, which he esteemed such even from everlasting."[34] Goodwin was drawing language not from Ephesians but from 1 Corinthians when he spoke of "the deep things of God."[35] In the second chapter of this letter, Paul puts great emphasis on how profound, secret, and inaccessible to human understanding the blessings of the gospel are. What has been made known to us in the gospel is "what God has prepared for those who love him" (v. 9 NIV) and far from being conformable to human wisdom, it is something that

> no eye has seen,
> nor ear heard,
> nor the heart of man imagined,

words which most Christians probably associate with heaven but which Paul clearly intends with reference to the present revelation of the gospel. If this divine wisdom has now been handed over to us in the gospel, it is by miracle, because the origins of these things lie so deep within the heart of God that only God can know them. The mystery of the gospel is locked up inside of God and can be communicated only by someone who is God. Paul underlines this three different ways:

> We impart a secret and hidden wisdom of God, which God decreed before the ages for our glory. (1 Cor. 2:7)

> These things God has revealed to us through the Spirit. For the Spirit searches everything, even the depths of God. For who knows a person's thoughts except the spirit of that person, which is in him? So also no one comprehends the thoughts of God except the Spirit of God. (1 Cor. 2:10–11)

> "For who has understood the mind of the Lord so as to instruct him?" But we have the mind of Christ. (1 Cor. 2:16)

The predestining Father determined this mystery; and the depth-searching Spirit has access to these depths because he is as intimate with God as my spirit is with me. But that same Spirit has revealed them to us, and we therefore have come into harmony with the mind of Christ, the one who knows the mind of the Lord.[36] For the present, let us ignore the implications of the threefoldness of the answer and simply note that the Spirit and Christ have brought out into the open a mystery that has its natural home at the center of God's heart, at the depth of his life. This opened secret is the gospel. It has such a profound and divine character

123

that even to make it known, God must give himself over for its revelation. That revelatory self-giving is perfectly in line with the content of the thing revealed, which is that God gives himself to us to be our salvation. He does not dispense blessings, but himself.

We have been led into pretty lofty thoughts by the material we are considering, but the soteriology of God's self-giving is immediately relevant to our lives with God. There is an evangelical spirituality that corresponds to the deeply personal nature of God's self-giving. It is a spirituality that focuses relentlessly on God himself and is on constant guard against the temptation to be distracted from God by his blessings, benefits, or gifts. A. B. Simpson's gospel song, "Himself," captures it perfectly:

> Once it was the blessing, now it is the Lord;
> Once it was the feeling, now it is His Word;
> Once His gift I wanted, now the Giver own;
> Once I sought for healing, now Himself alone.
>
> Once 'twas painful trying, now 'tis perfect trust;
> Once a half salvation, now the uttermost!
> Once 'twas ceaseless holding, now He holds me fast;
> Once 'twas constant drifting, now my anchor's cast.[37]

Depending on our taste in poetry, Simpson's lines may seem like overwrought emotion scanned out as pious doggerel. Depending on our individual tendencies in self-expression, the spirituality it expresses may seem histrionic and melodramatic. But this is the kind of language evangelicals have always used, and if they have often been able to say it with more decorum in a cultured and liturgical setting, they have also frequently said it so directly and emotionally that they made A. B. Simpson sound like a stuffy high-churchman by comparison. The modes of expression are many, but evangelical spirituality will always find a way to declare its adherence to God himself, emphasizing precisely the personal character of it. In view of the way God has thrown open his heart and turned his inner life inside out to be our salvation, how else could the people of the gospel respond? He speaks passionately to us, and we must answer.[38]

The gospel is that God is God for us, that he gives himself to be our salvation. In this sense, as John Piper has said in a series of meditations on God's love as the gift of himself: "God is the gospel."[39] He does not give us some thing that makes us blessed, but he blesses us by giving us himself. It is a great thing to have said this much: to have thought such grand thoughts about salvation that we have come to view it as God-sized, and to confront the fact that God gives nothing less than himself to be our salvation. But it is not yet enough, because we have not yet said it specifically enough to bring out its actual contours. It is high time to move from the size of the gospel, to the shape of the gospel. We have already had to sidestep this theme repeatedly in the present chapter, at the cost of remaining somewhat abstract and general in places where specificity was called for. Certain pressing questions must now be faced: if God gives himself to us, how is it that he has himself to give? If evangelical existence is the life of God in the soul of man, what is this life with which the living God is alive and which he can put into the human soul without obliterating its humanity? When God puts himself forward to be our salvation in person, who is this person? This God who is the gospel is God the Father, God the Son, and God the Holy Spirit. To these three we now turn.

125

4

THE SHAPE OF
THE GOSPEL

(Or, The Tacit Trinitarianism of Evangelical Salvation)

> But when the fullness of time had come, God sent forth his Son,
> born of woman, born under the law, to redeem those who were
> under the law, so that we might receive adoption as sons. And
> because you are sons, God has sent the Spirit of his Son into our
> hearts, crying, "Abba! Father!" So you are no longer a slave, but a
> son, and if a son, then an heir through God.
>
> GALATIANS 4:4-7

> When God designed the great and glorious work of recovering
> fallen man, and the saving of sinners, to the praise of the glory of
> his grace, he appointed, in his infinite wisdom, two great means
> thereof: The one was the giving his Son for them, and the other
> was the giving his Spirit to them. And hereby was way made for
> the manifestation of the glory of the whole blessed Trinity; which
> is the utmost end of all the works of God.
>
> JOHN OWEN[1]

Now that we have seen the gospel as God-sized, we are ready to see that
the Trinity has also given a particular threefold shape to the gospel. In
this chapter, we will look at the gospel as something that has had this
threefold shape impressed on it by the triune God. Speaking about "the
shape of the gospel" is, of course, speaking metaphorically. Literally, it
is physical objects that have shapes, contours, edges, and corners. The
metaphor of "shape" can help us perceive the metaphorical contours,

edges, and corners of the gospel. But shape is only metaphor, and it is high time we spoke as un-metaphorically as possible about the thing itself. The thing itself is the economy of salvation.

THE ECONOMY OF SALVATION

The economy of salvation is the flawlessly designed way God administers his gracious self-giving. When God gives himself to be the salvation of his people, there is nothing haphazard or random about it. God's agape is never sloppy. He has a plan, and he follows a procedure that is perfectly proportioned. Theologians call this well-ordered plan the economy of salvation.

The word *economy* can be an awkward one to use because in contemporary English it has come to sound like a word about money and markets. When we hear about economics, we think of the social science that studies the distribution of goods and services in human societies. An economy would be what an economist studies. But the word *economy* is much older than the (relatively young) science of economics. It comes from an ancient Greek compound word, *oikonomos*, made up of the words *oikos* (house) and *nomos* (law). An economy is the law that provides for orderly management of a household. The sense of the word may be better brought out by recalling the term "home economics," which makes explicit the reference to a home and suggests that the home economist is paying close attention to how all business is conducted for the good of the household. The word *economy* contains the far-reaching idea of the orderly arrangement of a shared life, which is a much broader concept than the modern science of money. Theology has retained the word in its older, wider sense, following the usage of ancient Greek writers like Aristotle, for whom an *oikonomos* was an administrator or steward over all a household's residents and property. It would be a useful word to reclaim just on these grounds.

Above all, though, *economy* is a word worth learning because it is an important word used in Scripture itself. Since it is usually obscured by readable English translations, it takes a little work to tease it out and bring it to our attention. We have already seen the single most important occurrences of the word in the New Testament. In our study of the first

THE SHAPE OF THE GOSPEL

chapter of Ephesians above, we translated Ephesians 1:10 as saying that God made known the mystery of his will "through an economy in which, when the times were fulfilled, he would sum up everything . . . under one heading: Christ!" There we went out of our way to preserve and highlight the word *oikonomia*, but at the cost of a rather poorly flowing English sentence. Better translators have made smoother sentences from it. The following translations are all responsible renderings of Paul's Greek sentences, but watch the transformation that the word *oikonomia* is put through in each of them:

> That in the dispensation of the fulness of times he might gather together in one all things in Christ. (KJV)
>
> . . . with a view to an administration suitable to the fullness of the times, that is, the summing up of all things in Christ. (NASB)
>
> . . . which he purposed in Christ, to be put into effect when the times will have reached their fulfillment—to bring all things . . . together under one head, even Christ. (NIV)
>
> . . . his purpose, which he set forth in Christ as a plan for the fullness of time, to unite all things in him. (ESV)
>
> And this is the plan: At the right time he will bring everything together under the authority of Christ. (NLT)

The first two translations give us strong and attention-getting nouns as translations for *oikonomia*: a "dispensation" and an "administration." The KJV's "dispensation" is based on the fact that the Latin word for *oikonomia* is *dispensatio*. The NASB's "administration" may have unfortunate bureaucratic connotations and introduces so many syllables that it loses readability points, but it has the virtue of showing us that there is a long, solid noun here in the text, to pay attention to and ask questions about. The NIV hides the word behind the verb phrase "to be put into effect." The ESV manages a smooth reading by shrinking *oikonomia* to the less massive "plan," and the NLT puts that word in a phrase that emphasizes it: "This is the plan."

The economy of salvation is not a ramshackle affair but a perfectly ordered domestic space. It is not a tumbledown shack but a manicured estate. In Ephesians, Paul plays on this "household" metaphor repeatedly: The economy (house-law, 1:10) is God's household (2:19) in which the Father (from whom all fatherhood is named, 3:15) builds us up together (2:20–22), we formerly homeless outcasts (2:19), to make us a dwelling of God by the Spirit (2:22).[2]

When Paul talks about God's economy, his point is that God is a supremely wise administrator who has arranged the elements of his plan with great care.[3] To watch God carry out this economy is to be instructed in the mystery of his will and to gain insight into the eternal purpose of his divine wisdom. Even those angelic beings, the "rulers and authorities in the heavenly places," are instructed in this "manifold wisdom of God" as they see it worked out now in God's household management of the church (3:10). Paul's own ministry, he says in 3:9, is "to bring to light for everyone what is the plan [*oikonomia*] of the mystery hidden for ages in God who created all things." What is made known in this economy is something "which was not made known to the sons of men in other generations as it has now been revealed to his holy apostles and prophets by the Spirit" (3:5). The instruction that men and angels receive is from coming to understand how God has arranged the elements of his plan. We can understand the eternal purpose of God, framed in his unfathomable wisdom, by paying close attention to this economy of salvation.

WHERE GOD EXPRESSES HIMSELF

There is a reason why we have so much to learn from attending to the economy of salvation. The reason is that God has carried out the central events of this economy with the definite intention of making himself known in them. The economy of salvation teaches us things because God intends it to. Specifically, God's intention is for the economy of salvation to teach us who he is. This is where the one true God identifies himself and reveals something ultimately definitive about who he is. Ephesians emphasizes the revelatory character of God's economy. We learn the character of God's wisdom by studying his ways in the administration of the unfolding history of salvation. We attend to his craftsmanship. We look for the marks of his workmanship to see what decisions he has made. In those decisions, we see God's self-revelation. It is in the central events of this economy that God has actively and intentionally expressed his character and identified himself. We are not merely saying that God, being by nature a great craftsman, leaves signs of his personal style of workmanship on everything he does and so has left marks of self-expression on the economy of salvation. No, when it comes to the great, defining events of the economy of salvation, it has been God's direct intention to do these things in order to make himself known to us.

In the old covenant, the central events were the choosing of Abraham, the exodus from Egypt, and the gift of the Promised Land. In these events God was doing something in history that brought about knowledge of him. "I will take you to be my people, and I will be your God," he declares in Exodus 6:7, with the result that "you shall know that I am the LORD your God, who has brought you out from under the burdens of the Egyptians." At the other end of Old Testament history, the Lord promises that he will bring his people back from exile and that this mighty act will result in sure knowledge of his identity and character: "And I will put my Spirit within you, and you shall live, and I will place you in your own land. Then you shall know that I am the LORD; I have spoken, and I will do it, declares the LORD" (Ezek. 37:14). Over and over, God links accurate knowledge of his character to recognition of a definite constellation of his mighty acts on behalf of his people.

But those old-covenant events all cry out for their divinely ordained fulfillment in the new covenant, where God completes his intention to make himself known. The book of Hebrews begins by announcing this breakthrough to a new level of God's self-expression toward us: "Long ago, at many times and in many ways, God spoke to our fathers by the prophets, but in these last days he has spoken to us by his Son" (Heb. 1:1–2). This Son is not simply a messenger who carries God's words, or an interpreter who explains God's ways. He is "the radiance of the glory of God and the exact imprint of his nature" (v. 3), and his being sent into the world is itself a mighty act of God to simultaneously save us and reveal himself. Together with its necessary completion in the outpouring of the Holy Spirit, the advent of the Son of God is the central event in which God has made himself known: "He has spoken to us by his Son."

A parable from contemporary life may clarify the way God makes himself known in the economy of salvation. Like all parables, it throws

THE DEEP THINGS OF GOD

light on a particular truth, but its illustrative helpfulness should not be pushed beyond the bounds of common sense. With that warning in place, here is the parable. A woman works for a business that provides her with a spacious cubicle office. The office includes everything she needs to get her job done. The computer, desk, chairs, conference table, filing cabinets, and bookshelves are all arranged to conduct the company's business professionally. There is framed art on the one fixed wall of the office and an area rug that really ties the whole room together. But the art and the rug both came to her through the company's central warehouse and were chosen by a purchasing committee to communicate the company's professional image. She has added a few touches to the cubicle that express her personality: two family photos beside her computer, a framed motto on the wall, and some knickknacks on a shelf. But one day she makes a new friend at the office and says to her, "You can't tell anything about who I am from this cubicle. Come to my home, and you will understand me." There, everything the friend sees is an expression of her personality. She bought that house because it suited her, and every furnishing in it is her choice and arrangement. To see her in her own domestic space is to know something about who she is, not just how she conducts company business. Her *oikonomia* is a self-expression in a way her professional space is not.

The analogy could be tweaked to make it more appropriate. We could say, for instance, that in the case of God, the happy land of the eternal Trinity is God's actual home, while the economy of salvation is his home away from home or the home he makes hospitably among his creatures. We could even call the immanent Trinity God's "family of origin." And we could add that, setting aside our wordplay with the term *oikonomia* (house-law), God's location for self-expression and revelation is not a living room or a location at all, but a series of events. But by the time we have made these changes, we have started turning the analogy into the reality. The reality is that the economy of salvation is God's intentionally communicative domestic arrangement, which he administers specifically to communicate his character and identity.

The economy of salvation has a meaningful form. If it were only the series of events that God undertook to save us, the economy might conceivably be a long, spread-out sequence of events, all with equal importance. But the economy also communicates. God has given form and order to the history of salvation because he intends not only to save us through it but also to reveal himself through it. The economy is shaped by God's intention to communicate his identity and character. If the history of salvation is also the way God shows us who he is and what he is like, then it makes sense that it would be a history with a clear and distinct shape. It may be vast, but it is well proportioned and does not suffer from sprawl. It features an obvious central point as the focus of attention. That obvious central point is the sending of Jesus, the Son of God anointed by the Holy Spirit. So even though the economy of salvation starts in the garden of Eden, spans hundreds of divine interventions, and is not concluded yet, it is still easy to discern its center and to read its total form. The center of the economy of salvation is the nexus where the Son and the Holy Spirit are sent by the Father to accomplish reconciliation.

WATCH JESUS AND THINK TRINITY

It might seem odd to point anywhere but to Jesus Christ as the center of the history of salvation. He is indeed, in person, the very center of the divine plan, and in fact we are not pointing elsewhere than to him for the revelation of God. But our goal is not just to put our finger on the center but to point to it in such a way that the total form of the economy also becomes apparent. To get that big picture, we have to see Jesus not in isolation but in Trinitarian perspective. He is sent by the Father, and everything he does is done in company with the Holy Spirit.

First, Jesus is sent by the Father. By his own testimony, everything Jesus does is the work of the Father. He does not act on his own initiative, and he is not carrying out his own plan. "I have come down from heaven, not to do my own will but the will of him who sent me" (John 6:38). He walks among us as the one who comes from the Father to reconcile us with the Father. There is no way of understanding the work of Jesus without taking the Father into account. To think about Jesus in isolation from the Father is to ignore Jesus' self-understanding: he is from the Father. His fellowship with the Father was the secret that sustained him and gave him his reason for living: "My food is to do the will of him who sent me and to accomplish his work" (John 4:34). If you have missed this aspect of what God is saying through the New Testament, I recommend speed-reading the Gospel of John and asking yourself what your dominant impression about Jesus is. It is bound to be his relationship with the Holy Father who sent him and is with him. As the nineteenth-century Anglican bishop Handley C. G. Moule summarized, "Nothing shines more radiantly in the New Testament than the eternal love of the Father for the Son."[4]

Second, Jesus works in company with the Holy Spirit. The cooperation of the Son and the Holy Spirit in the economy of salvation is an even richer subject for study, if possible, than the cooperation of the Father and the Son, because it expands our view of the scope of God's plan. When we look from Jesus to the Father, we see a great depth: the ultimate source, power, and purpose of the mission of Jesus. But when we look from Jesus to the Holy Spirit, we see a great breadth: the magnificent complexity and completeness of the economy. This scope becomes visible because of the way the Holy Spirit surrounds the ministry of Jesus on all sides. The work of the Spirit precedes the ministry of Jesus in that the Spirit is the one who brings about the virgin conception, the incarnation, and the forming and setting apart of Christ's human nature (Matt. 1:20; Luke 1:35). Lest we overlook the Holy Spirit's role at the beginning of Christ's earthly life, the ancient Apostles' Creed picks it out as one of the few things it mentions prior to the crucifixion: "conceived by the Holy Spirit, born of the virgin Mary, suffered under Pontius Pilate." Here the creed has good insight into the Gospels, which are silent about the Spirit's role in Christ's ministry for chapters on end but set the stage with a cluster of references to the Spirit at the beginning of the story of Jesus. This is obvious in Matthew and Luke with their accounts of the virgin conception, but even Mark's Gospel, which neither narrates the virgin conception nor mentions the Holy Spirit often, begins with a cluster of Spirit references (1:8, 10, 12).[5] The story of Jesus starts with the Holy Spirit.

His life and ministry also continue in the power of the Holy Spirit. Simply reviewing the biblical statements on this subject is powerful. R. A. Torrey's summary of Christian doctrine, *What the Bible Teaches*, gathers up the lines of biblical evidence helpfully:

1) Jesus Christ was begotten of the Holy Spirit. (Luke 1:35)
2) Jesus Christ led a holy, spotless life, and offered Himself to God, through the working of the Holy Spirit. (Hebrews 9:14)
3) Jesus Christ was anointed for service by the Holy Spirit. (Acts 10:38; Isaiah 61:1; Luke 4:14, 18)
4) Jesus Christ was led by the Holy Spirit in His movements. (Luke 1:4)
5) Jesus Christ was taught by the Spirit who rested upon Him. The Spirit of God was the source of His wisdom in the days of His flesh. (Isaiah 11:2; compare Matthew 12:17, 18)
6) The Holy Spirit abode upon Him in fullness and the words He spoke were the words of God. (John 3:34)
7) Jesus Christ gave commandments to His apostles whom he had chosen, through the Holy Spirit. (Acts 1:2)
8) Jesus Christ wrought His miracles in the power of the Holy Spirit. (Matthew 12:28; compare 1 Corinthians 12:9–10)
9) Jesus Christ was raised from the dead by the power of the Holy Spirit. (Romans 8:11)[6]

The Holy Spirit is also involved in the carrying out of Christ's work after his death, resurrection, and ascension into heaven. It is through the Holy Spirit that the work of Christ is applied to believers so that they are born again, become temples of God, and are empowered for discipleship. When Christ ascended into heaven, he sent the Holy Spirit to minister God's presence among his people. Indeed, when the Holy Spirit is poured out on Pentecost, his personal presence in salvation history after the finished work of Christ inaugurates a new era in God's ways with the world. Thus the work of the Holy Spirit surrounds the work of Jesus Christ, as he goes before and after the incarnate Son like a set of holy parentheses embracing the story of salvation in Christ.

The encouragement to watch Jesus and think Trinity can change the way we read Scripture and enable us to see things there that we may have overlooked before. When we turn our eyes upon Jesus and learn the habit of asking how the Father and the Holy Spirit are co-present with him, we can see that many of the most beloved biblical stories from the life of Jesus Christ have a Trinitarian background we had never noticed. Perhaps their presence is impossible to ignore at Christ's baptism in the Jordan, when the Spirit descends in the form of a dove and the Father speaks from heaven: "This is my beloved Son, with whom I am well pleased." But the baptism story should give us the interpretive key to the rest of the New Testament as well, because the Holy Spirit's anointing power is always on the incarnate Son, and the Father's good pleasure in his beloved is the secret of everything Christ does. We should always inquire after the hidden presence of the Spirit and the Father in the unhidden work of Jesus.

Attending to the Father's presence in the life of Christ makes us look up higher than we are used to. Attending to the Spirit's presence in the life of Christ makes us look back and forth further than we are used to. Taken together, the presence of the Father and the Spirit makes it clear how the life of Jesus is the focal point of the economy of salvation.

Diagram 4.1: The Work of the Trinity Centered on Jesus

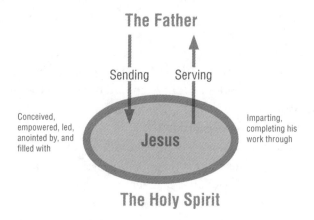

Seeing Jesus in the center of these divine actions is crucial for coming to understand the shape of the economy of salvation.

THE TWO HANDS OF THE FATHER

So far we have approached the economy of salvation from an intentionally Jesus-centered point of view. We started here on purpose, because the best way to come to understand the Trinity is to begin with the clarity and concreteness of Jesus the Son, sent by the Father in the power of the Spirit.[7] But once we have learned to perceive the Trinity at work in the life of Christ, there is another, complementary way of viewing the economy that can expand our vision even farther. That way is to turn our attention from Christ as the center of salvation toward the Father as the source of it. The Father is the one who sends Christ on his mission of salvation and also sends the Holy Spirit to complete the work. Viewed from this angle, the economy of salvation is something that has been molded into shape by the Father himself, through his two personal emissaries, the Son and the Spirit.

One of the greatest theologians of the early church, Irenaeus of Lyons (who wrote around the year 200), used a striking metaphor for this Father-centered view of things. He noticed that in the story of the creation of man in Genesis 2:7, "the LORD God formed the man of dust from the ground." Irenaeus noted God's direct, personal involvement in the making of man's body and soul. Against false teachers who preferred that God would have delegated to angels the dirty work of making the human body, Irenaeus insisted that God the Father did it himself, with his own two hands:

> It was not angels, therefore, who made us, nor who formed us, neither had angels power to make an image of God, nor any one else, except the Word of the Lord. . . . For God did not stand in need of these . . . as if He did not possess His own hands. For with Him were always present the Word and Wisdom, the Son and the Spirit, by whom and in whom, freely and spontaneously, He made all things, to whom also He speaks, saying, "Let Us make man after Our image and likeness."[8]

Of course Irenaeus did not mean that the Son and the Spirit were literally God's hands. In fact it is almost impossible to take the "two-hands" image literally, because to do so would be to reduce the Son and the Spirit to appendages of the Father. Irenaeus's point was that the Father, Son, and Holy Spirit are the one God who created man. But the image he suggests poetically, of the Father making man with his own two hands who are the Son and the Spirit, rivets our attention on God the Father as the source of all things, even as all things are worked out through the Son and the Spirit.

What this second-century theologian said about creation can help us in our goal of seeing the form of the entire economy of salvation. God did not leave the economy of salvation to take on its own shape, nor did he delegate its craftsmanship. The Father formed it himself with his own two hands. He was never without those two hands, the eternal Son and the eternal Spirit. And in the fullness of time he sent them on their missions into the world to bring us to himself. The economy of salvation, then, takes on its effective and meaningful shape when the Father sends the Son to be incarnate and the Spirit to be poured out (see Diagram 4.2).

Diagram 4.2: The Economy as the Two Hands of the Father

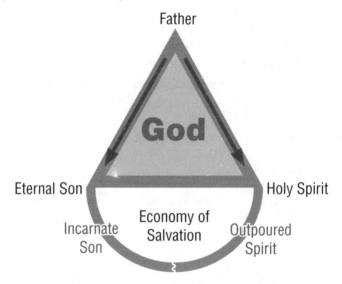

The Son and the Spirit are always together in carrying out the work of the Father. They are always at work in an integrated, mutually reinforcing way, fulfilling the Father's will in unison. Yet they are not interchangeable with each other, and they are not duplicating each other's work. In fact, the Son and the Spirit behave very distinctively in carrying out the concerted work of salvation. The Son is the Son and acts like the Son, while the Spirit is the Spirit and acts like the Spirit. Understanding them as the Father's two hands helps us see their unity (they both come from the Father for one purpose) and their distinctness (there are two hands, not one). God the Father did not send two emissaries who would do the same work twice. Because the Son and the Spirit are distinct, there is nothing redundant or even repetitive about their twofold work. We could describe their differences by saying the Son and the Spirit have distinct personalities, or that their personal styles show through in the way they carry out their distinct tasks. When we see their distinctness, we see the scope of the economy, which is where God reveals himself. Ninety percent of Trinitarian theology happens right here, where we come to understand the unity and distinction of the work of the Son and the Spirit, sent by the Father. Our task is to learn how to recognize this unity in distinction as revealed in the Bible and to describe it in a helpful, clarifying way.

The first clue to our task is obvious: the Son of God became incarnate and died for us, but the Holy Spirit did not. The Father sent the Son to take up the great work of incarnation and propitiation, while he sent the Holy Spirit to make that work possible in the first place (as we saw above, through the virginal conception and the anointing of the man Jesus Christ), and then to realize and complete the work after Christ had accomplished it. From this vantage point, we can perceive the distinctive profiles of the Father's two emissaries. Starting from here, we can even derive two entirely different vocabularies for the work of the Son and the work of the Spirit.[9] Push their unity and cooperation to the back of your mind for a moment while we examine their distinctness.

The Son and the Spirit are both ways that God keeps his promise to be "God With Us." But the Son is God With Us in the direct, personal sense that he is the eternal Son in human nature. The Spirit, on the other hand, is God With Us as the eternal Spirit dwelling among us as in a temple. The Son is God With Us by becoming one of us, but the Spirit is God With Us by living among us.

Think of the key words that are associated with the work of the Son and the Spirit. The right word for the Son's work is incarnation but for the Spirit it is indwelling. The Son becomes enfleshed, but the Spirit lives within. The Son of God took human nature to himself, personally taking on everything it means to be fully human. He was a divine person who had always had a divine nature, and without ceasing to be that eternal person with the divine nature he added to himself a complete human nature. So the incarnate Son became a human person in this particular sense: he was the eternal divine person who took on human nature. Incarnational theology is a deep subject and is too complex to explore in detail here. But the classic term used in that doctrine is *hypostatic union*, which means that Jesus was one person who possessed both God's nature and man's nature. The Son became human. The Holy Spirit, on the other hand, did not take human nature into personal union with himself. He did not become human. Instead, he indwells people.

The contrast becomes even clearer if you consider switching the categories between Son and Spirit. What if we said that the Son of God indwelled Jesus Christ instead of saying that he became Jesus Christ? That would be an entirely inadequate christology. It would make Jesus a human person filled with the Holy Spirit rather than the incarnate Son of God. Or what if we said that when the Holy Spirit comes to us, he becomes incarnate in us and takes on our nature? Again, that would be a severe misunderstanding of the Spirit's work and would lead to confusion about everything in the life of a Christian. Incarnation is not indwelling, but we need both if we are to experience God With Us.

When we look to the atonement, we also see the need for different vocabularies for the Son and the Spirit. Obviously the Spirit did not die for our sins, but there are less obvious implications of this fact. The work that Jesus Christ does for us is a vicarious, substitutionary work: he steps into the place that we occupy and offers himself to God in our place. As a propitiation for sin, the incarnate Son replaces us and bears the wrath of God on our behalf. The Spirit, on the other hand, does not substitute for us but empowers us. He does not take our place but puts us in our place. And in carrying out the great work of atonement, the Son completes the work once and for all in his death and resurrection, but the Holy Spirit takes that completed work and applies it to individual people.

Over and over in our Christian experience we note the difference between the Son and the Spirit. There are many things we say about the Son of God that we would never say about the Spirit. We are to be conformed to the image of the Son (Rom. 8:29), not the Spirit. We are told to be like Christ, and even to imitate God the Father in a certain sense (Eph. 5:1), but never to imitate the Holy Spirit. Again, there is one mediator between God and men (1 Tim. 2:5), and that is the man Jesus Christ, not the Holy Spirit. It may be tempting to extend these terms (*conformed*, *imitate*, *mediator*) to the Holy Spirit, from a sense of wanting to defend the full equality of the Spirit or to make sure the third person has the same honor as the first and second. We might even be able to argue that there is some metaphorical sense in which we imitate the Spirit or to extend the word *mediation* to describe the way the Spirit brings us to God through Christ. But that would be to speak very loosely and to ignore the categories that Scripture establishes. We would be in danger of missing the Spirit's distinctive work by confusing his work with Christ's. The best way to keep them unified is to see their difference; we distinguish in order to unite.

Chart 4.1: The Work of the Son and the Spirit

The Work of the Son	The Work of the Spirit
God with us, as one of us	God with us, dwelling among us
Incarnation	Indwelling
Hypostatic union	Communion
Assumes a human nature	Enlivens human persons
Substitutes for you	Regenerates you
Takes your place	Puts you in your place
Completes work all at once	Continues work constantly
Becomes a pattern for imitation	Forms us to fit that pattern
Is the one mediator	Unites us to the mediator
Accomplishes redemption	Applies redemption

ACCOMPLISHED BY THE SON, APPLIED BY THE SPIRIT

A classic way of looking at the two-handedness of God's work in salvation is the relationship between how the Trinity accomplishes redemption and how the Trinity applies that redemption to us. This idea of redemption accomplished and applied is a handy way of considering salvation in its objective and subjective aspects, even when the two phases of God's saving work are not correlated with the Son and the

Spirit.[10] Redemption would not reach its goal without being applied, but there would be nothing to apply if it were not already accomplished. But recognizing the Son and the Spirit, respectively, as the leading figures in the two phases enriches the idea even more. Christ the Son accomplishes redemption in his own (Spirit-created and Spirit-filled) work. The Holy Spirit applies that finished redemption to us in his own (Son-directed and Son-forming) work. The two works are held together by an inherent unity. The Son and the Spirit are both at work in both phases; nevertheless, the Son takes the lead in accomplishment, and the Spirit takes the lead in application.

Where can we turn for evangelical witnesses to this truth? We could turn to John Wesley, who drew a clarifying line between "what God does for us through his Son" and "what he works in us by his Spirit."[11] Or we could turn to John Owen, whose work *On Communion with God the Father, Son, and Holy Ghost* was an elaborate exploration of related themes.[12] Owen's influence extends down to J. I. Packer, who lists this as one of his five foundation principles in *Knowing God*:

> God is triune; there are within the Godhead three persons, the Father, the Son and the Holy Ghost; and the work of salvation is one in which all three act together, the Father purposing redemption, the Son securing it and the Spirit applying it.[13]

But one of the most helpful teachers on this subject is Puritan John Flavel (1627–1691). He was so committed to clear teaching on the subject that he wrote two different books. In the first book, *The Fountain of Life*, he described how God the Father made provision for salvation and then accomplished it in Christ. In the second book, *The Method of Grace*, he provided a full treatment of the way salvation actually takes hold of a human life. The first book is grace accomplished; the second book is grace applied. Many theologians have organized their teaching on salvation around this distinction, but Flavel stands out from the rest because of the Trinitarian character of his teaching. His book on the accomplishment of salvation is primarily focused on what the Son has done, while his book on the application of salvation is primarily focused on what the Spirit does. His *Fountain* and *Method* books are Jesus Christ and Holy Spirit books, respectively. That is, the first book describes the "grace provided and accomplished by Jesus Christ," while the second "contains the method of grace in the application of the great redemption to the souls of men" by the Holy Spirit.[14]

Flavel sees salvation worked out objectively in Christ, as God the Father loves the world and gives his Son (John 3); as he does not spare his Son and is therefore willing to give everything (Romans 8); as God is in Christ reconciling the world to himself (2 Corinthians 5). Nothing needs to be added to this complete salvation provided in the life, death, and resurrection of Christ. But it must be applied to each person who is to receive its benefits personally. And that application must also be a divine work, a work of the risen Lord who is not dead or done away with but is at the right hand of the Father. "From thence he shall come to judge the quick and the dead," and in the meantime, from thence he has sent the Holy Spirit.

Flavel is not trying to play the persons of the Trinity off against each other. He knows that the entire Trinity is at work in every aspect of salvation.[15] But he also wanted to distinguish between the work in which the Son is the primary agent and the work in which the Spirit is the primary agent. He wants to distinguish more clearly between them precisely so he can unite them more firmly. In one sense, God the Father applies salvation to believers in Christ himself, giving the incarnate Son, in his vicarious humanity, a complete salvation that is applied to "Christ as our surety" and "virtually to us in him."[16] God blesses the man Christ with the fullness of all blessings of salvation, and it overflows to us. This substitionary application, however, is actually effective in the divine-human person of Christ himself, but only "virtually to us." The actual (not merely virtual) application to us is "the act of the Holy Spirit, personally and actually applying it to us in the work of conversion." This is the method of grace: the Father acts toward Christ, the Spirit acts from Christ.

Flavel is insistent that the application of redemption by the Holy Spirit is mandatory, not merely optional. Without it, the work of the Father and the Son is of no avail:

The same hand that prepared it, must also apply it, or else we perish, notwithstanding all that the Father has done in contriving, and appointing, and all that the Son has done in executing, and accomplishing the design thus far. And this actual application is the work of the Spirit, by a singular appropriation.[17]

and again:

Such is the importance of the personal application of Christ to us by the Spirit, that whatsoever the Father has done in the contrivance, or the Son has done in the accomplishment of our redemption, is all unavailable and ineffectual to our salvation without this.[18]

The reason God's work waits on the fulfillment of the Spirit is that the Spirit is God. It would be insulting to say that "all that the Father has done . . . and all that the Son has done" is ineffectual until completed by some outside force. Flavel's point is that the Spirit is not some outside force, but a force internal to the being of God, of the same substance as God the Father and God the Son. Flavel pounds the point home:

It is confessedly true, that God's good pleasure appointing us from eternity to salvation, is, in its kind, a most full and sufficient impulsive cause of our salvation, and every way able (for so much as it is concerned) to produce its effect. And Christ's humiliation and sufferings are a most complete and sufficient meritorious cause of our salvation, to which nothing can be added to make it more apt, and able to procure our salvation, than it already is: yet neither the one nor the other can actually save any soul, without the Spirit's application of Christ to it. The Father has elected, and the Son has redeemed; but until the Spirit (who is the last cause) has wrought his part also, we cannot be saved. For he comes in the Father's and in the Son's name and authority, to complete the work of our salvation, by bringing all the fruits of election and redemption home to our souls in this work of effectual vocation.[19]

With the Spirit's work in our lives, then, the Trinitarian circuit is completed: the Spirit accomplishes our union with Christ, hides our life with Christ in God, and makes Christ become "unto us wisdom, and righteousness, and sanctification, and redemption" (1 Cor. 1:30 KJV). This is the Trinitarian method of grace whereby God brings us to himself by being himself toward us.

Is this Trinitarian understanding of grace still active in evangelicalism in more recent years? Flavel was a well-catechized, Oxford-educated Presbyterian with rather precise convictions of the Puritan Reformed type. We would expect him to have careful doctrinal distinctions at hand. But how has the Trinitarian method of grace fared in the hands of later evangelicals? Flavel's understanding of the Trinity in salvation was still alive and well in the nineteenth century in the theology of mass evangelist Dwight L. Moody. Moody presents a striking contrast to Flavel: his formal education probably did not extend beyond the fifth grade, he spoke to large audiences in simple terms, and his message tended toward the Arminian side of the evangelical spectrum. But we can tell that Moody's brand of evangelicalism presupposed a Trinitarian gospel as much as Flavel's did, because on a few occasions he made his underlying beliefs explicit. When he wanted to be more robustly theological, Moody had an interesting strategy: he would call a better-educated pastor to the platform with him and then interrogate him publicly on the subject at hand. One of his favorite interlocutors for these "Gospel Dialogues" was Marcus Rainsford (1820–1897), who was known "for his firm grasp of essential evangelical doctrine and for his peculiarly strong hold on the great foundation realities connected with the believer's standing in Christ." Moody valued Rainsford "for his clear cut definitions of doctrine and for his lucid and convincing statements of spiritual truth."[20]

In one of these Gospel Dialogues, Moody said to the audience, "I have tried to put the truth before you in every way I could think of. Now I want to put a few questions to Mr. Rainsford that relate to the difficulties that some of you have."[21] Whatever those difficulties may have been, Rainsford quickly laid out a distinction between Christ's work for us and the Spirit's work in us:

Mr. Rainsford: Christ's work for me is the payment of my debt; the giving me a place in my Father's home, the place of sonship in my Father's family. The Holy Spirit's work in me is to make me fit for His company.

Mr. Moody: You distinguish, then, between the work of the Father, the work of the Son, and the work of the Holy Ghost?

Mr. Rainsford: Thanks be to God, I have them all, and I want them all — Father, Son, and Holy Ghost. I read that my Heavenly Father took my sins and laid them on Christ; "The Lord hath laid on Him the iniquity of us all." No one else had a right to touch them. Then I want the Son, who "His own self bare my sins in His own body on the tree." And I want the Holy Ghost: I should know nothing about this great salvation and care nothing for it if the Holy Ghost had not come and told me the story, and given me grace to believe it.[22]

Shortly after this interaction, Moody asked Rainsford what the result would be if somebody received the word of God that very night. Rainsford replied, "The Father and the Son will make their abode with him; and he will be the temple of the Holy Ghost. Where he goes the whole Trinity goes; and all the promises are his."[23]

When the message of Trinitarian grace is simplified from the bulky tomes of a Flavel or an Owen to the Gospel Dialogues between a Moody and a Rainsford, is anything lost in the translation? The main points, I think, carry over quite well. Rainsford distinguishes Son and Spirit in order to unite them ("Thanks be to God, I have them all"), and in the process he uses Trinitarian categories to expand our view of the comprehensiveness of God's work. There is, however, one element of the message that is in danger of being forgotten: the distinction between the work of the Son and the Spirit belongs to a realm higher than our own personal experience.

Moody was an evangelistic genius whose campaigns spoke to the immediate experience of his audiences. But when we say that the Son accomplishes redemption and the Spirit applies it, we are first of all speaking about the economy of salvation and only subsequently about our own experience. If we forget this, then our thoughts can get tangled up in all sorts of merely experiential distinctions, like the distinction between objective fact and subjective appropriation, or between truth in general and truth "for me." Those distinctions lead to theological pseudo-problems if we try to use them in understanding the Trinitarian method of grace, and as a consequence, we think either of the Son's work as insufficient or the Spirit's work as an add-on. But the distinction between the work of the Son and the work of the Spirit is built into the Christian message. It is a distinction internal to the gospel itself, because it is internal to God himself. To rehearse it from the top: God in himself is Father, Son, and Spirit; so in the economy of salvation the Father sends the Son and the Spirit; so in our experience the Father accomplishes salvation for us in the Son and applies it to us in the Spirit.

Remembering that the only way to see the shape of the gospel is to see the shape of the economy of salvation, we can be grateful for thinkers like John Owen who wrote with such a comprehensive grasp of the economy. Calling the work of the Spirit "the second great head" of all the "gospels truths," Owen pointed out how closely related it is to the sending of the Son. The Father gives the Son "for us," that is, as a sacrifice for propitiation. But the same Father gives the Spirit "to us," that is, as an indwelling presence. Together, these two sendings manifest God's glory:

> When God designed the great and glorious work of recovering fallen man, and the saving of sinners, to the praise of the glory of his grace, he appointed, in his infinite wisdom, two great means thereof: The one was the giving his Son for them, and the other was the giving his Spirit to them. And hereby was way made for the manifestation of the glory of the whole blessed Trinity; which is the utmost end of all the works of God.[24]

Some theologians, noticing the distinctiveness of the Spirit's work in application of Christ's work, have gone so far as to talk about two economies, one of the Son and the other of the Spirit.[25] We stay closer to the storyline of Scripture, however, if we talk about the one economy of God and then go on to highlight its twofold character. God's work, in other words, is not two economies, but one twofold economy. This may seem like a minor difference in terminology, but it helps us account for why the two phases of salvation overlap so much. The Spirit, for example, is already active in the accomplishing of salvation in numerous ways: he brings about the incarnation by causing Jesus' conception, he empowers Jesus in his work, and he is the medium through which Jesus makes an offering of himself to the Father. Since the very name "Christ"

THE DEEP THINGS OF GOD

implies "Son of David anointed by the Spirit," it is apparent that without the Spirit there could be no Christ to accomplish salvation. So the Spirit is active in accomplishing redemption, but he acts by equipping the Son to do the work.

Similarly, knowing that we are looking at a single, twofold economy of God helps us recognize that the Son is still involved in the application of redemption in numerous ways. He is the risen and ascended one who sends the Spirit, and it is through the personal presence of the Spirit that Jesus himself also lives in the hearts of believers. So the Son is active in applying redemption, but he acts by equipping the Spirit to do the application. They are always mutually implicated, though in each phase one of them sets the other one up to take the leading role. Just as Christ (enabled by the Spirit) accomplished redemption, so the Spirit (making Christ present in faith) applies it. Nowhere in the twofold economy is there a simple departure or complete absence of one of the agents. We are always in the Father's two hands at once.

The work of the Son and the work of the Spirit, while distinct, are so intimately linked that it is hard to do justice to their profound unity. Consider, finally, the question of means and ends. Which of the two missions is the means and which is the end? Thinking in terms of redemption accomplished and applied, it is easy to consider the Spirit's work as the means of delivering the Son's work. In that case, the Son does the thing itself—reconciling God and man—and the Spirit serves his work by applying it to individual lives. Pentecost, in this view, happens in order to fulfill and extend Calvary and Easter. On the other hand, when we consider the intimacy of spiritual fellowship that the indwelling of the Holy Spirit involves, it begins to look as if all God's ways lead up to the sending of the Spirit.

If God's goal is to dwell among his people, the atonement was a necessary step to make that indwelling possible. The temple of human nature had to be cleansed to make it ready for the Spirit's indwelling. So the Son by incarnation prepared one perfect human temple, his own body, for the Spirit to be present in. And by atonement the Son purified the other temples, preparing them to receive the Spirit on the basis of the Son's finished work. "Christ redeemed us from the curse of the law by becoming a curse for us . . . so that we might receive the promised

148

Spirit through faith" (Gal. 3:13–14). Calvary and Easter, in this view, happen in order to make Pentecost possible. If we have to ask whose work is the means and whose is the end, our answer must be either that the question is badly formed, or that each of them is a means to the other. The Spirit serves the Son by applying what he accomplished, and the Son serves the Spirit by making his indwelling possible. Both Son and Spirit, together on their twofold mission from the Father, serve the Father and minister to us.

If we hear about the Trinity at all in relation to salvation, we are likely to hear something to the effect that "it takes the entire Trinity to save one soul." This is true, but not very specific. The real insight into God's plan and purpose awaits us when we learn to see specifically how the persons of the Trinity are distinctively at work in salvation: the Father sends his two emissaries, the Son accomplishes salvation, and the Spirit applies it. Anglican bishop Robert Leighton said it even more helpfully and precisely:

> We know that this Holy Trinity co-operates in the work of our salvation: the Father hath given us His Son, and the Son hath sent His Spirit, and the Spirit gives us faith, which unites us to the Son, and through Him to the Father. The Father ordained our redemption, the Son wrought it, and the Spirit reveals and applies it.[26]

From its ordaining, to its accomplishing, to its application, the economy of salvation is the one great plan of God to simultaneously save us and make himself known to us. As John Owen said, by giving his Son for us and giving his Spirit to us, the Father manifested "the glory of the whole blessed Trinity; which is the utmost end of all the works of God."[27] One sender, the Father, gives shape to salvation history by sending two emissaries, the Son and the Spirit, to carry out the plan of salvation. The Father's two hands give shape to the economy.

THE SON AND THE SPIRIT AMONG US

We are ready for the next step. The Son and Spirit do not just construct or configure the economy of salvation; they actually bring it into being by showing up. They constitute the history of salvation by their presence because it would not be here without their being in it. The plan of salvation is above all a plan for the Son and the Spirit to arrive among us in the fullness of time, and it is by being here that they give the economy its shape. Because the Father sends them on their joint mission, the Son and the Spirit are the way God is with us to transform our history of sin and ignorance into his history of salvation and revelation (see Diagram 4.4).

Diagram 4.3: The Son and the Spirit in the Economy

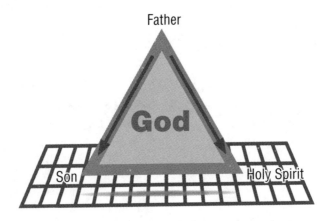

God the Father is intimately involved with the economy of salvation but not by being sent. Even when Jesus promised that the Father would come to those who love the Son, he did not say that the Father would be sent: "If anyone loves me, he will keep my word, and my Father will love him, and we will come to him and make our home with him" (John 14:23). Jesus went on to talk about how the Father had sent him (v. 25) and would later send the Holy Spirit in Jesus' name (v. 26). The Father loves by sending; the Son and the Spirit love by being sent. In the diagram above, the Father's indirect, or unsent, presence in the economy of salvation is indicated by the fact that the Son and the Spirit actually come to occupy places on the grid of salvation history, and the Father is the source who remains intimately and inwardly connected with them. "He who sent me is with me," said Jesus. "He has not left me alone, for I always do the things that are pleasing to him" (John 8:29). You could say the Father is not here, but it would be better to say he is here in the Son and the Spirit or he is here by sending them. The way God gives himself to us is that the Father gives the Son and the Spirit, sending them to redeem us and reveal the Trinity. In Trinitarian theology, the word for the sending of these two persons is *mission*. We can talk about their coming from the Father to us as their being sent on their respective missions, bearing in mind that the two missions are not separate from each other but mutually entwined in the ways we already explored.

So the Son and the Spirit fulfill the Father's will by taking their stand here among us. They do not just send messages, envoys, or influences; they show up in person. And when they show up in person, they behave as themselves. Their eternal personalities, we might say, are exhibited here in time. We can see this most clearly in the case of the incarnate Son, who should always be the focus of our attention. We need to understand Jesus as the eternal Son who behaves like the Son on earth as he does in heaven and in time as he does in eternity. He was always the co-eternal, co-equal Son of God who always delighted in the presence of the Father, and when he took on human nature to save us, he continued to be the co-eternal, co-equal Son of God, still delighting in the presence of the Father.

When the Word who was God and was with God in the beginning (John 1:1–2) took the astonishing step of becoming flesh and dwelling among us (John 1:14), what changed about him? A moment's thought shows that his divine nature did not change, since that would mean not only that he stopped being God, which is enough of a frightful and unbiblical conclusion, but also that there stopped being a God at all, since the divine nature itself would have changed into human nature. No, God remained God, and the Word remained God, when he became flesh. "Became," in the incarnation, cannot mean "transformed into," or "underwent a change in which he stopped being one thing and turned into another thing." When the Word became flesh he took human nature to be his own, and he added a complete, real human existence to his eternal self.[28]

But here is the crucial thing to notice, the great, open secret at the heart of the gospel of God: when the Word became flesh, the sonship of the second person of the Trinity did not undergo any change either.

It was the eternal Son, whose personal characteristic is to belong to the Father and receive his identity from the Father, who took on human nature and dwelled among us. His life as a human being was a new event in history, but he lived out in his human life the exact same sonship that makes him who he is from all eternity as the second person of the Trinity, God the Son. So when he said he was the Son of God, and when he behaved like the Son of God, he was being himself in the new situation of the human existence he had been sent into the world to take up.

Nobody has described this continuity better than Austin Farrer (1904–1968), the Anglican theologian who was a close friend of C. S. Lewis. Farrer pointed out that the Gospels do not portray Jesus as somebody who walked around behaving like he was God. Instead, they portray him as walking around behaving like the Son of God. "We cannot understand Jesus as simply the God-who-was-man. We have left out an essential factor, the sonship."[29] When we leave out that sonship, we may think we are affirming the deity of Christ more clearly ("he is God" is a simpler statement to teach and defend than "he is the Son of God"), but in fact we are obscuring the Trinitarian revelation. The loss is too great; we will miss so much that is right there in Scripture. "What was expressed in human terms here below was not bare deity; it was divine sonship," said Farrer.

> God cannot live an identically godlike life in eternity and in a human story. But the divine Son can make an identical response to his Father, whether in the love of the blessed Trinity or in the fulfillment of an earthly ministry. All the conditions of action are different on the two levels; the filial response is one. Above, the appropriate response is a co-operation in sovereignty and an interchange of eternal joys. Then the Son gives back to the Father all that the Father is. Below, in the incarnate life, the appropriate response is an obedience to inspiration, a waiting for direction, an acceptance of suffering, a rectitude of choice, a resistance to temptation, a willingness to die. For such things are the stuff of our existence; and it was in this very stuff that Christ worked out the theme of heavenly sonship, proving himself on earth the very thing he was in heaven; that is, a continuous perfect act of filial love.[30]

As Farrer said, it is impossible to imagine how God would act if God were a creature. To put the question that way is to force ourselves into constant, unresolved paradox: Would he act like the creator, or like a creature? What action could he take that would show him to be both? When the incarnate God walked on water, was he acting like the creator or the created? None of these questions are the kind of questions the New Testament puts before us. What the apostles want to show is that Jesus was the Son: he came, lived, taught, acted, died, and rose again as the Son of God. Everything we usually say about the two natures of Christ is true, because Jesus Christ is fully God and fully man. The Bible does not teach less than that, but it does teach more. While our temptation is to rush past his sonship to get to his deity, the Bible does the opposite, often rushing past his deity to dwell on his sonship. When the Word became flesh, John tells us, the apostles saw his glory, "glory as of the only Son from the Father, full of grace and truth" (John 1:14). The word of life that they heard, saw, and touched with their hands was the one who was "with the Father and was made manifest" (1 John 1:1–2).

The temptation to gloss over the fact that Jesus was the Son, in our hurry to get to the fact that he was God, is a temptation to be resisted. His sonship explains so much about what he did among us because it is the secret to his personal identity. "God" describes what Jesus is, but "Son" describes who he is. That is why the perception of his sonship takes us into the heart of the doctrine of the Trinity.

A cross-cultural illustration from the mission field is appropriate here. Missionary bishop Lesslie Newbigin (1909–1998) described the challenge of finding the right terms for proclaiming the gospel to a tribal culture for the first time. The missionary gathers information about what the tribe already understands about deity. After sorting through various local and territorial powers of the spirit world, he surfaces a concept of a strongest, highest, or oldest god above those lesser forces. This is much closer to the biblical idea of the one God, so it is a starting point. "Does one say that 'Jesus' is the name of that one God?" No, cautioned Newbigin, for that is not the main idea of the New Testament. "The truth is that one cannot preach Jesus even in the simplest terms without preaching him as the Son. His revelation of God is the revelation of 'an only begotten from the Father,' and you cannot preach him without speaking of the Father and the Son."[31] Newbigin's warning applies not only to other cultures but to our own, because we are tempted to regard the Trinitarian theology that is based on the sonship of Christ as "a troublesome piece of theological baggage which is best kept out of sight when trying to commend the faith to unbelievers."[32] Of course we don't need to be saying the word *Trinity* all the time in our evangelism and preaching. But if we squint at Christ's sonship and rush past his relation to the Father, we are missing what God has revealed about himself and settling for less than the full counsel of God.

What is so wonderfully clear with regard to the Son—that he is himself here with us just as he has eternally been himself in the happy land of the Trinity—is also true of the Holy Spirit. It is harder to perceive the distinct personality of the Spirit, though, partly because the Spirit is so successful in his work of focusing our attention on Jesus. Nevertheless, the same thing is true of both of them: when we meet the Son and the Spirit in salvation history, we meet divine persons. They are eternal, and there was never a time when they did not already exist as persons of the Trinity. Their coming into our history is not their coming into existence. But their coming into our history is an extension of who they have always been in a very specific, Trinitarian way.

Diagram 4.4: Eternal Processions and Temporal Missions

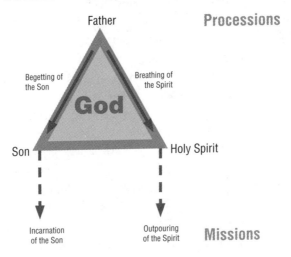

When the Father sends the Son into salvation history, he is doing something astonishing: he is extending the relationship of divine sonship from its home in the life of God down into human history. The relationship of divine sonship has always existed, as part of the very definition of God, but it has existed only within the being of the Trinity. In sending the Son to us, the Father chose for that line of filial relation to extend out into created reality and human history. The same is true for the Holy Spirit: when he is sent to be the Spirit of Pentecost, who applies the finished work of redemption and lives in the hearts of believers, his eternal relationship with the Father and the Son begins to take place among us. Having always proceeded from the Father in eternity, he now is poured out by the Father on the church.

There are helpful terms available for all this in the traditional theological categories of Trinitarianism. At the level of the eternal being of God, the Son and the Spirit are related to the Father by eternal processions. The Son's procession is "sonly," or filial, so it is called *generation*. The Spirit's procession is "spiritly," so it is called *spiration*, or, in a more familiar word, breathing. Those two eternal processions belong to God's divine essence and define who he is. The living God is the Trinity: God the Father standing in these two eternal relationships to the Son and the Spirit. We have already discussed this in some detail in the chapter on "the happy land of the Trinity," where we emphasized that the processions would have belonged to the nature of God even if there had never been any creation or any redemption. But now we come to the message of salvation itself and make the leap from God's eternal being to the temporal salvation he works out in the economy. The leap is an infinite one that only God could have made. By God's unfathomable grace and sovereign power, the eternal Trinitarian processions reach beyond the limits of the divine life and extend to fallen man.

Behind the missions of the Son and the Spirit stand their eternal processions, and when they enter the history of salvation, they are here as the ones who, by virtue of who they eternally are, have these specific relations to the Father. For this reason, the Trinity is not just what God is at home in himself, but that same Trinity is also what God is among us for our salvation. In an earlier chapter we mentioned some of the terms that theology has used for referring to the realm of the eternal processions: the ontological Trinity, the essential Trinity, the Trinity of being, or the immanent Trinity (immanent meaning "internal to" itself). Now we can say that what is present in the economy is that Trinity, as the Father sends the Son and the Spirit to be who they are here in our midst, to save us and reveal God to us.

The eternal Trinity is truly present in the gospel Trinity. This changes everything about our salvation, our knowledge of God, and our experience of God, because it takes us straight to the center of God's revealed ways. This is how God gives himself to us: by the Father giving the Son and the Spirit. This is how God is with us: in Christ and the Spirit of Christ. This is how we know God: as he truly is, as Father, Son, and Holy Spirit. The whole field of Christian life and thought is thus open for biblical, Trinitarian exploration. But there is also a relatively minor point that is worth noting, and it has to do with where our minds go when we think of the doctrine of the Trinity. It is easy to fall into the habit of thinking that "Trinity" points to some set of facts about God which, while true, have nothing to do with us. When most Christians hear the word *Trinity*, their immediate mental response is to reach for an analogy: Is the Trinity kind of like a shamrock, or like the three states of matter (solid, liquid, gas), for instance the one substance H^2O being ice and water and steam? They do this, I think, because of a mental habit of associating the Trinity with a logical problem, the problem of reconciling three and one. But while there is a time and a place for coming to terms with that problem, and while analogies can offer some limited help on that occasion, we have learned something different from the shape of the economy of salvation. We have learned to associate "Trinity" with the incarnate Son and the outpoured Spirit.

When we talk about Jesus, sent by the Father to work in the Spirit, we should know that we are talking about the Trinity. Our thoughts and affections should jump to the Gospels and the gospel, the story of Jesus and the present encounter with him, rather than to shamrocks and steaming icebergs. The whole point is that the presence of the Son and Spirit themselves, sent by the Father into the economy of salvation, is the Trinity. The eternal Trinity is the gospel Trinity. These persons in the gospel story are not what the Trinity is like—they are the Trinity. We will see how this changes everything about how we look for the signs of the Trinity in the various elements of the church's life and work. For now, it is enough to underline the new mental associations, the whole new habit of associative thinking, that we gain from attending to the economy. Away with tropical icebergs! Shamrocks begone! In the gospel we have God the Trinity.

ADOPTION INTO THE TRINITY

Recovering the explicitly Trinitarian theology of our evangelical fore-bears can provide us with some new ideas, categories, and terminology to use in understanding the gospel. Talking in terms of eternal processions and temporal missions may be novel for our generation, but it was the common stock of evangelical theology until fairly recently. New to us, these ideas will be reinvigorating for evangelical life and thought. But the most exciting thing about recovering the Trinitarian depth of the gospel is that it equips us to use familiar terms with a greater understanding of what they have really meant all along. Classic evangelical Trinitarianism, once we have recovered it for contemporary use, restores some of our most familiar and conventional terms for salvation to their original depth and power. The most important instance of this restoration is the way this Trinitarian background makes the biblical doctrine of adoption come to life.

Adoption is a central biblical description of how God saves. It emphasizes the quality of the new relationship that God brings us into, a relationship of having been made into his children. In explicitly Trinitarian terms, this means that God brings us into the relationship of sonship that has always been part of his divine life. When we become sons of God, we are joined to the sonship of the incarnate Son, which is in turn the human enactment of the eternal sonship of the second person of the Trinity. Sonship was always within God, and it came to be on earth as it is in heaven, in the person of the incarnate Christ. Every time we hear the biblical proclamation that we have been made God's children, we should hear the deep incarnational and Trinitarian echoes of this good news: "See what kind of love the Father has given to us, that we should be called children of God; and so we are" (1 John 3:1). Paul

157

declares, "God sent forth his Son . . . so that we might receive adoption as sons. And because you are sons, God has sent the Spirit of his Son into our hearts, crying, 'Abba! Father!'" (Gal. 4:4–6). Paul's way of putting it is especially helpful because it also refers to the work of the Holy Spirit in bringing about our sonship. The Spirit is the one who baptizes us into Christ, forms us into sons on the pattern of his sonship, and even takes up residence within us as the principle of sonship that enables us to call on God as Father.

Diagram 4.5: Trinitarian Adoption

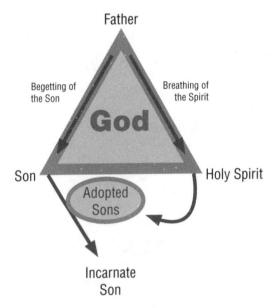

When the eternal Son becomes the incarnate Son, his eternal, filial relation to the Father takes on a human form. He does not become a different person but remains the Son. His procession from the Father extends into a mission from the Father. Thus divine sonship appears among humans, in Christ. The Holy Spirit, as we have already seen, is involved in this mission of the Son to be incarnate. He brings about the conception of Jesus and empowers Christ in his ministry, among other things. But the role of the Spirit is especially important in incorporating believers into this sonship of Christ. It is the Spirit of adoption (Rom.

8:15), or the Spirit of the Son (Gal. 4:6), who makes us children of the Father. He puts us into the place of sonship.

This is how "the two hands of the Father" work simultaneously to bring us into fellowship with God: the Son opens up the path of human sonship, and the Spirit puts us into it. This two-handedness of adoption was the main idea of an important article in *The Fundamentals*, that interdenominational publication that marked the conservative evangelical revolt against modernism in the early years of the twentieth century. Published serially in twelve volumes between 1910 and 1915, the publications were sent free of charge to Christian workers around the world. The 1917 republication of *The Fundamentals*, under the editorial hand of R. A. Torrey, consisted of ninety essays printed in four volumes.[33] Torrey put the essays into an orderly sequence in this edition, making *The Fundamentals* a popular synthesis of conservative biblical scholarship, theology, and apologetics.

The Fundamentals have sometimes been criticized for a lack of theological breadth, as they focused on the handful of doctrines that were under attack by modernism. In ninety chapters on a range of disputed issues, for example, there is not a chapter on the Trinity. Uncharitable interpreters of *The Fundamentals* (and there have been hardly any sympathetic scholarly interpretations in recent decades) have taken this conspicuous absence as evidence of the narrowness and imbalance of *The Fundamentals* project. But the uncharitable reading is too facile to fit the case. Lacking a Trinity chapter, *The Fundamentals* nevertheless exhibit a robust evangelical Trinitarianism precisely at this point of the doctrine of salvation by adoption. This is best exemplified in Charles Erdman's essay "The Holy Spirit and the Sons of God."[34]

Erdman begins this essay by pointing out that "due importance has not been given to the peculiar characteristic of the Pentecost gift in its relation to the sonship of believers."[35] After describing the "sonship in glory" that Jesus enjoyed, Erdman goes on to say that "when the disciples were baptized with the Spirit on the day of Pentecost they were not only endued with ministering power, but they also then entered into the experience of sonship."[36] Working out that experience of sonship in the believers, according to Erdman, was the proper task of the Holy Spirit for at least two Trinitarian reasons. First, the Holy Spirit forms believers into sons because his work is based on the completed work of Christ the Son: "through the heavendescended Spirit the sons of God are forever united with the heavenascended, glorified Son of God." Second, the Spirit forms believers into sons because he always works toward that perfect sonship that he knows to belong to Christ: "the sum of all His mission is to perfect in saints the good work He began, and He molds it all according to this reality of a high and holy sonship."[37] The perfection of Christ "was preeminently the life of a Son of God and not only of a righteous man; of a Son ever rejoicing before the Father, His whole being filled with filial love and obedience, peace and joy."

The Trinitarian background of adoption is striking. The Heidelberg Catechism raises the question, "Why is Christ called the only begotten Son of God, since we are also the children of God?" and answers it, "Because Christ alone is the eternal and natural Son of God; but we are children adopted of God, by grace, for his sake."[38] The catechism is concerned to point out the absolute difference in the way this sonship is experienced by these two very different kinds of sons. Christ, and Christ alone, is the Son of God by nature and from eternity. Believers, on the other hand, are made to be sons by adoption, through the gracious decision of God, for the sake of Christ the Son. The difference is infinite. But alongside that difference is the striking element of similarity, indeed of sameness, and that sameness the relation of sonship.

Bishop Robert Leighton described the greatness of this adoption in God's overall plan by saying, "For this design was the Word made flesh, the Son made man, to make men the sons of God."[39] As any responsible interpreter of this topic must do, Leighton underlined the difference: "It is a sonship by adoption, and is so called in Scripture, in difference from His eternal and ineffable generation, who is, and was, the only begotten Son of God." But Leighton also emphasized that this adoption is something deeper than a mere "outward relative name" as in human adoption or "that of men." Divine adoption comes from deeper in God's identity and penetrates deeper into the being of the redeemed than human adoption can. We see this in two ways in Scripture. First, God's adopted children are also said to be regenerated or born again from him (1 John 1:13). Second, they are said to have received the Spirit:

A new being, a spiritual life, is communicated to them; they have in
them of their Father's Spirit; and this is derived to them through
Christ, and therefore called His Spirit. Gal. 4:6. They are not only
accounted of the family of God by adoption, but by this new-birth
they are indeed His children, partakers of the Divine nature.[40]

There is an important strand of the evangelical tradition that seems
almost to dare itself to say the highest things possible about the sonship
that believers enter into through the work of the Spirit and how it is
the same sonship as Christ's. Leighton seems to have been a partici-
pant in this tradition. One of the most strident was Robert S. Candlish
(1806–1873), whose book *The Fatherhood of God* argued that our
relationship to the Father was in "substantial unity" with the sonship
of the human nature of Christ and that "the only difference between our
enjoyment of sonship and Christ's was that Christ enjoyed the privileges
of sonship before we do, but not in a different manner." This must be
saying too much. But Sinclair Ferguson, commenting on this incautious
language, could not bring himself to lodge any complaint more serious
than the warning that "perhaps Candlish went beyond what is written, but it is not easy to show that he went against what is written."[41]
At all costs, we do not want to diminish God's glory by claiming an
unwarranted intimacy with him, one that ignores our permanently subordinate position as creatures or minimizes our alienated condition as
sinners. But we also want to confess the God-sized, God-shaped greatness and goodness of the actual salvation brought to us in the gospel.
Doing so has brought us to the place where we can and must say that
God the Son became man so that men could become sons of God.

In fact, once the Trinitarian background of adoption emerges into
plain sight, these high, almost extravagant, claims for our sonship must
be made. There is something intoxicating in the insight that we are sons
of God in God the Son. It transposes our understanding of salvation
into a higher key, transfigures our notions of what God has done for us
in Christ and the Spirit into something we can hardly look at directly,
and transforms our relationship with God into a conscious enjoyment
of filial blessing. We have been looking to see why the evangelical tradition has said that "the things of the gospel are depths," even "the deep

things of God." Trinitarian adoption brings into our view the ultimate grounds for saying this: sonship is on earth as it is in heaven. The clear dividing line between God's essence and his actions is still in place. There is never any compromise of the blessedness and self-sufficiency of God in the happy land of the Trinity. There is still an infinite distinction between who God is in himself and what he freely chooses to do for us. But adoption is the mightiest of God's mighty acts of salvation, and without transgressing the line between the divine and the created, God does reach across it and establish a relationship more intimate than we could have imagined. In adopting children, God does something that enacts, for us and our salvation, his eternal being as Father, Son, and Spirit among us. Eternal sonship becomes incarnate sonship and brings created sonship into being. In this case, what God does is who he is.

"Really, thought becomes giddy," said Marcus Rainsford, "and our poor feeble minds weary, in contemplating truths like these, but they are resting places for faith." Rainsford (whom we met as Dwight Moody's interlocutor in the Gospel Dialogues) spoke for evangelical Trinitarianism when he said that these things are not secrets that we have somehow managed to pry our way into but are things that the Son intentionally made known to us by speaking about them to his Father in front of his disciples: "It was in order that our faith might be strengthened, our hope established, and our love deepened, that the Lord uttered these words to His Father—not in private, but in the hearing of His disciples."[42]

Can this kind of theological intoxication be squared with a sober doctrinal perspective? Yes, it can. In fact, the genius of evangelical Trinitarianism is that it has undertaken to define a safe context for these high and holy truths of salvation. Other traditions in theological history have been able to perceive these infinite depths stretching away behind salvation, but they have been less cautious in their descriptions of them and less consistently Trinitarian. Christian mystics down through the centuries have said astonishing things, many of them crossing the line into the indefensible. All the language of mystical rapture, ineffable bliss, beatific vision, uncreated energies, and deification has been employed to communicate something of what is given to us in adoption into the Trinity. But evangelical Trinitarianism has frequently endeavored to retain the depth of the insight while limiting the excesses. Recall James Denney's remark, "I'd rather be found in Christ than lost in God."[43] Evangelical Protestantism has often issued strict warnings against mystical excesses, but this is not because of a low view of salvation or a philistinish restriction of theological vision. Indeed, it is the skyscraping Trinitarian soteriology of the evangelical tradition that has required its own recurrent anti-mystical warnings. The great evangelical tradition warns itself against mysticism constantly, because it runs so close to it, as Adolph Saphir pointed out: "The mystic writers will always be a useful protest against the mere 'form of godliness,' and the letter that killeth; but the minds that feel most attracted by them need most to be on their guard in reading them."[44] We wouldn't warn ourselves about mysticism if we weren't inclined to it.

How has evangelical theology kept this high doctrine of salvation from veering off into insupportable giddiness? First, through our habitual biblicism, which prefers to restrict itself to the language of Scripture as much as possible, avoiding elaborate technical terminology. Even the terms we learned above, like *mission* and *procession*, are at the very edges of what evangelicals will be able to embrace wholeheartedly. A few such terms are necessary to help us specify what we mean by the scriptural words we use, but in general we want to use as few as possible. That is because, second, we prefer to repeat and confirm the biblical language itself, and to be able to read our doctrine of salvation straight off the pages of the Bible when possible. Short interjections for clarification are permissible, and minor detours to gather together some systematic-theological connections can be beneficial, but for the most part we prefer our doctrine of salvation, like our Trinitarianism, to be stated in the Bible's own terms.

Third, it is no coincidence that we reserve our most astonishing claims about intimacy with God for this particular section of the doctrine of salvation, the Trinitarian section. This is the only safe place to make such claims. Any system of theology that makes extravagant claims about union with God had better avoid talking about God's essence or attributes directly, lest it fall into the transgression of blurring the boundary between God and creatures. Calvin, in the Trinity chapter of his *Institutes*, says that even "God, to keep us sober, speaks sparingly of his essence" when making himself known to us, and we ought to speak even more circumspectly when describing our union with God.[45] What we can safely talk about, however, is the Father, Son, and Holy Spirit. Their fellowship and cooperation in our salvation gives us the guidelines and distinctions we need for strong statements about salvation as a kind of union with God. It is remarkable how consistent the evangelical tradition has been about juxtaposing these two things: that salvation brings great intimacy with God and that such intimacy requires a Trinitarian context. One of the most popular refrains of nineteenth-century evangelicalism was this one:

> So near, so very near to God,
> I cannot nearer be;
> For in the person of His Son,
> I am as near as He.
>
> So dear, so very dear to God,
> More dear I cannot be;
> The love wherewith He loves the Son,
> Such is His love to me.[46]

We should probably add that whenever a union with God is proclaimed in non-Trinitarian terms, evangelical testimony becomes shrill and insupportable. People expect to be close to God in some undefined way and try to come to terms with this misunderstood promise without the guidelines of adoption (procession becomes mission, enabling adoption).

Fourth, evangelicalism at its best has understood how to put this nonspeculative, biblical, and Trinitarian account of adoption into the proper relationship with other key ideas about salvation, the ideas for which evangelicalism is more famous. I am thinking of atonement and justification in particular. It is possible to talk about adoption in a way that obscures the necessity of the atonement, as if God had only to reach out and embrace us with fatherly love and no costly sacrifice involved. It is also possible to emphasize adoption in a way that bypasses justification with its legal categories and its concern for righteousness.

Again, it is remarkable how consistently successful the evangelical tradition has been about praising adoption without detracting from these key ideas. One example will have to suffice here. J. I. Packer has called adoption "the highest privilege that the gospel offers: higher even than justification."[47] Packer is aware that "this may raise eyebrows," so he defends his view by saying that justification is the primary blessing and even the fundamental blessing of salvation. But it is not the highest blessing. "Adoption is higher," says Packer, "because of the richer relationship with God that it involves."[48] Since he obviously does not want to denigrate justification or to propose anything novel, Packer goes on to quote from the classic work on justification by Buchanan: "According to the Scriptures, pardon, acceptance, and adoption, are distinct privileges, the one rising above the other in the order in which they have been stated. . . . The privilege of adoption presupposes pardon and acceptance, but is higher than either."[49] In fact, Packer proposes that the New Testament could be summed up in the three words "adoption through propitiation."[50]

Nothing in this presentation of Trinitarian adoption is new. The only thing I may be pressing in an unusual way is that salvation (by adoption through propitiation) is deeper than we think and that evangelicals have long believed it in its depth. If we have forgotten the Trinitarian depth of our doctrine of salvation, it is only in very recent years: since the Reformers; since the Puritans; since the Victorians; since the first Fundamentalists; since J. I. Packer and Sinclair Ferguson, who are still with us.

We have seen, in this line of thought, that the Trinity is the gospel. More expansively said: the good news of salvation is that God, who in himself is eternally the Father, the Son, and the Holy Spirit, has become for us the adoptive Father, the incarnate Son, and the outpoured Holy Spirit. God the Father sent the Son to do something for us and the Spirit to be something in us, to bring us into the family life of God. God, who is eternally triune in himself in the happy land of the Trinity, gives himself to us to be our salvation, giving the economy of salvation a triune shape that reveals who he is, and making the Father, Son, and Spirit present in our own lives. And along the way, we have seen that these truths are not exotic or unheard of but have been embraced by evangelicals for centuries.

The great French Protestant preacher Adolphe Monod (1802–1856) spoke on this subject while on his dying bed in words that cannot be surpassed for their clarity and force:

> The relation of the Father, the Son and the Holy Spirit to man corresponds to a relationship in God between the Father, the Son and the Holy Spirit; and the love which is poured out to save us is the expression of that love which has dwelt eternally in the bosom of God. Ah! The doctrine then becomes for us so touching and profound! There we find the basis of the Gospel, and those who reject it as a speculative and purely theological doctrine have therefore never understood the least thing about it; it is the strength of our hearts, it is the joy of our souls, it is the life of our life, it is the very foundation of revealed truth.[51]

5

INTO THE SAVING LIFE
OF CHRIST

*(Or, What's Trinitarian about a Personal Relationship
with Jesus)*

When I accept Christ as my Savior, my guilt is gone, I am indwelt
by the Holy Spirit, and I am in communication with the Father
and the Son, as well as the Holy Spirit—the entire Trinity.
FRANCIS SCHAEFFER

The Father's love gave Christ to them, Christ's love gave Himself
for them, and the Holy Ghost's love reveals and applies to them
the salvation of God.
MARCUS RAINSFORD

Is the gospel mainly about Jesus Christ or mainly about the Trinity? That
is a question so badly formulated that it would not deserve an answer,
except that it undeniably gives voice to a tension that is widely felt in
evangelical circles and beyond. One of the reasons for the ambivalence
that some evangelicals feel toward the doctrine of the Trinity is that it
can seem to be a distraction from the simple message about salvation in
Christ. And evangelicals are famous for being focused on Jesus Christ
and the conscious experience of personal salvation by receiving Christ
as Savior. We have already seen the divine scope and the Trinitarian
shape of the economy of salvation. Now we need to see, as clearly as
possible, that the gospel of the Trinity is not an alternative gospel to
the experience of personal salvation through Christ. There are not two

167

THE DEEP THINGS OF GOD

different messages here but a single proclamation of good news that is simultaneously Christ-centered and Trinity-centered. There is never any need to play the doctrine of the Trinity off against salvation in Christ, because they are centered on the same reality. The more Trinity-centered we become, the more Christ-centered we become, and vice versa.

CHRIST-CENTERED, NOT FATHER-FORGETFUL OR SPIRIT-IGNORING

The main reason that a Christ-centered message can never be in real tension with a Trinity-centered message is that the two messages are concentric. When you declare that Jesus Christ is the center of your message, you are committing yourself to proclaim him and whatever is central to his own concerns. But Jesus himself is always centered on the work of the Father and the Spirit, so successfully focusing on Christ logically entails including the entire Trinity in that same focus. It is incoherent to hold to Jesus without simultaneously holding to the Father and the Spirit. Unfortunately, while it is incoherent, it is not impossible. Many people fall prey to this temptation of trying to grasp Christ in abstraction from the Father and the Spirit.

In his own ministry Jesus apparently found himself confronting the same tendency. John's Gospel reports repeatedly that Jesus talked over the heads of his listeners when he taught about his relationship to the Father and the Spirit. "They did not understand that he had been speaking to them about the Father," interjects the narrator at John 8:27; and again at John 7:39, "This he said about the Spirit, whom those who believed in him were to receive, for as yet the Spirit had not been given, because Jesus was not yet glorified" (John 7:39). From explanations like this, the reader gets the impression that Jesus was teaching about the Trinity, but his disciples had not yet learned how to see Jesus himself in Trinitarian perspective. Similarly in Acts 1:6–8, the disciples come to the risen Christ and ask, "Lord, will you at this time restore the kingdom to Israel?" Jesus' reply is striking, not only because it sets aside their expectations about the timeline for the kingdom, but also because it points them away from their expectations about what Jesus will do, to the work of the Father and the Spirit: "It is not for you to know times or seasons that the Father has fixed by his own authority. But you will receive power when the Holy Spirit has come upon you, and you will be my witnesses . . ."

Of course Jesus is not telling the disciples to stop focusing on him. We are at all times to "[look to] Jesus, the founder and perfecter of our faith" (Heb. 12:2). But we are to look to him in a way that lets us see him situated in his relationships to the Father who sent him and the Spirit whom he sends. Unless we see Jesus in this way, we fail to see him as who he actually is. The consequences are inevitably confusion and a loss of spiritual power, usually brought about by substituting Jesus into a role that ought to be filled by the other persons of the Trinity. For example, there is a metaphorical sense in which Jesus plays a fatherly role towards believers. But the main thrust of the New Testament message is certainly not that Jesus is our father; it is that the Father of Jesus is our Father. To substitute Jesus for the Father is to miss the plain meaning of the Bible by ignoring his Father. This is to focus on Jesus in a way that detracts from his own message. The problem is not in being too Christ-centered, but in using Christ-centeredness to enable an unbiblical Father-forgetfulness.

Another example is the tendency to think of Jesus as the one who lives in our hearts without making reference to the Holy Spirit's role as the direct agent of indwelling. Once again, there is a grain of truth to this: Jesus does dwell in the hearts of believers, and a handful of passages in the New Testament describe our relationship to Jesus this way (especially Eph. 3:16–17). But the dominant message of the Bible is that we are in Christ, not that Christ is in us. And on those few occasions when Christ is said to be in us, the work of the Spirit is nearly always mentioned. This is not a theological subtlety noted only by overly precise theologians but a special emphasis of Scripture. Billy Graham, who has certainly popularized a powerful message about accepting Jesus into your heart, identified this indwelling work of the Spirit in salvation as something that needed special emphasis:

> One point about the relation of the Holy Spirit and Jesus Christ needs clarification. The Scriptures speak of "Christ in you," and some Christians do not fully understand what this means. As the

God-man, Jesus is in a glorified body. And wherever Jesus is, His body must be also. In that sense, in His work as the second person of the Trinity, Jesus is now at the right hand of the Father in heaven. . . . For example, consider Romans 8:10 (KJV), which says, "If Christ is in you, the body is dead because of sin." Or consider Galatians 2:20, "Christ lives in me." It is clear in these verses that if the Spirit is in us, then Christ is in us. Christ dwells in our hearts by faith. But the Holy Spirit is the person of the Trinity who actually dwells in us, having been sent by the Son who has gone away but who will come again in person when we shall literally see Him.[1]

Once again, it is not wrong to affirm that Jesus lives in our hearts, but it is wrong to ignore the Holy Spirit's role in that indwelling.

It is interesting to see how this signature evangelical teaching about Christ living in our hearts has devolved and degraded over the years. If you trace it to its origin, it is a relentlessly Trinitarian message, as we have already seen in Billy Graham's presentation of it in the 1970s. An earlier presentation of the message of Jesus in our hearts—one that the Billy Graham team made extensive use of—is Robert Boyd Munger's widely reprinted 1951 sermon, "My Heart—Christ's Home." Munger begins with Ephesians 3:16–17 and then says, "Without question one of the most remarkable Christian doctrines is that Jesus Christ himself through the Holy Spirit will actually enter a heart, settle down and be at home there. Christ will live in any human heart that welcomes him." Munger definitely describes the indwelling of Christ as being "through the Holy Spirit" in this opening sentence. In the next few pages, he describes Christ's ascension and the subsequent descent of the Spirit that made the indwelling possible: "Now, through the miracle of the outpoured Spirit, God would dwell in human hearts."[2]

From this clearly Spirit-honoring beginning point, Munger goes on to develop the homey application that made his sermon a classic, as Christ the guest is shown through each room of the heart-house, extending his lordship into every part. Even that element of Munger's sermon can be traced further back to John Flavel's 1689 book *Christ Knocking at the Door of Sinners' Hearts, or, A Solemn Entreaty to Receive the Saviour and His Gospel*. Flavel, whose radically and consistently Trinitarian theology we saw in the previous chapter, places Jesus decidedly in the context of the Father and the Spirit. Flavel's book is even based (like Munger's) on Jesus' saying in Revelation 3:20, "Behold, I stand at the door and knock." He carefully distinguishes the original intention of that passage (a warning to a church) from its legitimate extended sense (a personal invitation to sinners), and then dilates on the personal application: "Thy soul, reader, is a magnificent structure built by Christ; such stately rooms as thy understanding, will, conscience, and affections, are too good for any other to inhabit."

With the Trinitarian background in place, the message of Jesus knocking on the door of a sinner's heart is a recognizably Trinitarian gospel. It is not Father-forgetful or Spirit-ignoring in its classic exponents such as John Flavel, Robert Boyd Munger, or Billy Graham. Surely these three witnesses count as an evangelical pedigree and can bolster our confidence in the theology presented through countless flannelgraph images of Christ knocking on the door of a fuzzy, felt hearthouse. Surely with this Trinitarian lineage in place, we can affirm that all the flannelgraphs are true! But we have to admit that the Trinitarian connections are fairly easy to lose. They may have been there in Flavel, Munger, and Graham, but they are often lost in translation, especially in recent decades. Jesus is still presented as knocking on the heart's door, but too often in a Father-forgetful and Spirit-ignoring way.

Just as we can lapse into substituting Jesus for our heavenly Father, we can replace the Spirit with Jesus when we talk about the divine indwelling. Taken together, these two errors constitute an unfortunately common distortion of the biblical message. They replace the Trinity with Jesus, or they center on Jesus in a Father-forgetful, Spirit-ignoring manner. Jesus becomes my heavenly Father, Jesus lives in my heart, Jesus died to save me from the wrath of Jesus, so I could be with Jesus forever. Once again, there is no such thing, in Christian life and thought, as being too Christ-centered. But it is certainly possible to be Father-forgetful and Spirit-ignoring. At their best, and from their roots, evangelicals have avoided that. In recent decades, though, it requires vigilance to make sure we are presenting the evangelical message with recognizable Trinitarian connections. What Would Jesus Do? He would do the will of the Father in the power of the Spirit. He would send the Spirit to bring us to the Father.

UNION WITH CHRIST

Being properly Christ-centered always entails being Trinity-centered. Everyone who receives the salvation described in the New Testament is saved by being joined to Christ as the incarnate, atoning second person of the Trinity. But when we go on to work out our understanding of that salvation, we need to keep the full scope of the economy of salvation in place. When it comes to soteriology, the doctrine of salvation, there is a watershed that marks some as believers of one type and some as believers of another type. The watershed is a Trinitarian grasp of union with Christ.

The New Testament idea of salvation is that God has dealt with us by dealing with Jesus Christ: the life, death, and resurrection of Christ are the place where God the Father took hold of human nature to save it, dealt with sin decisively, and poured out his Spirit without reserve. Then and there God and man became intimately united and worked out the grievances that threatened to overturn their covenant relationship. In Christ, God was so overwhelmingly active and available that once and for all the second half of the covenant was kept: "I will be your God and you will be my people." It all happened in the life, death, and resurrection of Jesus Christ.

Since salvation is all accomplished in the life of Jesus, our salvation is a matter of being joined to him or united to him, or as Paul says succinctly: being "in Christ." God apparently has two steps for saving people: (1) accomplish salvation in Christ; and (2) put people into Christ. As Paul says in 1 Corinthians 1:30, "because of him you are in Christ Jesus," which could be rendered "by God's doing you are in Christ," or as the KJV has it, "of him are ye in Christ Jesus." This fact of union with Christ is the core of Christian soteriology. John Calvin put it classically when, having finished a thorough treatment of the work of God in Christ, he opened the third book of *The Institutes* with these words:

> We must now see in what way we become possessed of the blessings which God has bestowed on his only-begotten Son, not for private use, but to enrich the poor and needy. And the first thing to be attended to is, that so long as we are without Christ and separated from him, nothing which he suffered and did for the salvation

of the human race is of the least benefit to us. To communicate to us the blessings which he received from the Father, he must become ours and dwell in us. Accordingly, he is called our Head, and the first-born among many brethren, while, on the other hand, we are said to be ingrafted into him and clothed with him, all which he possesses being, as I have said, nothing to us until we become one with him.[3]

Note the Trinitarian contours here: the Father puts all the blessings of salvation onto the incarnate Son, and the Spirit unites us to that. It is not enough to say that faith links us to the benefits of Christ, because we must "climb higher and examine into the secret energy of the Spirit, by which we come to enjoy Christ and all his benefits."

Salvation begins and ends in union with Christ, and all the blessings of salvation flow naturally from that union. This should be familiar territory to anybody who understands the gospel. But the Trinitarian shape of this application of redemption guards against numerous mistakes. Mainly, it lodges the saving life of Christ in the work of the Father and the Spirit, and thus keeps us from falling back into a faux Christocentrism that is both Father-forgetful and Spirit-ignoring. But it also keeps us from declining into a couple of defective understandings of what salvation is.

Deficient soteriology type A: rather than centering everything on the life, death, and resurrection of Jesus Christ, some people conceive of salvation as essentially a here-and-now encounter in which they cry out to a higher power who hears their cry and performs an act of deliverance. The higher power is Jesus, and he has feelings of love toward them. How is this present act of deliverance related to the life of Jesus back then? At best, this soteriology thinks of the past event as a transaction that gives the present Christ his rights or abilities to save now, perhaps by settling an account with God. The emphasis of this soteriology falls on the emotional attitude of this present higher power toward the believer: "Jesus loves me."

One way to see the difference between this soteriology and the biblical one is to mark how Paul speaks of the love of Jesus for the believer: "I have been crucified with Christ. It is no longer I who live, but Christ who lives in me. And the life I now live in the flesh I live by faith in the Son of God, who loved me and gave himself for me" (Gal. 2:20). The present-encounter soteriology says "Jesus loves me" in the present tense, but Paul hangs everything on the past tense of "Jesus loved me." The present-encounter soteriology (like all soteriological self-misunderstandings by Christians) is maddeningly close to the truth: we do cry out to the powerful and present Jesus who does love us and will save here and now. But he saves us now and loves us now because he is the same yesterday and today, and because God the Holy Spirit places us into what God the Father has done in Christ so that we go to the cross and come out of the tomb in him. Galilee, Gethsemane, and Calvary are not just distant events in the prior biography of our present Savior. Christ is present to us through the Spirit, in the power of that finished work, and our salvation has the shape of dying and rising with him.

This brings us to deficient soteriology type B: This way of viewing salvation is focused on finding the right church with the right sacraments. Jesus started a spiritual organization that is still in existence, and it administers water baptism and Communion with bread and wine. Locating this church from among the plethora of options and getting into contact with the proper sacraments is what matters. There is less to say about this soteriology because its inadequacy is more obvious. It's the classic case of the sacramental tail wagging the soteriological dog: if this is the way sacraments matter then nothing else matters, and there is no such thing as a doctrine of salvation that isn't identical with locating the right sacraments. It is mainly worth mentioning because it succeeds in emphasizing what the present-encounter soteriology leaves out, which is a reference to the saving life of Christ.

What is so frustrating about this deficient soteriology is that it is obsessed with tasting and handling the Christ-ordained rituals, the very meaning of which is union with Christ: baptism in water means burial and resurrection with Christ; the bread and wine mean actual partaking of the body and blood of Christ rather than notional assent to facts about him. Yet these symbols can so easily become opaque and threaten to mean themselves rather than the things they signify. People who lapse into this soteriological misunderstanding are very close (much closer in many cases than the rival soteriology considered above) to recognizing union with Christ. In fact they recognize the form but misunderstand the content. The right soteriology comes from a Christocentrism that is not in contradiction to a Trinity-centeredness. There are two movements or trajectories to consider here: one movement is the dying and rising with Christ, our mortification and vivification by being identified with his death and resurrection. That is the Christocentric focus. The second movement is the long line that traces how we are saved when God the Spirit unites us to what God the Father has done in the life of God the Son. That is the Trinitarian focus. It is based on the Trinitarian shape that the economy of salvation has. It is the horizon against which we must understand salvation in Christ. The deficient soteriologies can be overcome by a Christocentric perspective that is not Father-forgetful or Spirit-ignoring. May the eyes of our hearts be opened so we can see the power of God toward us who believe, in accordance with the power which he worked in Christ when he raised him from the dead and seated him at his own right hand (Eph. 1:18–21).

THE TRINITARIAN THEOLOGY OF FRANCIS SCHAEFFER

As we focus on the way all this Trinitarian theology comes into our own experience, it is high time we turn to another case study of classic evangelical teaching that presents these various elements in their proper proportions and with an eye toward experiencing it. Look at Francis Schaeffer's words from his 1972 book *True Spirituality*. In the chapter entitled "The Supernatural Universe" he says:

> Little by little, many Christians in this generation find the reality slipping away. The reality tends to get covered by the barnacles of naturalistic thought. Indeed, I suppose this is one of half a dozen questions that are most often presented to me by young people from Christian backgrounds: where is the reality? Where has the reality gone? I have heard it spoken in honest, open desperation by fine young Christians in many countries. As the ceiling of the naturalistic comes down upon us, as it invades by injection or by connotation, reality gradually slips away.

Schaeffer was in earnest about this cry for reality. He was not just reporting the "honest, open desperation" of "fine young Christians" who came to him in the early seventies; he had also asked these questions himself, in almost the same language, twenty years before. In the very next sentence he gives the answer as he had found it:

> But the fact that Christ as the Bridegroom brings forth fruit through me as the bride, through the agency of the indwelling Holy Spirit by faith—this fact opens the way for me as a Christian to begin to know in the present life the reality of the supernatural. This is where the Christian is to live. Doctrine is important, but it is not an end in itself. There is to be an experiential reality, moment by moment.[4]

It would be easy to overlook one of the most important elements in this answer: the Trinitarian element. The road to spiritual reality, according to Schaeffer, is through an experienced reality of God but specifically of the fact "that Christ . . . brings forth fruit through me . . . through the agency of the indwelling Holy Spirit." The reality Schaeffer invites us to understand and experience is a Trinitarian reality, an experience of God the Father through the Son and the Spirit. And the God whom Schaeffer points to in all his most popular writings, the God who is there and is not silent, is not God in general, but God the Holy Trinity. Schaeffer goes on, becoming more insistently Trinitarian as he develops the thought:

> This experiential result, however, is not just an experience of 'bare' supernaturalism, without content, without our being able to describe and communicate it. It is much more. It is a moment-by-moment, increasing, experiential relationship to Christ and to the whole Trinity. We are to be in a relationship with the whole Trinity. The doors are open now: the intellectual doors, and also the doors to reality.[5]

Schaeffer attributes his effectiveness in later ministry to his encounter with the Trinity. In his 1974 position paper for the Lausanne congress on evangelization, Schaeffer tells the story of the deep period of doubt and perplexity in his life in 1951 and 1952. Troubled by the lack of spiritual reality in the Christian groups he worked with, Schaeffer began asking what was missing, and why. He thought his way all the way back to his original agnosticism and put all his beliefs and commitments back on the table for renegotiation. He paced back and forth for months or took long walks when the weather permitted. He notified his wife, Edith, that if he didn't find what he needed in Christianity, he would reject it and then do something else with his life. His conclusion:

> I came to realize that indeed I had been right in becoming a Christian. But then I went on further and wrestled deeper and asked, "But then where is the spiritual reality, Lord, among most of that which calls itself orthodoxy?" And gradually I found something. I found something that I had not been taught, a simple thing but profound. I discovered the meaning of the work of Christ, the meaning of the blood of Christ, moment by moment in our lives after we are Christians—the moment-by-moment work of the whole Trinity in our lives because as Christians we are indwelt by the Holy Spirit. That is true spirituality.[6]

Writing about this turning point in his life, Schaeffer later said: "Gradually the sun came out and the song came. Interestingly enough, although I had written no poetry for many years, in that time of joy and song I found poetry beginning to flow again . . . admittedly, as poetry it is very poor, but it expressed a song in my heart which was wonderful to me."[7] And there is a bit of poetry, first published in 1960 and later reprinted in the preface to 1974's *No Little People*, which captures what Schaeffer was seeking and what he found:

> To eat, to breathe
> to beget
> Is this all there is
> Chance configuration of atom against atom
> of god against god
> I cannot believe it.
> Come, Christian Triune God who lives,
> Here am I
> Shake the world again.

The "Christian Triune God who lives" did answer that prayer and shook the world through Schaeffer's ministry.

In 1951 Francis Schaeffer had an encounter with the Trinity that revolutionized his life. It sparked the phase of his ministry for which we all remember him and put him in touch with a sense of spiritual reality he had lacked before: "a moment-by-moment, increasing, experiential relationship to Christ and to the whole Trinity. We are to be in a relationship with the whole Trinity." But when this change came over him, he didn't sit down and write a treatise on the Trinity; instead, he famously started writing about everything else under the sun. As a result, if you want the details of Schaeffer's Trinitarian view of salvation (his soteriology), you have to piece it together from a few places scattered around his writings. The most programmatic statement of Schaeffer's Trinitarian soteriology is in his book *True Spirituality*.[8] He connects the dots this way:

> The Holy Spirit indwelling the individual Christian is not only the agent of Christ, but he is also the agent of the Father. Consequently, when I accept Christ as my Savior, my guilt is gone, I am indwelt by the Holy Spirit, and I am in communication with the Father and the Son, as well as of the Holy Spirit—the entire Trinity. Thus now, in the present life, if I am justified, I am in a personal relationship with each of the members of the Trinity. God the Father is my Father; I am in union with the Son; and I am indwelt by the Holy Spirit. This is not just meant to be doctrine; it is what I have now.[9]

If you want even more detail on Trinitarian salvation, you have to follow Schaeffer into the land of direct, personal Bible study. His basic course in Bible knowledge has been published as the series *Basic Bible Studies*.[10] The striking simplicity of these studies is underlined by the direct appeal Schaeffer makes to the reader:

> It would be my advice that each time you do these studies, you speak to God and ask Him to give you understanding through the use of the Bible and the study together. If someone pursues these studies who does not believe that God exists, I would suggest that you say aloud in the quietness of your room: "O God, if there is a God, I want to know whether You exist. And I ask You that I may be willing to bow before You if You do exist."[11]

What else would you expect from a Christian writer whose message was summed up in the affirmation, "He is there, and He is not silent"?

According to Schaeffer, every Christian who wants to understand salvation and the Christian life is obligated to come to grips with the biblical revelation on the subject: "It is central and important to our Christian faith to have clearly in mind the facts concerning the Trinity." His *Basic Bible Studies* were designed to deliver those facts.

The first point in Schaeffer's Bible study on the Trinity is that the God of the Bible is personal: God has plans that he considers in advance and then carries out with purpose (Eph. 1:4). Not only does he think but he takes action, real action in space and time (Gen. 1:1). And not only does he think and act, but he feels. He loves the world (John 3:16). "Love is an emotion. Thus the God who exists is personal. He thinks, acts, and feels, three distinguishing marks of personality. He is not an impersonal force or an all-inclusive everything. He is personal. When He speaks to us, He says 'I' and we can answer Him 'You.'"

One of Schaeffer's favorite phrases for the personhood of God was that he is "personal on the high order of Trinity," and the next step in his basic Trinitarian Bible study is to state all the biblical evidence about unity and diversity in the God of the Bible. The Old Testament teaches, and the New Testament reaffirms, that there is only one God (Deut. 6:4; James 2:19). "But," Schaeffer goes on, "The Bible also teaches that this one God exists in three distinct persons." His first line of evidence for this claim is the divine plurals used in the language of the Old Testament: "Who will go for us?" (Isa. 6:8); "Let us make man in our image" (Gen. 1:26); "Let us go down there and confuse their language" (Gen. 11:7). "In this verse, as in 1:26, the persons of the Trinity are in communication with each other."[12]

These Old Testament plurals would not be enough to prove the triunity of the one God all alone. They are odd enough to require some explanation: Why would a consistently monotheistic revelation use words like *we*, *us*, and *ours*? And they might point to a certain fullness or richness of God's inner life. But solid Trinitarianism has to wait until the Son and the Spirit are directly revealed in the events of the New Testament. What Schaeffer primarily wants us to learn from these passages, however, is not triunity itself but the fact that it preexists creation.

Combined with a few New Testament insights ("You loved me before the foundation of the world," said Jesus to his Father in John 17:24), these plurals show that "communication and love existed between the persons of the Trinity before the creation."[13] And that mattered a lot to Schaeffer, because it means that when God reveals himself as Father, Son, and Spirit, he is revealing who has always been.

When he turns to the New Testament, Schaeffer highlights the baptism of Christ (Matt. 3:16–17) because of the clarity with which each of the three persons is shown there. He also points to a few of the passages where all three persons are named in a single verse: Matthew 28:19; John 15:26; and 1 Peter 1:2.[14]

With this biblical doctrine of God as Schaeffer's foundation, his soteriology is explicitly Trinitarian. Under the heading of salvation, the Trinity is not the very first thing Schaeffer teaches. That priority is reserved for a classic Protestant statement of the biblical doctrine of salvation by grace alone through faith alone. But from that all-important point of entry, the very next thing Schaeffer wants to say is that what this justification introduces us into is a new relationship, or web of relationships, to the triune God:

> This new relationship with the triune God is, then, the second of the blessings of salvation, justification being the first. This new relationship, as we have seen, is threefold:
> 1) God the Father is the Christian's Father.
> 2) The only begotten Son of God is our Savior and Lord, our prophet, priest and king. We are identified and united with Him.
> 3) The Holy Spirit lives in us and deals with us. He communicates to us the manifold benefits of redemption.[15]

In summary, commenting on 2 Corinthians 13:14, Schaeffer says, "The work of each of the three persons is important to us. Jesus died to save us, the Father draws us to Himself and loves us, and the Holy Spirit deals with us."[16]

After the believer is placed in a saving relationship with the persons of the triune God, three consequences follow: (1) relationship to brothers and sisters in the church; (2) assurance of salvation; and (3) a Christian life characterized by the process of sanctification. In these studies Schaeffer devotes several sections to sanctification, equipping his readers with a good survey of the things they will need to know to live an intelligent Christian life. He highlights the difference between the event of justification and the process of sanctification, which is "a flowing stream involving the past. . . , the present, and into the future."[17] Salvation, as he had said in *True Spirituality*, "is a single piece, and yet a flowing stream."[18] Schaeffer also rounds out his teaching on sanctification with a great deal of practical advice about how Christians are to deal with sin and with an introduction to the basic spiritual disciplines.

True to Trinitarian form, though, one of the main things Schaeffer wants to say is that sanctification is a project of the entire Trinity, and he does so by surveying the way each of the three persons is related to Christian holiness. God the Father is active in our sanctification as the one who will accomplish it, and who sets the standard of it: "May the God of peace himself sanctify you" and "equip you with everything good that you may do his will, working in us that which is pleasing in his sight" (1 Thess. 5:23; Heb. 13:20–21).

Elsewhere Schaeffer says of the Father's role, "When we accept Christ as our Savior, we are immediately in a new relationship with God the Father. . . . But, of course, if this is so, we should be experiencing in this life the Father's fatherliness."[19]

God the Son is involved in our sanctification in that it is the purpose for which he died: "Christ loved the church and gave himself up for her, that he might sanctify her, having cleansed her by the washing of water with the word . . . gave himself for us to redeem us from all lawlessness and to purify for himself a people for his own possession who are zealous for good works" (Eph. 5:25–26; Titus 2:11–14).[20]

God the Spirit is the holy one who makes us holy: "you were washed, you were sanctified . . . by the Spirit of our God . . . [and] are being transformed . . . from glory to glory. . . [by] the Lord, who is the Spirit . . . [and we are saved] through sanctification by the Spirit and faith in the truth" (1 Cor. 6:11; 2 Cor. 3:18; 2 Thess. 2:13 NIV, NASB).[21]

Most of this richly Trinitarian understanding of salvation recedes into the background of Schaeffer's writing. Outside of the *Basic Bible Studies*, he does not often work through the details of Trinitarian soteriology. But Schaeffer always spoke from a depth of insight that flowed from his 1951 experience of the reality of the Trinity in salvation. He wrote and spoke with a sense of God's presence that was deeply personal and which he did manage to communicate to sympathetic listeners in all that he taught after 1951. Schaeffer's Trinitarian awakening left its mark on his work in the strong sense of the personhood of God that colored all his expressions. It may be hard for evangelical Christians to hear the phrase "a relationship with God" as a radically Trinitarian claim, but that is how the language functioned for Schaeffer. Whenever he said "relationship," you can bet there was Trinitarianism ringing in his ears: "Our relationship is never mechanical and not primarily legal. It is personal and vital. God the Father is my Father; I am united and identified with God the Son; God the Holy Spirit dwells within me. The Bible tells us that this threefold relationship is a present fact, just as it tells us that justification and Heaven are facts."[22]

Of course, as the story of Schaeffer's 1951 Trinitarian awakening makes clear, not every Christian is aware of the Trinitarian depths waiting beneath their spiritual lives. "It is," Schaeffer warned, "possible to be a Christian and yet not take advantage of what our vital relationship with the three persons of the Trinity should mean in living a Christian life. We must first intellectually realize the fact of our vital relationship with the triune God and then in faith begin to act upon that realization."[23] And immediately after this warning he invited his readers to review the Basic Bible Study on the three new relationships that constitute the Christian life.

One of the most remarkable characteristics of Schaeffer's teaching on the subject of the Trinity, and the reason we have investigated it in some depth here, is how it consistently combined two virtues: simplicity and depth. Over and over in his teaching on the Trinity, Schaeffer uses the phrase "When we accept Christ as Savior" and then describes some things that follow it. That phrase "accept Christ as Savior" is a comfortable phrase for evangelicals and also a clear central point to emphasize for unbelievers. If one of Schaeffer's innumerable conversations took a sudden turn in the direction of immediate personal application, Schaeffer was never far from the direct presentation of the gospel: accept Christ as Savior. If someone asked him in real earnest, What must I do to be saved? he would not lead them on a twisting dialectic through the innards and gizzards of sacred and secular thought: he would say "accept Christ as Savior." That's the simplicity.

But Schaeffer also brought the depth: look at the second half of any of his "accept Christ" sentences:

> "Now that we have accepted Christ as our Savior, God the Father is our Father."[24]
>
> "When we accept Christ as our Savior, we are immediately in a new relationship with God the Father. . . . But, of course, if this is so, we should be experiencing in this life the Father's fatherliness."[25]
>
> "When I accepted Christ as my Savior, when my guilt was gone, I returned to the place for which I was originally made. Man has a purpose."[26]
>
> "When I accept Christ as my Savior, my guilt is gone, I am indwelt by the Holy Spirit, and I am in communication with the Father and the Son, as well as of the Holy Spirit—the entire Trinity."[27]

The simplicity ("accept Christ") leads into the depth ("I am in communication with the Father and the Son, as well as of the Holy Spirit—the entire Trinity.") This depth is the spiritual reality that Schaeffer heard young people lamenting the absence of; it is the depth he was missing in 1951 when he called everything to a halt and reevaluated his status as a believer. "It is a moment-by-moment, increasing, experiential relationship to Christ and to the whole Trinity. We are to be in a relationship with the whole Trinity. The doors are open now: the intellectual doors, and also the doors to reality."[28]

Remember that at that time he asked God, "But then where is the spiritual reality, Lord, among most of that which calls itself orthodoxy?" And Schaeffer didn't get a thunderbolt from the sky, or a special revelation, or a second work of grace, or a Pentecostal baptism in the Spirit, or a new revelation that nobody else had ever heard. No, his experience was in fact an insight into what was already his: "Gradually I found something. I found something that I had not been taught, a simple thing but profound. I discovered the meaning of the work of Christ, the meaning of the blood of Christ, moment by moment in our lives after we are Christians—the moment-by-moment work of the whole Trinity in our lives because as Christians we are indwelt by the Holy Spirit. That is true spirituality."[29]

That was Schaeffer's Trinitarianism: always poised between the simplicity and the depth, able to draw from each as he or his audience required, he presented the deeper experience of the Trinity as an invitation to come and live out what all Christians implicitly believe: "It is . . . possible to be a Christian and yet not take advantage of what our vital relationship with the three persons of the Trinity should mean in living a Christian life. We must first intellectually realize the fact of our vital relationship with the triune God and then in faith begin to act upon that realization."

EXPERIENCING FATHER, SON, AND HOLY SPIRIT

Schaeffer's encounter with the Trinity, like Nicky Cruz's and the others we have seen so far, was a definite experience, a breakthrough in his life. But it is important to avoid the trap of reducing his new encounter with the Trinity to the category of experience. When evangelical Christians come to understand the Trinitarian soteriology we have been describing in this book, they tend to describe it as a moment of insight that changes everything about their life and faith. At the very least, they see it as a breakthrough to a new level of depth in the things they had known before. But there are some good reasons for avoiding the category of experience when talking about these great Trinitarian themes.

First, if we were to begin talking about "having a Trinitarian experience" or beginning to "experience the Trinity," it would sound like a new step to take, a next step in a sequence of steps. But that would be to focus attention in the wrong place. All these Trinitarian realities we have been exploring are contained within the good news of salvation and are already true about the gospel, whether we know and understand them or not (or, as we said earlier, whether we know that we know them or not). The evangelical Trinitarianism we have been describing in the last few chapters is not primarily an advance in experience but in insight. It changes everything, not by introducing you into something that was not previously true but by showing you the significance of something that has been true all along. Salvation is Trinitarian, whether you know it or not; breakthroughs can happen when you move from not knowing to knowing.

No doubt when we do come to see the Trinitarian depth underlying the gospel, we do go on to have an experience. The progress in understanding brings about a fresh encounter with God and an experience with him. But the second reason to be cautious about calling it an experience is that the category of experience is such a sticky one. An experience is a kind of virtual reality, whether the thing that provoked it was real or not. An experience of something is itself something; but a different something than the original something. As a result, experiences can be sticky like flypaper, stopping us at a certain level and not letting us go on to the thing itself. Evangelicals, who have a genius for cultivating authentic experience, also have a knack for reducing things to the level of experience.

Diagram 5.1: God in Salvation History and Experience

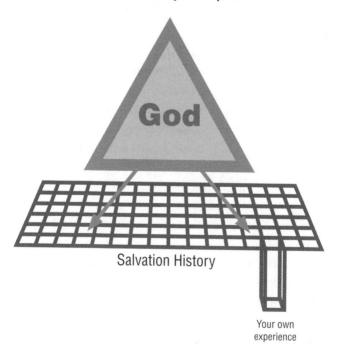

Salvation History

Your own
experience

Third, experience is too small a category for what we have described here. The Trinity simply cannot fit into the little experiences we are capable of having, with the biographical and psychological limits they impose. There is something incongruous about pointing to a moment in our lives and saying the eternal Trinity is there, as if God could be found within that moment analytically. Our little conversions, awakenings, and renewals simply cannot bear the burden of being the place where God is to be known in his majesty as Father, Son, and Spirit. When God makes himself known, he puts himself into the economy of salvation, not into our experience. The infinite God is present in the vast and comprehensive economy of salvation, to show himself and save us. With our little lives and their experiences, we fit into a subsection of that economy, and God's glory comes through to us in ways that fit our limited capacities.

The evangelical writers who have insisted on this most vehemently are precisely the ones who have testified to the greatest experiences with God. The more profoundly they have experienced the Trinitarian depths of God's salvation, the more careful they have been to insist that God is bigger than their experiences of him. Oswald Chambers is a good case in point. He warned, "As Christian workers we must never forget that salvation is God's thought, not man's; therefore it is an unfathomable abyss. Salvation is not an experience; experience is only a gateway by which salvation comes into our conscious lives. We have to preach the great thought of God behind the experience."[30] Chambers wrote like this because he was jealous to keep the experience of the gospel from turning into the gospel of experience, which is not good news after all. But he also insisted that what we experience in our lives is a real glimpse of God's great work. He compared our experiences to a pinhole through which a vast landscape is seen: "When a soul comes face to face with God, the eternal Redemption of the Lord Jesus is concentrated in that little microcosm of an individual life, and through the pinhole of that one life other people can see the whole landscape of God's purpose."[31]

Perhaps we can also make the point about experience by using another familiar evangelical teaching aid:

Diagram 5.2: The Engine, Car, and Caboose of Salvation

What we have learned about the kind of evangelical Trinitarianism that changes everything is that God's own eternal being as the Trinity is what matters most; it is the one thing better than the good news. But the good news, God's free choice to be himself for us by sending the Son and the Spirit into the economy of revelation and salvation, is the crucial link between who God is and what he does to save us. We find our places within that economy of salvation, and our experience of God in the gospel also comes along for the ride. This is the proper order of evangelical talk about the Trinity and the gospel. It should always be at least implicitly observed, and sometimes that order should be made explicit.

THREEFOLD ASSURANCE

As we learn to order our understanding of Trinitarian salvation, there are many advantages for evangelical thought. One of the greatest is the way the difficult doctrine of the assurance of salvation can find its proper home. The doctrine of assurance can be slippery. Even among those Protestant evangelical traditions that have recognized the necessity of formulating a doctrine of assurance that answers to the biblical witness about faith's confidence, there has long been a candid acknowledgment that the doctrine must simultaneously face opposite directions. It must assure me that I, even I, am saved; but it must do this by pointing away from me to an objective ground. To state the doctrine too objectively is to leave the believer as an onlooker to a redemptive spectacle that assures him with absolute confidence that somebody is saved but leaves open, disturbingly open, the question whether he is that somebody. To state the doctrine too subjectively, however, directs the believer's attention to phenomena of his own biography, experience, and consciousness, where the ground of salvation cannot be seen. A

well-ordered doctrine of assurance must underwrite the confident confession that even though I am condemned if considered in myself, I am
not in fact in myself but in Christ, where I, truly I, am saved.

In a flourishing Christian life, this confident repose on God shows
itself as an effortless and un-self-conscious equipoise: gazing on the
Savior and glancing at the self, the believer is saved and assured of
being saved in one simple motion. Let the redeemed of the Lord say so!
But when a Christian begins to lose confidence in salvation, the idea
of assurance becomes an idea without a home. In the next few pages,
I will show that assurance has a home in the Trinitarian salvation we
have been exploring. This is one of the most difficult parts of the book,
and some readers may want to skim over it on their way to the Bible
and prayer chapters. But others who are troubled about assurance of
salvation can find a new and helpful way of thinking about assurance
in light of the Trinity.

To many theologians it has seemed that assurance of salvation is
best described as assurance of faith and therefore should be included
in the description of faith itself, since to have assurance is just to know
that one believes the promise of someone worth believing in. On this
analysis, assurance is faith roused to self-consciousness, or faith knowing itself as faith. This answer is surely correct, so long as it can be
consistently distinguished from a confidence in the exercise of faith,
or the felt experience of having faith. When assurance is considered as
a kind of intensification of faith or as a subjective reflex of the act of
faith, it is too easily assimilated to the risings and fallings of religious
experience and subject to all the temperamental vicissitudes of that
experience. The summons to assurance then becomes an exhortation to
grasp the promise of salvation with a passionate inwardness that is the
measure of faith.

In reaction to this, some theologians bundle assurance and faith
together and then link them to an external source of authority. One
obvious external source is the authority of the church, especially its
competence to deliver truthful doctrines and valid sacraments. Faith
and its assurance then quickly become reduced to implicit faith in the
church's authority. Much medieval religion, however correct in substance it may have been, relied too heavily on believing whatever the

church taught, even without knowing what that was. Calvin rightly ridiculed this as "ignorance blended with humility," a mixture unworthy of the name of faith.

Another possibility is the appeal to biblical authority to ground assurance. Since Scripture is the record of God's promise, it is certainly right to appeal to it in this way. But in a way that is structurally similar to the appeal to church authority, the appeal to the authority of Scripture is only as successful as salvation it specifies. Unless that content is made explicit, the appeal to the divine authority of Scripture is a mere placeholder marking out where the argument should go.

These three attempts are variations on the theme of grounding assurance in an intensification of faith: first in the intensified experience of faith, second in the authority of the church that proposes what to believe, and third in the Scriptures as the authoritative record of God's promises that are to be believed. We might label these three solutions in their pure forms as the pietist, the Catholic, and the fundamentalist solutions. None of them is entirely mistaken, but they have in common a tendency to leave the content of the promise unstated. On their own they end by collapsing into either the objective or subjective ranges of the spectrum.

A heroic effort to ground assurance in God's eternal predestinating election is characteristic of the Reformed theological tradition. This has many merits to recommend it. First, it marks a definite advance by naming the content of salvation: God's gracious election. Second, it recognizes the requirement for a truly objective starting point for assurance: you don't get much more objective than monergistic predestination! But precisely in this success, it leaves open too much space between the objective and subjective poles of assurance. The question of assurance— How can I know that I am saved?—is not so much resolved as restated in the famous form: How can I know that I am among the elect? This bluntness is no help in the search for assurance.

The best Reformed thinkers, in contrast, have always kept their explorations of election within the wider framework of adoption, indwelling, and an effectual call worked out in the course of history, along with a full enjoyment of the manifold benefits of union with

Christ. Reformed soteriology has proven its capacity for a great inclusiveness of multiple biblical themes.

The classic Protestant view of assurance, however, emphasizes justification. "I should be assured of my salvation because God has unilaterally, forensically justified me in pronouncing me righteous on the grounds of Christ's redeeming work." As a proposed doctrinal home for assurance, justification is very promising: it is biblically well attested, it is highly objective, and it is specific about what salvation is. In its specificity it is sharply focused and served as a perfect point of conflict with the Roman Catholic theology that denied assurance of salvation. The Reformers rightly identified justification as the right place to draw the line, and assurance followed in its train.

However, this great virtue of the Reformation account of justification carries a particular disadvantage when it comes to its application to the doctrine of assurance: it is a focusing maneuver, specifying in the most precise and pointed way the element of salvation on which everything turns. That is appropriate for a dispute over the nature of God's mighty act of justifying the ungodly and the surgical work of excising the overgrown claims of human merit within salvation. But it is less helpful for the doctrine of assurance, because the movement of thought required for describing assurance is not the movement of focusing but the expansive and inclusive sweep of reciting the many blessings of salvation. As we have already seen, the Trinitarian account of salvation is able to deliver that expansiveness and inclusiveness. That makes Trinitarianism the natural home for the doctrine of assurance. Some of the benefits of locating assurance within this explicitly Trinitarian context include the following.

First, it ensures a greater objectivity than any other option. Back behind the economic sending of the Son and the Spirit, though in line with them, is the eternal immanent Trinity. The way this soteriology directs our attention to God's absolute aseity, independence, and blessedness is unprecedented. And it does so without some of the distorting consequences of appealing first to God's inscrutable sovereignty in election. It gets behind even that eternal counsel to the only thing behind the eternal counsel, the very bedrock of the being of God: his being as Father, Son, and Holy Spirit.

Second, it takes the encounter between the believer and Jesus and puts it in the broader context of the Father, Son, and Spirit acting concertedly for each other's glory, and then as a subordinate end, for our salvation. While a confession of the encounter between Jesus and me is integral to evangelical faith, it must happen against the horizon of Jesus and his Father. Trinitarian salvation is intensely personal but allows us to construe the word *personal* as an indication of the infinite depth of the divine life rather than as a pointer to our richly developed inwardness in its religious manifestation. It enables believers to respond with proper gratitude to God's action on our behalf, without degenerating into a monotonously self-referential and inwardly focused piety.

Third, this Trinitarian view of salvation is routed through the economy of salvation and moves from God to salvation history before contacting me and my own experience of salvation. This requires me to see my Christian experience as serving God's larger ends, employing me as a witness to God's spreading glory. The economic presences of the Son and the Spirit are, after all, missions, a word that was first of all a technical term in Trinitarian theology before it was a description of cross-cultural world evangelism. Our participation in the twofold mission of the Son and the Spirit is not only our salvation but our employment in the mission of God.

Finally, an explicitly and elaborately Trinitarian soteriology commends itself as a hospitable location for the doctrine of assurance in that robust confidence in God and his salvation flourish there. The reason for this is that, as we have seen, the Trinity is the gospel. Trinity and gospel are not just connected in some distant way, as two ideas that can be related to each other by a long train of reasoning. The connection is much more immediate than that. Seeing how closely these two go together depends on seeing both Trinity and gospel as clearly as possible in a large enough perspective to discern their overall forms. When the outlines of both are clear, we should experience the shock of recognition: Trinity and gospel have the same shape! This is because the good news of salvation is ultimately that God opens his Trinitarian life to us. Every other blessing is either a preparation for that or a result of it, but the thing itself is God's graciously taking us into the fellowship of Father, Son, and Holy Spirit to be our salvation.

Trinitarian salvation, then, is the proper home for the assurance of salvation. American Presbyterian theologian Benjamin Morgan Palmer's excellent little book *The Threefold Communion and the Threefold Assurance* drew these connections in a powerful way:

> What amazing security does this view give to the whole system of grace, seeing that it cannot fail in a single point except through a schism in the Godhead itself. The hand trembles that writes the daring suggestion; which is only saved from blasphemy by the assurance that he who searches the heart knows it is written only to give the most intense emphasis to the truth which it declares.

Palmer goes on: "Well may the Psalmist of old sweep with his fingers the strings of the Hebrew lyre to the tune of the sixty-second Psalm (vs. 6, 7): 'He only is my rock and my salvation: he is my defence; I shall not be greatly moved. In God is my salvation and my glory; the rock of my strength and my refuge is in God.'"

Marcus Rainsford, the interlocutor with Moody in the Gospel Dialogues, was also alert to the benefits of the Trinitarian background for the doctrine of assurance. He said:

> This is precious truth, but it stands upon a rock. The Father has as much interest in the salvation of the redeemed as Christ has, and Christ and the Holy Ghost have as much interest in them as the Father has. The Father's love gave Christ to them, Christ's love gave Himself for them, and the Holy Ghost's love reveals and applies to them the salvation of God. [32]

And he made the same point again in an equally Trinitarian way:

> We are taught in Scripture that our security flows from three great facts. The Father has loved us with an everlasting love—a love that never changes; Christ, who died for our sins, is now at God's right hand in resurrection glory and ever lives to make intercession for us, pleading His work finished and accepted; and God the Holy Ghost dwelleth in us. [33]

6

HEARING THE VOICE
OF GOD IN SCRIPTURE

*(Or, The Tacit Trinitarianism of Evangelical
Bible Reading)*

We cannot speak, think, and feel too highly of Scripture in its vital
connection with Christ and the Spirit.

ADOLPH SAPHIR

And we also thank God constantly for this, that when you received
the word of God, which you heard from us, you accepted it not as
the word of men but as what it really is, the word of God, which is
at work in you believers.

1 THESSALONIANS 2:13

The Bible has always been the focus of evangelical spirituality, and
evangelicals have always been Bible people. They may not be famous
as Trinitarians, but they are famous for biblicism. In this chapter, we
will examine evangelical commitment to the Bible and see that here,
too, a powerful but understated Trinitarianism has always been at
work. Because evangelicalism's image is so resolutely biblicist, it is
more important here than ever that we not only see that evangelical
approaches to Scripture have a Trinitarian dynamic under them but that
we also meet historical evangelicals who have known this to be true.

COMMUNION AND AUTHORITY

Evangelicals know to expect the voice of God to reach them in the
words of Scripture and have long approached the Bible as a real means

of grace, as a channel through which God himself will meet us here and now. The expectation of a personal encounter with God through devotional reading of the Bible is sometimes considered to be at odds with the high view of Scripture—its authority, verbal inspiration, and inerrancy—which is also characteristic of evangelical doctrines of Scripture. The pious personal encounter can be viewed as being in tension with the propositionally centered and authority-focused accounts of Scripture. There is a kind of "hot vs. cold" contrast according to which evangelicalism is depicted as divided between warm, pietistic biblicism on one side and icy, rationalistic, propositionalist orthodoxy on the other.

The two approaches to Scripture belong together, and what binds them together is a tacit Trinitarianism that has exerted formative influence on evangelical doctrines of Scripture. Evangelicals developed their high view of Scripture's authority out of the conviction that in these writings the voice of God is heard and that contemporary readers can hear that voice precisely because the mode of original inspiration was likewise a divine speech act with a Trinitarian cadence. In chronological order, then, Trinitarian inspiration of the text underwrites Trinitarian encounter through the text, which is finally recognized in a confession of verbal inspiration. Rendering explicit the tacit Trinitarianism of evangelical approaches to the Bible provides an alternative account of why evangelical bibliology came to be committed to verbal inspiration—not for sub-Trinitarian reasons of bare formless authority but for reasons of corresponding to the form of Scripture as the words of the Father articulated in the Son and carried by the Holy Spirit. Evangelical doctrines of Scripture have attempted to confess that where the voice of God is heard, particular words are not a matter of indifference.

As the nineteenth-century theologian Benjamin Morgan Palmer argued, in this book "the words of the Father are delivered by the Son, through the power of the Spirit; if this be not enough to clothe the written Word with all the dogmatic authority we ascribe to it, it is hard to see how the claim to any prerogative can ever be established."[1] Evangelicals do in fact ascribe complete dogmatic authority to the written Word, and that is because this book is the one in which "the words of the Father are delivered by the Son, through the power of the Spirit." They read the Bible as if it is the word of God, because it is. It is not merely a written authority in the bare, authoritarian way that a sub-Trinitarian doctrine of revelation and Scripture could underwrite. Scripture is a field of divine action, and the agents are the Father, Son, and Spirit.

To make this case, we will call on three witnesses from evangelical history. First, we will look at a popular Bible expositor from the nineteenth century, Adolph Saphir. Second, from the series of books called *The Fundamentals*, I have selected the longest of the ninety chapters, entitled "Life in the Word," by Philip Mauro. Third, we will catch evangelicals singing their doctrine of Scripture by examining a hymnal compiled in 1911 by the celebrated preacher G. Campbell Morgan, which contains fifty hymns on Scripture for use in Bible schools. Saphir, Mauro, and Morgan testify to a tacitly Trinitarian approach to Scripture that undergirds the high doctrine of Scripture characteristic of evangelicalism. I have tried to pick representative evangelicals, though I admit to finding representatives in whose work the Trinitarianism emerges to become more explicit than tacit. I also chose evangelicals from one hundred years ago, because, while they had their own problems, they did not have our problems. They exhibit an approach to Scripture that had not yet been tested by the onslaught of high modernism or muddled with existentialist neo-orthodoxy and the evangelical reaction against it.

"THAT HE HIMSELF MAY THROUGH HIS WORD SPEAK"

Our first witness is Adolph Saphir (1831–1891). He is now mostly forgotten, so his name does not carry much authority. But his words are the weightiest of all our witnesses. Saphir was a highly regarded nineteenth-century preacher and Bible expositor. His entire family converted from Judaism to Christianity when the Scottish Free Church sent missionaries to Hungary in 1843. Saphir studied in Berlin, Glasgow, Aberdeen, and Edinburgh. He entered the ministry in 1854, and after time as a missionary to Jews in Hamburg he was pastor of churches in Glasgow and in London from 1861 to 1888. From these parishes he carried out an influential writing ministry.

Saphir's approach to Scripture could be drawn from any of his writings, but I will focus on his masterpiece, *The Hidden Life: Thoughts on Communion with God.*[2] R. A. Torrey said of this book, "It is one of the most helpful books in English literature on the subject of prayer and the deeper Christian life. By many it is regarded as unequalled." It is a series of meditations on James 4:8, "Draw near to God, and he will draw near to you." Saphir wants to invite Christians to a direct encounter with God through Scripture. Notice the tension built into that phrase: the encounter with God is direct, but it is through Scripture.

Saphir teaches and rejoices in sound doctrine, but he constantly warns his readers not to confuse sound doctrine with the experienced reality of God drawing near. He says, "The most subtle idolatry and image-worship is when the soul rests in doctrine, however true. When delighted with the profound and comprehensive scheme of Scripture truth, it forgets that this is but the abstraction, the theory, the shadow of great and living realities."[3] To the contrary, Saphir says:

> Draw nigh to God, and He will draw nigh to you—He Himself, although He may use various channels and instruments; it may be Paul, or Cephas, or Apollos; it may be affliction or prosperity; it may be through the voice of Nature or of Providence; it may be through the word or the example of a Christian; yet it is God Himself.[4]

You may be disconcerted by this list of instruments used by God for drawing nigh. Fear not. Saphir has no intention of using "direct encounter with God" to level all instruments to the same plane, demoting Scripture to the same status as nature or providence. He goes on:

> But of all instruments and channels the written Word is of the utmost importance; it stands supreme. It is through Scripture, eminently, that God draws nigh to the soul. But let us never mistake the reading of the Scripture for that real drawing nigh of the living God, towards which it is the great help, and of which it is the great witness. Scripture is not the substitute for God's drawing nigh to us, it is only the channel; the written Word of the past must become the living Word of the present.[5]

What is the relation between "the written Word of the past" and "the living Word of the present"? It is a dangerous dichotomy, but Saphir's whole point is not to dichotomize but to distinguish in order to unite:

> God speaks in and through the Word. It is not that God spake long ago, and that the record of His acts and words, His revelation, was embodied in a perfect manner, and preserved for us in Scripture. This is true. But God gave us the Bible, not to be silent now and let the Bible speak instead of Him, and be a guarantee for Him, but that He Himself may through His word speak, comfort, and confirm the soul, filling it with His light and love.[6]

To bring home his point about the direct communication that God speaks in Scripture, Saphir uses the metaphor of translation:

> God draws nigh in the Word. Do we know what it is to read the Bible in the original? It does not mean in Hebrew or Greek. God speaks neither Hebrew nor Greek. This is the original language of Scripture—the love of God to the soul: "I have loved thee with an everlasting love: therefore with loving-kindness have I drawn thee." And all God's vocabulary is summed up in Jesus—Alpha and Omega, He is the Word. When God takes the written Word back from the paper into His own mouth, then we read the original; then it is again God-breathed, and the word which cometh out of His mouth shall not return void.[7]

The doctrinal content of Scripture is real and unaltered, but Saphir highlights its effect in reaching its hearers and bringing them into an encounter with God himself. As in its origin, Scripture is in its effect Trinitarian: "And thus it becomes to us an engrafted, implanted Word, inseparably connected with the Father, with the living Savior, and with the indwelling Spirit. God reveals Himself continually to us in the Word—God in Christ and by the Holy Ghost."[8]

In the nineteenth century, evangelicals with a high view of Scripture were increasingly criticized as being book worshipers, or bibliolaters. Saphir knew better than to take this charge seriously on the lips of liberal theologians:

> The charge of Bibliolatry (worship of the Bible) has been of late frequently preferred against those who maintain the supremacy

of Scripture. As far as this objection is urged by those who do not fully and clearly acknowledge the Divine authority and inspiration of Scripture, it is easily refuted. But as far as we ourselves are concerned, we may do well to consider whether our opponents are not giving utterance to a truth which they themselves do not fully see, and warn us against a danger the existence of which we are apt to overlook. In other words, never mind whence and for what purpose the charge of Bibliolatry is made—consider the thing itself; is there such a tendency, such an evil, such a danger? I know that many Christians will reply at once, "We cannot value, and reverence, and cherish the Bible sufficiently." And this is quite true. The danger is not of a reverence too deep, but of a reverence untrue and unreal.[9]

Saphir then put forth a rule for esteeming Scripture rightly, and it is a rule that appeals to the tacit Trinitarianism of hearing God's voice in Scripture:

We cannot speak, think, and feel too highly of Scripture in its vital connection with Christ and the Spirit; but there may be a way of viewing Scripture by itself apart from Christ and the Holy Ghost, and transferring to this dead book our faith, reverence, and affection; and this surely would come under the category of idolatry— substituting something, however good and great in itself, or rather in its relation to God, in the place of the living God.[10]

Again, Saphir draws out his christological and pneumatological presuppositions:

By Bibliolatry I understand the tendency of separating, in the first place, the Book from the Person of Jesus Christ, and in the second, from the Holy Ghost, and of thus substituting the Book for Him who alone is the light and guide of the Church.[11]

Saphir warns that it is entirely possible to devolve from being pious to being "God-estranged text-worshippers," and as an illustration of this result of bibliolatry he cites a Rabbinic saying from his own Jewish background: "Now that God has given the Law, He has no more need and right to interfere by further revelations." Saphir warns that "under the pretence of honouring the Bible, they virtually treated God as one who had ceased to live and rule among them."[12] He identifies the inevitable result of this declension as the accelerated hardening of religion into dead rationalism:

> And now the rule of man began. For if instead of God we have the Bible, the task of commentators, interpreters, casuists, commences. For the text is obscure, the commentary distinct; the text is severe, the casuist accommodating; the text is deep and many-sided, the interpreter shallow and one-sided; the text desires inward truth and radical cure, the tradition heals the hurt of the daughter of my people superficially and falsely. In course of time the tradition came to be regarded as more valuable, more necessary, more practical, than the Bible. Naturally so. Without a living God, viewing the Bible as God's substitute, a clear and detailed interpretation of the code is in reality of greater importance than the code itself.[13]

For Saphir, it was all or nothing: either Scripture is the word of God in the full and direct meaning of that packed theological phrase, or it plummets to the level of sponsoring a book religion with commentators and legal argumentation as the functional authority. Christianity, on the other hand, is communion with God. And the only way to draw near to God is in the confidence that God draws near to us in the inspired Word of Scripture, where we truly meet him.

LIFE IN THE WORD

If we expected to find a severe and wooden doctrine of Scripture, one that emphasized sheer authority and overlooked the life-giving power of Scripture as a means of grace, we certainly did not find it in the romantic Saphir. But perhaps he is a bad representative of the evangelical tradition. Surely we would find a stricter, less communion-based approach to Scripture elsewhere among the evangelicals. For example, the turn to fundamentalism must have narrowed this approach, right?

The Fundamentals was a very important set of books. As mentioned earlier, they were published serially, ninety chapters in twelve volumes over the course of several years. The longest chapter in the series is by

Philip Mauro and is entitled "Life in the Word."[14] Mauro (1859–1952) was a successful lawyer who converted to Christianity under the preaching of A. B. Simpson. He had a knack for grabbing headlines: he was on the *Carpathia* when it came to the rescue of the *Titanic's* survivors; he prepared legal briefs for the Scopes trial and wrote a 1922 book called *Evolution at the Bar*; and he witnessed to Thomas Edison.

Among the other eighty-nine chapters of *The Fundamentals* are presentations on inspiration and inerrancy and numerous chapters on specific historical-critical issues. But the doctrine of Scripture is most elaborately spelled out in Mauro's chapter. What, therefore, is the doctrine of Scripture in *The Fundamentals*? It is summed up and organized around the word *life*. Mauro says: "It is clear, then, that when we read, 'The Word of God is living,' we are to understand thereby that it lives with a spiritual, an inexhaustible, an inextinguishable, in a word a divine, life. If the Word of God be indeed living in this sense, then we have here a fact of the most tremendous significance."[15] Mauro unpacks that significance by working through a list of characteristics of being alive. "We look then at the Written Word of God to see if it manifests characteristics which are found only in living things, and to see if it exhibits, not merely the possession of life of the perishable and corruptible sort with which we are so familiar by observation, and which is in each of us, but life of a different order, imperishable and incorruptible."[16] Indeed, Mauro says, Scripture has the following characteristics of life:

- It has perennial freshness.
- It is non-obsolete and always contemporary.
- It is indestructible.
- It is a discerner, a "critic," of hearts and minds (Heb. 4:2).
- It is remarkably translatable.
- It lodges in hearts and grows.
- It transforms other life.

But Mauro dwells especially on how the Bible gives life: "Indeed, the great purpose of the Written Word is to impart life—even eternal (that is to say divine) life—to those who are dead through trespasses and sins."[17] Mauro distinguishes between living, life-giving truth, that is, the truth which makes the Bible the word of God, and every other kind of truth:

> Never yet has any man been heard to testify that he had been the wretched and hopeless slave of sin, and had continued in spiritual darkness, fast bound in misery and vice until his eyes were opened by the great truth that two and two make four, or that three angles of a triangle are equal to two right angles; and that thereby his life had been transformed, his soul delivered from bondage, and his heart filled with joy and peace in believing.[18]

What, finally, are the implications of the life of the Bible? "Thus the Word of truth becomes, in some inscrutable way, the vehicle for imparting that life of which the risen Christ, the Incarnate Word, is the only Source."

Let me specify how Mauro's doctrine of Scripture is Trinitarian. I would like to avoid using the word *Trinitarian* in too expansive a way. Mauro's example of evangelical Bible reading is Trinitarian in that, through the category of "life," he accounts for the divinity of Scripture by appeal to the Son and Spirit in salvation. Mauro was no Saphir and did not manage to bring the christological and pneumatological threads so closely together in his argument. Exegesis did drive him into this territory, but it is oblique:

> Other Scriptures testify with equal clearness to the great and glorious truth that those who are begotten of the Spirit, through the incorruptible seed of the Word, receive a nature of the same sort as that of the Divine Source of their life. In the eighth chapter of Romans there is a section devoted to the sons of God in whom the Spirit dwells (verses 9–16); and of these it is declared that God predestinated them "to be conformed to the image of His Son, that He might be the first-born among many brethren" (verse 30).[19]

If Saphir verged on the mystical, Mauro was more directly conversionist. Certainly Saphir's Trinitarianism is more elaborate and more profound than Mauro's. But while the particular Trinitarian contours are less prominent in Mauro, what is just as obvious is that the

Scriptures take their high place of authority precisely because of their power in giving life.

LOVE SONGS TO THE BIBLE

From Saphir in the 1870s to Mauro circa 1915, there may have been some loss of the thickness of conservative evangelical Trinitarianism. There was in fact some narrowing and hardening of evangelicalism as it entered the fundamentalist/modernist rapids, though nothing so severe or total as is usually depicted. For our third witness, we turn to the great tradition more directly, through evangelical hymnody. George Campbell Morgan (1863–1945) used to be more famous than he is now. Best known as the pastor of Westminster Chapel in London, he also worked in the United States with Dwight L. Moody's many projects and taught widely in Bible institutes such as Moody and Biola. One contemporary called him "the hardest working preacher in Christendom."

Morgan could make himself at home in many denominational settings: his father was a Baptist pastor, while Morgan sought (but was refused) ordination from the Methodists and eventually was ordained as a Congregationalist, though he later pastored in a Presbyterian church. I am invoking G. Campbell Morgan not so much as an author as for his editorial judgment. In 1911 he edited a hymnal, *The Song Companion to the Scriptures*, which he described this way in the preface:

> This Hymn-book has been prepared to meet the demand created by the growth of the Bible-school movement. While many excellent Hymnals are extant, suitable for the regular services of the Church, for special Conventions and Meetings for the deepening of the spiritual life, and for Evangelistic Services, no book has been provided specially suited to the needs of assemblies gathered specifically for the study of the Divine Library.
>
> The plan, as indicated by the Contents Pages, is purely Biblical. A very special feature is that of the large number of hymns on the Word of God, which have been gathered with extreme care.[20]

Morgan scoured all available sources and managed to come up with a "large number of hymns on the Word of God." He found, in fact, fifty hymns on the Word of God. Fifty love songs to the Bible! If this is not bibliolatry, what is? If this is not replacing the living God with a stable text, what would be? Let me alarm you before I soothe you.

Hymn 100 is John Newton's "Precious Bible," while in Hymn 114, John Fawcett sings:

> How precious is the Book Divine,
> By inspiration given!
> Bright as a lamp its doctrines shine
> To guide our souls to heaven.

Fawcett goes on to attribute all sorts of saving actions directly to the book:

> Its light, descending from above,
> Our gloomy world to cheer,
> Displays a Saviour's boundless love
> And brings His glories near.

"It shows to man his wandering ways," he says, and, "When once it penetrates the mind / It conquers every sin. . . . Life, light and joy it still imparts."

Hymn 106, by Thomas Kelly (1769–1855), sings directly to the personified book:

> Precious volume! What thou doest
> other books attempt in vain:
> Plainest, fullest, sweetest, truest,
> All our good from thee we gain.

And "Precious volume! All revealing, / All that we have need to know." Kelly is also the author of Hymn 134, which begins by testifying:

> I love the sacred Book of God,
> No other can its place supply—
> It points me to the saints' abode;
> It gives me wings, and bids me fly.

The second stanza is again speaking to the personification of the book itself:

Blest Book, in thee my eyes discern
The image of my absent Lord:
From thine instructive page I learn
The joys His presence will afford.

A critic who approaches the evangelical tradition with suspicion could surely find in these lines all the evidence necessary to declare that this hymnal is primary evidence of the evangelical displacement of the living God by a book: the "Blest Book" shows the believer "the image of my absent Lord." What can this mean but that Jesus is gone and he left behind a document? On the other hand, Kelly's hymn goes on to reflect on what will happen when "my absent Lord" returns with "the joys" of "His presence":

Then shall I need thy light no more,
For nothing then shall be concealed;
When I have reached the heavenly shore
The Lord Himself will stand revealed.

When 'midst the throng celestial placed
The bright original I see,
From which thy sacred page was traced,
Blest Book! I've no more need of thee.

The whole hymn is an exploration of the relationship between the book and the Lord. Kelly speaks to the personified "Blest Book" only about how it brings Christ before his attention, and after saying that there will come a day when he'll have no more need of the Bible because Christ will be directly present, Kelly concludes:

But while I'm here thou shalt supply
His place, and tell me of His love;
I'll read with faith's deserving eye,
and thus partake of joys above.

The fact is that far from bibliolatry, when we catch evangelicals in the act of singing about their Bible, we catch them singing to and about God, and increasingly we hear them singing about the Son and the Spirit. In Hymn 125, Horatius Bonar sings:

> Thy thoughts are here, O God,
> Expressed in words Divine,
> The utterance of heavenly lips
> In every sacred line.

And he goes on:

> Each word of Thine a gem
> From the celestial mines;
> A sunbeam from that holy heaven
> Where holy sunlight shines.
> Thine, Thine this Book, though given
> In man's poor human speech,
> Telling of things unseen, unheard,
> Beyond all human reach.

Bonar knows that one need not make an idol of the Bible to be able to say, "What Scripture says, God says."

Morgan includes Mary A. Lathbury's "Break Thou the Bread of Life," which includes the lines:

> Break Thou the Bread of life,
> Dear Lord, to me,
> As thou didst break the loaves beside the Sea;
> Beyond the sacred page
> I seek Thee, Lord:
> My spirit pants for Thee, O living Word.

The personalism of Lathbury's "Beyond the sacred page" echoes the eschatological tones we heard in Kelly's "Blest book, I've no more need of thee." And in Hymn 103, T. T. Lynch sounds like Adolph Saphir when he writes, "Christ in his Word draws near; hush, moaning voice of fear, he bids thee cease."

Many of these hymn writers are willing to play on the similarity between the incarnate Word and the written Word, which raises the question of whether they are aware of what they are doing when they make this move. It seems increasingly likely that they are doing this in full cognizance of the difference when we note the way other authors in the collection handle the difference between Word and Word. Listen to the way W. W. How (Hymn 105) traces the connection between the incarnate Word and the written Word: "O Word of God incarnate, O wisdom from on high, O truth unchanged, unchanging, O light of our dark sky; We praise Thee for the radiance that from the hallowed page, A lantern to our footsteps, shines on from age to age." The author praises Jesus for providing the guidance of the Scriptures for his people:

> The church from thee, her master,
> Received the gift divine,
> And still that light she lifteth,
> O'er all the earth to shine.
> It is the golden casket
> Where gems of truth are stored;
> It is the heaven-drawn picture
> Of Thee, the living Word.

Here, How pictures Scripture as the "golden casket" in which are stored gems of truth, given radiantly by the Word incarnate.

The believer's dependence on God's Trinitarian action to make himself directly known in Scripture is a recurring theme in several hymns, including the anonymous Hymn 112: "A glory in the Word we find, when grace restores our sight; but sin has darkened all the mind, and veiled the heavenly light. When God's own spirit clears our view, how bright the doctrines shine! Their holy fruits and sweetness show the author is divine. How blest are we, with open face, to view thy glory, Lord, and all thy image here to trace, reflected in thy word."

With increasingly explicit Trinitarianism, William Cowper's hymn "The Spirit and the Word" (113) says:

> The Spirit breathes upon the Word,
> And brings the truth to sight,
> Precepts and promises afford
> A sanctifying light.
> A glory gilds the sacred page,
> Majestic, like the sun,
> It gives a light to every age,
> It gives, but borrows none.
> The hand that gave it still supplies
> The gracious light and heat,

Its truths upon the nations rise
— They rise, but never set.

Charles Wesley's presence is strong in this miniature hymnal-within-a-hymnal about the Bible, and his hymns are, as always, marked by pronounced theological literacy. In Hymn 101 he sings to the Holy Spirit, "Come, Divine Interpreter, Bring us eyes Thy Book to read, Ears the mystic words to hear, words which did from thee proceed." He cannot decide whether the decisive action of revelation is properly Christological or pneumatological, so he writes entire hymns alternately to Christ the Prophet and the Holy Spirit of truth. Hymn 123 runs:

Come, o thou prophet of the Lord,
Thou great interpreter divine
Explain thine own transmitted word,
To teach and to inspire is thine,
Thou only canst thyself reveal —
Open the book and loose the seal.

Whate'er the ancient prophets spoke
Concerning thee, O Christ, make known,
Chief subject of the sacred book,
Thou fillest all, and thou alone
Yet there our Lord we cannot see
Unless thy spirit lend the key.

Now, Jesus, now the veil remove
The folly of our darkened heart,
Unfold the wonders of thy love,
The knowledge of thyself impart
Our ear, our inmost soul we bow,
Speak lord. Thy servants hearken now.

Wesley's Hymn 127 is also a powerful invocation of the Holy Spirit, who inspired the Scriptures to be their interpreter:

Spirit of truth, essential God,
who didst thy ancient saints inspire,

shed in their hearts thy love abroad,
and touch their hallowed lips with fire;
our God from all eternity, world without end, we worship thee.

Still we believe, almighty Lord,
whose presence fills both earth and heaven,
the meaning of the written word
is by thy inspiration given.

Thou only dost thyself explain
the secret mind of God to man.
Come then, divine interpreter,
the scriptures to our hearts apply,
and taught by thee, we God revere,
him in three persons magnify;
in each the Triune God adore,
who was and is forevermore.

Morgan frequently places Christ and Spirit hymns side by side, because it is just good tacit Trinitarian theology to recognize that the Spirit makes Jesus Christ present to us as the Word of the Father and that hearing the voice of God in Scripture is a single, concerted, Trinitarian event. Morgan's editorial hand also shows up in the architecture of the hymnal. Having found these fifty hymns on the Word of God, he arranges them very thoughtfully within an overall Trinitarian structure. First, he signals his intention by opening the hymnal with Section 1: "The Holy Trinity," which contains five songs on the Trinity. The next three sections are:

2: "The Revelation: The Father" (twelve hymns);
3: "The Revealer: The Son" (seventy hymns from advent to second advent);
4: "The Interpreter: The Holy Spirit."

This long section of hymns on the Holy Spirit, the Interpreter, is divided into two sections: fifty on the Interpreter "In the Scriptures," followed by twenty-one on the Interpreter "In the Heart." Morgan not only had a keen editorial eye for the Trinitarianism implicit in evangelical

Bible reading but also understood how it fit into the overall pattern of Christian truth.

THE VOICE OF THE TRINITY IN
SOLA SCRIPTURA

Time would fail us to trace the way evangelicals have been driven to a high view of Scripture by their conviction that the Trinity is at work in these texts. Glen Scorgie once described A. W. Tozer's approach to Scripture as one that "eloquently describes the evangelical soul's desire to hear God speak in the present tense and personally." For Tozer, "it is this present Voice which makes the written Word all-powerful. Otherwise it would be locked in slumber within the covers of a book. . . . That God is here and that He is speaking—these truths are back of all other Bible truths." Scorgie adds: "In my opinion, Tozer's vision embodies all that neo-orthodox theologian Karl Barth dreamed of, and more, and manages to do this while keeping the orthodox doctrine of Scripture intact."[21]

It is certainly true that evangelicals know to expect the voice of God to be heard in the words of Scripture and that the Bible is a real means of grace. Evangelicals may have some dysfunctional, subjectivistic ways of expressing this truth, and we may cultivate the experience in short-sighted ways, even using it as a prop for our anti-intellectualism. But we are fundamentally right. This book is a channel through which God himself will meet us again and again in personal encounter. The voice of God in Scripture is the breath of the Spirit carrying the word of the Father. Scorgie goes on:

> Evangelical Christians have always recognized that the inspired Scriptures are the chief "instrumental means" by which God communicates with us in a direct and intensely personal fashion. It is the main vehicle for the voice of God, as it penetrates from eternity like a shaft of laser light. As an eternal voice, it retains the quality of eternity itself. It is always living and in the present tense.[22]

A strong stance on the inspiration and authority of Scripture has been made possible by a strong stance on the illumination and power of Scripture. J. I. Packer once wrote, "The givenness of Jesus Christ is bound up with the givenness of New Testament theology, which is (so I urge, following its own claim as mainstream Christian tradition has always done) nothing less than the Father's own witness through the Spirit to the Son."[23]

7

PRAYING WITH THE GRAIN

(Or, The Tacit Trinitarianism of All Christian Prayer)

When you pray, say "Father . . ."
LUKE 11:2

The whole threefold life of the three-personal Being is actually
going on in that ordinary little bedroom where an ordinary man
is saying his prayers.

C. S. LEWIS

You don't have to get your Trinitarian theology all sorted out before
you can pray to the Trinity. Our God hears prayers. He does not wait
for us to pass the theology test before he listens to us praying. God the
Father knows what we need before we ask (Matt. 6:8); God the Son is a
high priest who can sympathize with our weakness, giving us confidence
to draw near the throne of grace (Heb. 4:15–16); and God the Spirit
knows how to pray even when we do not, interceding for us with groanings too deep for words (Rom. 8:26). Whether or not we understand
the doctrine of the Trinity, God has his Trinitarian theology in good
working order long before we show up, and our prayers are founded
on the Father, the Son, and the Spirit.

HOW PRAYER ACTUALLY WORKS

It is because of God's triunity that we have communion with God in
prayer. Once we understand that the Christian life is constituted by the
Trinity, we have an opportunity to pray in a way that is consistent with

that constitution. If the Spirit unites us to the Son and reconciles us to the Father, we have an invitation to pray accordingly: to the Father, through the Son, by the Holy Spirit. This is not just the "theologically correct" way to pray but a way of praying that draws real spiritual power from being aligned with reality. The reality is that Christian prayer is already tacitly Trinitarian, whether we recognize it or not. Aligning with it means praying with the grain instead of against it.

Wood has a grain to it. The long fibers that make up a piece of wood all run in one direction, and a wise woodworker will always find the direction of that grain before starting to work. He can work along the grain or cut across it, but he avoids planing or sanding against that grain because that is to invite a clash with the directionality built into the piece of wood. Paper has a grain to it as well, which is why you can tear straight lines down the page but not across it. Cat fur has a grain, and if you stroke a cat against that grain, the results are not good for felines or humans. When you work with the grain of the wood, or the paper, or the cat, things go well. When you go against the grain, either because you are oblivious to the structural forces involved or because you consider them negligible, things do not go as well.

The act of prayer has, metaphorically speaking, a grain to it. Prayer has an underlying structure built into it, complete with a directionality that is worth observing. This grain is Trinitarian, running from the Spirit through the Son to the Father. It is a built-in logic of mediation, designed that way by God for reasons deeper than we are likely to fathom. But we do not need to understand it in order to benefit from its solid structural integrity. Nor do we need to take special lessons in praying in a properly Trinitarian fashion. The possibility of praying in a more Trinitarian way is all promise and no threat, all invitation and no danger. Christian prayer is already thoroughly, pervasively, structurally Trinitarian whether you have been noticing it or not. The only thing you have to add is your attention, to begin taking notice of what's Trinitarian about prayer.

Prayer is a great blessing, but it can be daunting and difficult when you stop to think what is involved in a finite, sinful creature reaching out to an infinite, holy God. When we recall the distance and dissimilarity between us and God, it is easy to wonder whether we have the ability to pray and whether coming into God's presence is a good idea anyway. Perhaps it is that pressure that leads us to behave so poorly in our attempts at prayer: mouthing thoughtless clichés that even we don't know the meaning of; tongue-tied; repetitious; distractible; with wandering minds that only succeed in coming back to self-centeredness as a reliable point of departure. Not only does God know that prayer is daunting, but it is even a biblical doctrine that we are not in ourselves equipped for: Romans 8:26 says, "We do not know what to pray for as we ought." That same passage goes on to say that "the Spirit himself intercedes for us with groanings too deep for words. And he who searches hearts knows what is the mind of the Spirit, because the Spirit intercedes for the saints according to the will of God." And within a few verses, a second intercessor appears: "Christ Jesus is the one who died— more than that, who was raised—who is at the right hand of God, who indeed is interceding for us" (Rom. 8:34). Christian prayer has double intercession built into it. The Father not only welcomes prayers, but he has provided mediation and perhaps even mediation of the mediation. Your prayer life is secure in the two hands of the Father.

That built-in logic of mediation is the grain of prayer. We are directed to pray to the Father in the name of Jesus, and it is customary to do that by ending prayers with the formula "in Jesus' name." But there is a thought experiment that you can do to see more clearly the direction of the grain of prayer. If you try praying backwards, you will find yourself beginning with the formula, "in Jesus' name," as an introduction to set up everything you are about to say. This calls attention to the fact that all Christian prayer is offered under this sign: "Not by my authority or according to my fitness or deserving of a hearing, but on the basis of the finished work of Jesus Christ I approach God." Now consider that even if you were praying to Jesus, you would still be approaching God the Son on the same basis: not by your own authority but on the basis of the finished work of Christ. Even when you pray to Jesus, you pray in Jesus' name, because Christian prayer has a built-in logic of mediation, a directionality, a grain. That grain becomes more evident when you do something that runs a little bit against the grain, like petting a cat from tail to head. But when you are alert to the direction of the grain you can intentionally work along it. It is possible to pray with the grain, observing the directionality and the logic of mediation built into the Christian approach to God.

TO THE FATHER, THROUGH THE SON, BY THE SPIRIT

The direction of prayer's grain is presupposed and suggested in a fragmentary way throughout all of Scripture. But it is classically stated in Ephesians 2:18: "For through him we both have access in one Spirit to the Father." Christian prayer, as a subset of Christian communion with God, is an approach to God the Father, through God the Son, in the Holy Spirit. John Owen called this passage "a heavenly directory," and Horatius Bonar teased out a theology of worship from it:

> The whole Trinity has to do with our return and reception. The Father throws open His presence chamber, the Holy of Holies where He dwells; the Son provides the way for our restoration, by answering in His death all the ends that could have been served by our exclusion; and the Holy Spirit conducts us into the Father's presence along the new and living way.[1]

Bonar's interpretation of the passage is typical of most evangelical treatments of it. In the context of the overall argument of Ephesians, this statement is directly concerned with the joining of Jews and Gentiles in one unified way of access to God. Paul is seeing the Gentiles included alongside the Jews in the fulfillment of the ancient promises. But Paul states his case so expansively that later interpreters are warranted in making more general application to the entire economy of salvation. When John Bunyan defined true prayer, he built his definition around this Trinitarian structure from Ephesians 2. Bunyan's complete definition runs:

> Prayer is a sincere, sensible, affectionate pouring out of the heart or soul to God, through Christ, in the strength and assistance of the Holy Spirit, for such things as God hath promised, or according to the Word, for the good of the church, with submission, in faith, to the will of God.[2]

What difference does it make to begin cultivating an alertness to the

Trinity in our prayer? Here is the difference it makes: it builds on what is already actually going on in prayer. We have an opportunity to bring our experience and our awareness into alignment with the structure of the economy of salvation. It might be wise to restrain ourselves from saying much more than that, but it is possible to say one thing more. Since the economy of salvation, as we have seen, is the one sure revelation of God's triunity, then our alignment with it is also an alignment with what has been revealed about the eternal being of God. Not only are we coming to God the Father in a way that echoes the salvation-historical enfolding of the Gentiles into the promises to Abraham, but we are coming to God the Father in a way that retraces the path of his sending the Son and the Spirit to reveal himself and redeem us. Prayer thus opens up to an eternal Trinitarian vista. There is always already a conversation going on among Father, Son, and Holy Spirit. When we pray, we are joining that conversation. We have been invited to call on God as Father, invited by a Spirit of sonship that cries out "Abba, Father" as the eternal Son does.

This insight leads to a second advantage of attending to the Trinitarian dynamic of Christian prayer. It takes the pressure off us to make prayer happen. Not only are the Son and the Spirit involved as intercessors in our prayers, but there is also a communicating life in the very being of God that is analogous to prayer. We are invited to enter that eternal conversation in an appropriately lower, creaturely way, but the heavenly analogue of prayer is already going on in the life of God rather than waiting for us to get it started. If you have ever become weary of working up the right response in prayer or worship, you can glimpse the relief of being able to approach prayer and worship with the knowledge that the party already started before you arrived.

The third advantage of praying with the grain of Christian mediation is that it aligns your prayer life in particular with your spiritual life in general. That is, your Christian existence is a life that has been brought to the throne of the Father by the work of the Son in the power of the Spirit. Your prayers are verbal actions that follow the same path: to the Father, through the Son, in the Spirit. Consciously Trinitarian prayer is an invitation to align your words with the more all-encompassing reality of your life as God has constituted it. Andrew Murray points to these multiple, mutually aligned domains when he says, "In each act of worship, each step of growth, and each blessed experience of grace, all the Three Persons are actively engaged." He goes on to indicate how these areas will harmonize beautifully with each other when they are all echoing with faith in the Trinity:

> Would you apply this in the life of holiness, let faith in the Holy Trinity be a living practical reality. In every prayer to the Father to sanctify you, take up your position in Christ, and do it in the power of the Spirit within you. In every exercise of faith in Christ as your Sanctification, let your posture be that of prayer to the Father and trust in Him as He delights to honour the Son, and of quiet expectancy of the Spirit's working, through whom the Father glorifies the Son. In every surrender of the soul to sanctification of the Spirit, to His leading as the Spirit of Holiness, look to the Father who grants His mighty working, and who sanctifies through faith in the Son, and expect the Spirit's power to manifest itself in showing the will of God, and Jesus as your Sanctification. If for a time this appears at variance with the simplicity of childlike faith and prayer, be assured that as God has thus revealed Himself, He will teach you so to worship and believe. And so the Holy, holy, holy will become the deep undertone of all our worship and all our life.[3]

Our life in Christ is an all-encompassing reality, and individual acts of personal, verbal prayer are one part of it. But attending to the Trinitarian grain of prayer can be spiritually powerful and productive. Every act of devotion can be self-consciously a microcosm of the entire spiritual life. Perhaps this kind of alignment of life with devotion is the high possibility behind the command to "pray without ceasing" (1 Thess. 5:17).

PRAY LIKE A SON OF GOD

Christians are people who talk to God like they are Jesus Christ. Calling God "Father" is a great privilege, one that can have no possible grounding in our own merit. But we do it because Jesus the Son invites us to join him in his prayer to his Father. Christian prayer is a family thing, and it is only open to sons of God. This is the greatest application of the theology of Trinitarian adoption we examined in a previous chapter. We pray by borrowing the sonhood of the true Son and talking to the Father. When you approach the throne of grace and call on God as your father, God the Father receives you because you pray in the family style that you learned from the Son: "Our Father in heaven, hallowed be your name" (Matt. 6:9). God the Father is our Father in a complex, saving sense: Father of Jesus by nature, Father of sinners by grace and adoption. And you are "predestined to be conformed to the image of his Son, in order that he might be the firstborn among many brothers" (Rom. 8:29). How are we to act like sons of God?

> For all who are led by the Spirit of God are sons of God. For you did not receive the spirit of slavery to fall back into fear, but you have received the Spirit of adoption as sons, by whom we cry, "Abba! Father!" The Spirit himself bears witness with our spirit that we are children of God, and if children, then heirs—heirs of God and fellow heirs with Christ, provided we suffer with him in order that we may also be glorified with him. (Rom. 8:14–17)

The adoptive Spirit that God gives us will lead us to call God "Abba, Father." And that Spirit will not lead us to enslavement and fear, but oddly it will cause us to groan or perhaps will groan for us: "The Spirit himself intercedes for us with groanings too deep for words" (Rom. 8:26). We obey and are shaped by this Holy Spirit of sonship to the Father.

This life of prayer as sons should certainly be a reminder of our privilege and our need at the same time. One of the most powerful meditations on the two-edged character of praying like the Son of God was written by William Tyndale (1492–1536). Tyndale is famous as a Bible translator, but he was also the author of a number of doctrinal and practical treatises suffused with biblical insight. A real gem, one of his smaller pieces is a strange commentary on the Lord's Prayer.[4] Tyndale writes a meaty introduction, and then he puts forth the theology of the Lord's Prayer in the form of a dialogue between the sinner who prays the prayer and the God who hears it. As the prayer is put on the lips of this character named "the synner" (sixteenth-century orthography for "sinner"), each word takes on gravity and profundity. So the synner says to God:

Oure father which arte in heven
what a greate space ys betwen the and us:
How therefore shall we thy children here on erth
baneshed and exiled from the in this vale of misery and wretchedness
come home to the in to oure naturall countre?

It is an extended gloss on the two words "Father" and "heaven," dwelling especially on the great distance implied in the Father's location in heaven: there is "greate space betwen" the Father's home far away in "oure naturall countre" and the current location of the Father's children here in this "vale of misery and wretchedness." As Tyndale works on this theme of distance, he seems to be casting the sinner in the role of the prodigal son, far from his father's house, wasting his substance in the far country.

These meditations alone would be a valuable commentary on the right use of the Lord's Prayer. But as Tyndale unfolds the treatise on the Lord's Prayer, a surprising thing happens: God replies! Responding to the synner who has called on him as Father, God says:

The child honoureth hys father
and the servaunt hys master.
Yf I be youre father where ys myne honouore.
Yf I be youre lorde where ys my feare. Malachias i.
For my name thorowe you and by youre meanes ys blasphemen
rayld apon and evyll spoken of. Esaias lii.

It is a stinging rebuke and enough to wake up anybody who sleepily mumbles their way through a rendering of the Lord's Prayer. God is positively standoffish here. He pushes back and demands from the synner much greater clarity, a much starker confrontation than the opening address suggests. And the synner replieth:

Alas O father that ys trueth.
we knowledge oure synne and treaspace
nevertheless yet be thou a merciful father
and deale not wyth us according to oure deservynges
neither judge us by the rigorousness off thi lawe
but geve us grace that we maye so lyve
that thy holy name maye be alowed and sanctified in us.
And kepe oure hertes

that we nether do speake
no
that we not once thynke or purpose any thinge
but that which is to thyne honoure and prayse
and above all thinges make thy name and honoure to be soughte of
us and not
oure awne name and vayne glory.
And off thi myghty power bringe to passe in us
that we maye love and feare the as a sonne hys father.

The whole prayer continues in this vein, and it becomes apparent that the exercise, especially God's stern and sustained rebuke, constitutes an educational process for the synner. He repeatedly starts his sentences with "Alas that ys trueth," and always casts himself on God's mercy rather than his own deservynges. He asks that God would bringe to passe in him, by his own myghty power, a proper filial reponse: "that we maye love and feare the as a sonne hys father."

God keeps pushing back, response after response. The next sentence is: "How can myne honoure and name be ahalowed amonge you when your hertes and thoughtes are all wayes enclined to evyll"—as if God were saying, "What gives you the right to wish for my name to be hallowed?" And so on with God's will being done and his kingdom coming on earth as in heaven. Just who do you think you are to be asking these things in prayer when your hertes and thoughtes are all wayes enclined to evyll?

It is an odd, arresting treatise on prayer. In the introduction Tyndale explains what he is doing. The synner prays, but "God answereth by the lawe, as though he wolde putt hym from hys desyre." But the point of this law-speech ("Why do you call me Father if you do not behave like a son?") is not to exact filial behavior or pressure the synner into acting as righteously as Jesus. It is to make the synner see the greatness of his need: "Marke this well and take it for a sure conclusion. When god commaundeth us in the lawe to do any thinge he commaundeth not therefore that we are able to do yt but to bryng us un to the knowledge of oureselves that we might se what we are and in what miserable state we are in and knowe our lack that thereby we shuld torne to god and to knowlege our wretchednes un to hym and to desyre him that of his mercy he wold make us that he biddeth us be."

Tyndale's theology, with a few Anglo modifications, is Luther in English. So he uses the law to drive the synner to the gospell, which functions altogether differently: "The gospell entyseth draweth and sheweth from whence to fetche helpe and coupleth us to God thorowe fayth." Faith grasps the gospell, and only faith can pray. "Prayar ys the effecte and worke off fayth," but "they never praye which fele not the workynge of the lawe in their hertes." In this case, the law meets us as the rebuke that we do not behave as sons of God; the gospel meets us in adoption; and the law comes back again to teach us right conduct in our new, gospel lives.

John Bunyan provided a shorter version of the same fearful dialogue:

> O how great a task is it, for a poor soul that becomes sensible of sin and the wrath of God, to say in faith, but this one word, "Father!" I tell you, however hypocrites think, yet the Christian that is so indeed finds all the difficulty in this very thing, it cannot say God is its Father. O! saith he, I dare not call him Father; and hence it is that the Spirit must be sent into the hearts of God's people for this very thing, to cry Father: it being too great a work for any man to do knowingly and believingly without it (Gal. 4:6).[5]

And in our own century Oswald Chambers engaged in mock dialogue with a Christian who raised different objections to praying to the Father: "But I don't feel that God is my Father." Chambers's response was, "Jesus said, 'Say it—say Our Father,' and you will suddenly discover that He is." He goes on, "Don't pray according to your moods, but resolutely launch out on God, say 'Our Father,' and before you know where you are, you are in a larger room. The door into a moral or spiritual emancipation which you wish to enter is a word. Immediately you are prepared to abandon your reserve and say the word, the door opens and in rushes the Godward side of things and you are lifted on to another platform instantly."[6]

PRAYER ON EARTH AS IT IS IN HEAVEN

If sonship is our access to praying to the Father, we might ask if the eternal Son prays to the eternal Father, or if there is something going on between the Father and the Son that we catch a glimpse of in the creaturely analogy of prayer. J. C. Ryle posed the question this way: "How and in what manner does Christ exercise His priestly office?" And he answered:

> This is a deep subject, and one about which it is easy to make rash statements. The action of one of the Persons of the blessed Trinity in heaven is a high thing, and passes man's understanding. The place whereon we stand is holy ground. The thing we are handling must be touched with reverence, like the ark of God. Nevertheless, there are some things about Christ's priestly office which even our weak eyes may boldly look at; and God has caused them to be written plainly for our learning. The secret things belong unto the Lord our God: but those things which are revealed belong unto us and to our children . . . (Deut. 29:29.) Let us see.[7]

Andrew Murray, no less pious than Ryle, was a bit more aggressive in making statements about the eternal being of God in its Trinitarian dimensions. In the seventeenth chapter of *With Christ in the School of Prayer: Thoughts on Our Training for the Ministry of Intercession* under the heading "Prayer in Harmony with the Being of God," Murray argued:

> And so there was in the very Being and Life of God an asking of which prayer on earth was to be the reflection and the outflow. It was not without including this that Jesus said, "I knew that Thou always hearest me.' Just as the Sonship of Jesus on earth may not be separated from His Sonship in heaven, even so with His prayer on earth, it is the continuation and the counterpart of His asking in heaven. The prayer of the man Christ Jesus is the link between the eternal asking of the only-begotten Son in the bosom of the Father and the prayer of men upon earth. Prayer has its rise and its deepest source in the very Being of God. In the bosom of Deity nothing is ever done without prayer—the asking of the Son and the giving of the Father.[8]

Can a merely unitarian God answer prayer? Murray said no. He poses some questions:

> One of the secret difficulties with regard to prayer—one which, though not expressed, does often really hinder prayer—is derived

from the perfection of God, in His absolute independence of all that is outside of Himself. Is He not the Infinite Being, who owes what He is to Himself alone, who determines Himself, and whose wise and holy will has determined all that is to be? How can prayer influence Him, or He be moved by prayer to do what otherwise would not be done? Is not the promise of an answer to prayer simply a condescension to our weakness? Is what is said of the power—the much-availing power—of prayer anything more than an accommodation to our mode of thought, because the Deity never can be dependent on any action from without for its doings? And is not the blessing of prayer simply the influence it exercises upon ourselves?[9]

Murray was a Dutch Reformed theologian with a high view of God's all-determining sovereignty, and he was quite serious about the objection. He goes on:

In seeking an answer to such questions, we find the key in the very being of God, in the mystery of the Holy Trinity. If God was only one Person, shut up within Himself, there could be no thought of nearness to Him or influence on Him. But in God there are three Persons. In God we have Father and Son, who have in the Holy Spirit their living bond of unity and fellowship. When eternal Love begat the Son, and the Father gave the Son as the Second Person a place next Himself as His Equal and His Counsellor, there was a way opened for prayer and its influence in the very inmost life of Deity itself. Just as on earth, so in heaven the whole relation between Father and Son is that of giving and taking.[10]

So the fact that God eternally exists as Father and Son (in the unity of the Holy Spirit) means that there is an opening, a space prepared, for the structure of asking-and-granting that is prayer:

Just as the Sonship of Jesus on earth may not be separated from His Sonship in heaven, even so with His prayer on earth, it is the continuation and the counterpart of His asking in heaven. The prayer of the man Christ Jesus is the link between the eternal asking of the only-begotten Son in the bosom of the Father and the prayer of men upon earth. Prayer has its rise and its deepest source in the very Being of God. In the bosom of Deity nothing is ever done without prayer—the asking of the Son and the giving of the Father.[11]

Crucial for Murray was to resist the urge to think of some will of God that is antecedent to the Son and the Father, or some decision that was made behind the back of the Trinity, in the oneness of God that is not already triune. There is no such God, so there is no such divine will. The divine will is Trinitarian and is worked out according to the asking-and-granting structure revealed in the Son:

> This may help us somewhat to understand how the prayer of man, coming through the Son, can have effect upon God. The decrees of God are not decisions made by Him without reference to the Son, or His petition, or the petition to be sent up through Him. By no means. The Lord Jesus is the first-begotten, the Head and Heir of all things: all things were created through Him and unto Him, and all things consist in Him. In the counsels of the Father, the Son, as Representative of all creation, had always a voice; in the decrees of the eternal purpose there was always room left for the liberty of the Son as Mediator and Intercessor, and so for the petitions of all who draw nigh to the Father in the Son.[12]

I do not know how unitarian theists pray or how they think the all-determining God can leave open a space in his eternal counsels to take their wills into account. Murray argued that this is a real problem for anyone who would approach such a God with petitions or intercessions. But he found the solution to the problem in the triunity of God, which, far from being the source of intellectual difficulties, is the solution to many problems:

> It is in the daybreak light of such thoughts that the doctrine of the Blessed Trinity no longer is an abstract speculation, but the living manifestation of the way in which it were possible for man to be taken up into the fellowship of God, and his prayer to become a real factor in God's rule of this earth. And we can, as in the distance, catch glimpses of the light that from the eternal world shines out on words such as these: "Through Him, we have access by one Spirit unto the Father."[13]

THE DEEP THINGS OF GOD

TONGUE-TIED BY TRINITARIAN PRAYER

Not everybody experiences the doctrine of the Trinity as something helpful to their prayers. Quite the contrary, many Christians are getting along just fine saying prayers to God without a single Trinitarian thought in their heads, and when a well-meaning theologian asks them to take the Trinity into account, things fall apart. They thank the Father for dying on the cross, they thank Jesus for sending his only Son, and they suddenly realize that they have no clear ideas whatsoever about the Holy Spirit. Befuddled, they retreat to just praying to God-in-general, but find no comfort there because now they can't imagine what God means in Trinitarian terms and wonder who they've been talking to all these years. So here is the theology quiz that always comes up when we start thinking about the Trinity and prayer: Who do I pray to? The Father? The Son? The Spirit? God? The Trinity? All of the above?

Here is the theologically correct answer: pray to the Father, in the name of the Son, through the power of the Holy Spirit. Most New Testament prayers follow that pattern. There are a few prayers to Jesus in the New Testament and, as far as I know, no recorded prayers to the Holy Spirit. But the Son is a divine person, and the Spirit is a divine person, and you can pray to them. But don't forget what we've seen in the logic of mediation about the way the Spirit and the Son occupy the offices of intercessor and mediator to bring us before the Father. There is a current that runs that direction, and when you know that, you can immerse yourself in that current. It is the logic of how prayer is actually working anyway. Think about it: if you are in the habit of praying to Jesus, are you approaching Jesus the eternal Son of God on the basis of your own merits and deserving? No. Then on what basis? On the basis of his propitiation and mediation. Even prayer to Jesus has to be prayer in Jesus' name. So you can see how that current of mediation runs in that direction, and you can be aligned to it by praying habitually to the Father in Jesus' name.

Of course you don't have to. You can pray to Jesus or the Spirit, or you can pray to God in general without thinking any of these Trinitarian thoughts. There is no good biblical case to be made against praying to the Son or the Spirit, no matter how strong the case for praying to the Father is. But it does raise the counter-question, Why would you want to deviate from the clear biblical pattern? The Bible is very clear: pray to the Father. It is true that there is considerable biblical warrant for praying to the Son. In fact, it is almost impossible to meditate on the presence of the risen Christ without turning to him in prayer. Many parents have decided they should teach their children to pray to Jesus because Jesus is so concrete and personal for young minds to focus on in their prayer. I cannot say if this is sufficiently wise from a developmental standpoint to warrant systematic deviation from the examples in Scripture or to sidestep the logic of Trinitarian mediation and teach children to pray against the grain. If you do choose to teach your children to pray to Jesus, you should have a plan for when you are going to introduce them to the biblical model of prayer.

Prayer to the Holy Spirit is even more difficult, for though the Spirit is a person who is God and therefore is someone who can be worshiped and prayed to, there are no biblical instances of prayer to the Spirit. Graham Cole's observation is worth quoting at length:

> To pray to the Spirit is not wrong theologically, but if that practice displaces prayer to the Father in the name of the Son in reliance upon the Spirit, then there may be another sort of problem that emerges. The problem is that of disproportion. . . . The gospel may also be spoiled by a lack of due weight in theological emphasis, by giving an element in it either too much or too little accent. A biblical truth may be weighted in a way that skews our thinking about God and the gospel. Arguably, to make prayer to the Holy Spirit the principal practice in Christian praying would be such an error. The Holy Spirit may be prayed to. He is God. But the Holy Spirit is not to be prayed to in such a way as to mask the mediatorship of Christ and our location in Christ as members of his body. For to pray to the Father in the name of the Son in reliance upon the Spirit is to rehearse the very structure of the gospel.[14]

"To rehearse the very structure of the gospel" is a good goal to incorporate into every act of prayer, and it is as easy as obeying the clear examples of praying primarily to the Father, in the name of the Son, in the power of the Holy Spirit. In one sense, you already pray rightly, no matter how you do or do not consciously consider the persons of the Trinity in your prayers. You are in fact being brought to the Father through the Son in the Spirit. Whether you make the investment of praying with the grain is an open invitation to enter into the deep things of God wholeheartedly.

Vagueness in prayer is to be avoided, and once you have considered the personal presence of the Father, Son, and Holy Spirit, you may not be able to go back to praying with the undifferentiated word *God*. It may cease to sound to you like a name once you have given sustained attention to the names of the persons of the Trinity. Robert Speer wrote in his *Fundamentals* essay "God in Christ the Only Revelation of the Fatherhood of God":

> I suspect that prayer has been just a sham to many of us, or a thing that we have done because other people told us it was the thing to do. We never got anything out of it; it never meant anything to us. We might just as well have talked to stone walls as to pray the way we have prayed. We went out and said, "God," and we might just as well have said, "hills," or "mountains," or "trees," or anything else. Why have we not gone into the school of Christ and learned there, alike from His practice and His doctrine, what real prayer is and how a man can do it. You cannot find a single prayer of Christ addressed to God, not one; nor can you find a single prayer of Christ's in which He so much as mentions God.[15]

There is one final way that Trinitarian theology can seem like an obstacle rather than an aid to prayer: the Holy Spirit can seem alarmingly nondescript. As soon as we begin meditating on the three persons, we discover how difficult it is to form a clear impression of the Spirit as somebody, as a person with a personality that can be on par with God the Father and Jesus Christ. This is no cause for alarm. Though it is always wrong to be Spirit-ignoring, there is no reason to think we should be Spirit-focused in the sense of directing our thoughts to him most of the time. The Spirit's work is to glorify the Son, so the more the Spirit permeates your life, the clearer a grasp you will have of the Son. The more you have the Spirit, the more you will talk about Jesus Christ; the more you will call Jesus Christ "Lord," by the Holy Spirit, to the glory of God the Father.

TRINITARIAN PRAYER ACCORDING TO C. S. LEWIS

C. S. Lewis discusses the Trinity in various places throughout his writings, including—suggestively—in his fiction.[16] But his most comprehensive treatment of the Trinity comes in the context of prayer and is focused in a very practical way on a kind of theological analysis of the built-in directionality of Christian prayer. The passage comes at the end of *Mere Christianity* in Book 4, entitled "Beyond Personality: Or First Steps in the Doctrine of the Trinity." These eleven short chapters, originally delivered as popular addresses to general audiences over the radio, spell out Lewis's understanding of what it means for Christians to believe in the Trinity.

To begin with, Lewis presents the doctrine of the Trinity as an invitation to experience God. Trinitarian theology is more about living than learning: we learn it only in order to live it. Of course there's thinking to do when it comes to the Trinity; it is a doctrine, after all, which means a teaching, something to be instructed in, to reflect on, and to seek understanding concerning. But that quest for understanding is not an end in itself or an exercise in pure speculation; it is in service of a living encounter with the living God. So Lewis leads his readers through a fairly challenging set of theological constructions: the eternal generation of the Son, the relation of time to eternity, the distinction between biological life and spiritual life, etc. But he never allows us to lose sight of the goal: union with God in Christ. "I warned you," he says at one point, "that Theology is practical. The whole purpose for which we exist is to be thus taken into the life of God. Wrong ideas about what that life is, will make it harder."[17] Lewis undertakes to equip us with right ideas about the life of God, to remove certain barriers to our participation in it.

Lewis begins, as he often does, with a rather cavalier comparison between Christianity and all the competing views. Ask people if they believe in a personal God, he says, and plenty of them will be quick to tell you that they believe God must be much more than just a person. God must be beyond merely personal, must be somehow super-personal. Christianity agrees with that. But without further specification, this claim of super-personality evaporates into sub-personality. Instead of envisioning a God who is more than just a person, modern religion-at-large (what Lewis calls "Christianity plus water") ends up with an impersonal God, a God who is not even a person. Only Christianity has backed up its claim with a concrete description of what it might mean for God to be "beyond personality." "If you are looking for something super-personal," he says, "something more than a person, then it is not a question of choosing between the Christian idea and the other ideas. The Christian idea is the only one on the market."[18]

"The Christian idea" is of course the Trinity: that the one God is Father, Son, and Holy Spirit, three persons in one being. Before Lewis gets into the question of why Christians have historically felt compelled to believe this doctrine—of what led us to say such a thing in the first place—he knows that his audience is already shifting around in their seats wondering if it is even possible to think coherently of three persons as one God. After all, it is a rare apologist who is lucky enough to be the first to tell someone about the Trinity. Most people within earshot of Christendom have heard about it before, somewhere. And most people are subconsciously convinced that the whole doctrine has something to do with the mystical connection between an abstract three and an abstract one. Lewis wisely reckons with the fact that he is likely to lose his audience at the first mention of the number three and that having lost them, he will never be able to get them to the heart of the matter. He wants to tell them about the mystery of coinherence but knows that he must first set their minds at ease about the puzzle of incoherence. So he makes a quick, pointed attempt to explain, not how the one God can be three persons, but why it is that we cannot really understand how this is so.

This is a famous passage, and Lewis argues his way through it very tidily.[19] He uses the language of the three dimensions, exploring the relationship between the higher, more complex dimensions and the lower, simpler ones. Lines are one-dimensional things, but when they are taken into the second dimension, they can be combined to form a square. Squares are two-dimensional, but if they are transposed into the third dimension, six of them can coexist as one cube. As you progress to dimensions that are "more real and more complex," you do not leave behind the lower dimensions; you combine them in ways that were unimaginable in the lower dimensions. This example from geometry helps us picture the situation in theology: as far as we can see, one person means one being, and three persons means three beings. We can no more conceive of three persons in one being than a two-dimensional resident of Flatland could conceive of six squares somehow being combined into one single form. "In God's dimension," though, it is possible and actually the fact that these three persons are one being in a way that we cannot conceive in terms of our own less complex, less real world.

Lewis doesn't mean to say that this is exactly how God is related to our concept of being and personhood. He offers the model in an attempt to help us imagine more precisely why we cannot imagine what God is. We know God is a Trinity of persons because God's self-revelation to us leads us to believe so, not because of this multi-dimensional geometry. Lewis gives us a rational explanation of why we will just have to live with something beyond rational explanation. The unity of these three persons in one being makes sense but in a way that we cannot grasp fully, so Lewis equips us to live with a high tolerance for mystery, while finally refusing to posit a real, final contradiction between faith and reason. This is a model of apologetic procedure: although Christianity is made up of a few central mysteries, when we are arguing for the faith, we shouldn't just slap people in the face with an insult to their rationality; we should not require a *sacrificium intellectus* as the first toll booth on the road to faith. Nor should we dumb down the content of Christianity to something that makes so much sense that there's nothing left of it but common sense, which has no need to be divinely revealed. Lewis presents the mystery and offers a way of grasping the contours of its mysteriousness, putting forth the many-dimensions argument not as a proof but as a demonstration of the plausibility of the mystery.

Thinking along with his listeners, Lewis goes on to ask: Why go to the trouble of pushing up against the limits of our understanding and trying to come to terms with this incomprehensible God? What good is talking about this God we cannot understand? Lewis poses this question to himself and then replies: "Well, there isn't any good talking about Him. The thing that matters is actually being drawn into that three-personal life, and that may begin any time—tonight, if you like."[20] Here is a motif with which longtime Lewis readers are familiar: the occasional breakthroughs from theology to direct invitation. You can almost hear the choir softly humming "Just as I Am." It is a short step between the two modes of speech, because as Lewis sees and expounds the Trinity, the doctrine is in itself already the invitation to experience God.

Having dealt summarily with the mathematical problem, at least enough to set his listeners at ease about that old distracting riddle, Lewis moves on to his positive exposition of the mystery itself. He begins with what patristic theology called the economy of salvation: the history of God's dealings with the world. This history of salvation can be considered from two approaches: one more personal and immediate, the other more objective and world-historical. In a few hundred well-chosen words, Lewis conducts us through both, beginning with the personal and then moving back to its objective foundation. Having already mentioned that the point of human existence is to be drawn into God's three-personal life, he launches into a classic passage, describing this experience:

> An ordinary simple Christian kneels down to say his prayers. He is trying to get into touch with God. But if he is a Christian he knows that what is prompting him to pray is also God: God, so to speak, inside him. But he also knows that all his real knowledge of God comes through Christ, the man who was God — that Christ is standing beside him, helping him to pray, praying for him. You see what is happening. God is the thing to which he is praying — the goal he is trying to reach. God is also the thing inside him which is pushing him on — the motive power. God is also the road or bridge along which he is being pushed to that goal. So that the whole threefold life of the three-personal Being is actually going on in that ordinary little bedroom where an ordinary man is saying his prayers. The man is being caught up into the higher kind of life — what I called Zoe or spiritual life: he is being pulled into God, by God, while still remaining himself.[21]

Christian life, as Lewis describes it, is a matter of "being taken up into the life of the Trinity." This seems like rather strong language, and we are tempted to imagine that it is a description of the experiences of a few people who are special, outstanding examples of saintliness.

PRAYING WITH THE GRAIN

But Lewis makes it clear that he is describing the "ordinary, simple Christian." This strong language applies to even the most pedestrian among us, we ordinary souls who are not especially prone to flights of mystical rapture. The ordinary Christian life is lived as an experiencing of the Trinity. Lewis fleshes this out by looking at the same process from two perspectives: from one point of view, we are being pulled into God. Another way of saying the same thing is that God is condescending to draw near to us, to move into our time and space. The ordinary little Christian in that passage is not so much caught up into heaven as heaven is coming down to him: "The whole threefold life of the three-personal God is going on in that ordinary little bedroom." The three persons of the Trinity are really present to us, with us, and for us, in our lives and in this earthly history.

Having drawn our attention to this Trinitarian structure of Christian life, Lewis immediately leads us back to its foundation in the revelation of Jesus Christ. The three ways we experience God correspond to the three ways God has revealed himself in the history of salvation:

> That is how Theology started. People already knew about God in a vague way. Then came a man who claimed to be God; and yet he was not the sort of man you could dismiss as a lunatic. He made them believe Him. They met Him again after they had seen Him killed. And then, after they had been formed into a little society or community, they found God somehow inside them as well: directing them, making them able to do things they could not do before. And when they worked it all out they found they had arrived at the Christian definition of the three-personal God.[22]

Now this is a very rough way of describing the revelation of the Trinity, but it is basically correct. There is a way in which, in the big picture, the story of the Christian experience of the Trinity is the story first of God the Father, then of the incarnation of the Son, and finally of the descent of the Holy Spirit at Pentecost.[23]

The strengths of Lewis's six-sentence account of salvation history are obvious and can be summed up in the fact that in answer to the question, What is the Trinity? he responds in the only way that is finally possible for Christianity: he tells the story of God in Christ. In addition, he gently reminds us that the doctrine itself was not handed to the church by God ready-made but was the product of rational reflection on the experience of God's threefold revelation: "When they worked it all out they found they had arrived at the Christian definition of the three-personal God." Many evangelical Christians, assured by their pastors and teachers that the Trinity is a biblical doctrine, expect to find it explicitly formulated on the pages of Scripture. They are often disappointed and sometimes scandalized to learn that the Trinity is latent, but not blatant, in the Bible. Lewis directs us to the whole shape of the story rather than to a few triadic proof texts.

Equally obvious are the weaknesses of Lewis's "quick and dirty" account of the economy of salvation. For one thing, it is somewhat bizarre to reduce the rich history of God's covenant with Israel into the sentence, "People already knew about God in a vague way." There is nothing vague about the God of Abraham, Isaac, and Jacob (or for that matter, of Hagar and Rahab and Esther). Of course Lewis knew this perfectly well and only ventured such a wild simplification in the interest of weighing each word and keeping his sentences light. An even greater danger of misunderstanding looms, however, in the way in which the three persons of the Trinity come on stage one after another: Father, then Son, then Spirit. If this were a play, one actor could play all three parts. Such a description could be misinterpreted as the heresy of modalism, which pictures the one God as putting on different masks for different tasks (or worse yet, as appearing in different modes for different moods). Modalism arises whenever a theologian stops halfway to the doctrine of the Trinity and tries to preserve God's unity by committing serial monotheism. God in this case would appear first as the Father in order to create, then as the Son in order to redeem, and finally as the Spirit in order to indwell and fulfill.

But Lewis is no serial monotheist; he is a committed and consistent Trinitarian thinker. To clarify his meaning and banish any hint of modalism, he takes recourse to the ancient doctrine of the eternal generation of the Son. He goes out of his way to make sure we understand that the Father has never been without the Son, that there was never a time before the coming forth of the Son from the Father. From all eternity, in the unity of the Holy Spirit these three have been in communion with each other. God is eternally the Trinity, three persons in one being since before the foundation of the world. Lewis devotes seven pages to clarifying this doctrine, even inserting a short excursus on the relationship of eternity to time by way of clearing away conceptual difficulties arising from the doctrine.[24] Seven pages is a heavy investment in a book like *Mere Christianity*, where every word counts. Lewis obviously felt that it was important to anchor his economic Trinitarianism in the eternal nature of God's being and to provoke his listeners to reflect on this classic doctrine. If all he wanted to do was refute modalism, he could have given a few more sentences to his description of Jesus' life and relationships with the Father and the Spirit, perhaps by calling attention to the prayers of Jesus.

The best way to swat down modalism is with a brief mention of Christ's baptism, at which all three persons of the Trinity come on stage at the same time. But instead Lewis carried out a more far-reaching maneuver, taking this opportunity to show how the history of salvation has its basis in the eternal threefold life of God in eternity. When Christians say "God is love," they mean that "the living, dynamic activity of love has been going on in God for ever and has created everything else."[25] Lewis's description of this love climaxes in his account of the Holy Spirit, whom he describes in the standard Western terminology: "The union between the Father and Son is such a live concrete thing that this union itself is also a Person. I know this is almost inconceivable."[26] Love between humans is not like that; when I invite a couple to my house for dinner, I set two extra plates on the table; one for him and one for her. I do not set a third plate on the table for their mutual love, because their mutual love is not itself a person. The Father and the Son are more real and more personal than us, however, and in some ineffable way, the Western church affirms, the love between them is itself a full, distinct, subsistent person. The eternal love going on within the Trinity is like a complex life, or a drama, or a dance, and it is personified in the Holy Spirit.

So Lewis bases his exposition of the Trinity on the history of salvation, the economy, in our personal experience as well as in the big picture. We know that God is Father, Son, and Holy Spirit because that is how God is present to us in the history of salvation. Jesus Christ, the Son of God incarnate, came to save us, sent by the Father and empowered by the Holy Spirit, who he then, after his ascension, sent to his disciples. Anyone who knows the story of Jesus knows there are these three central characters in his story: the Trinity. That is the big picture, the economy of salvation. What makes Lewis's treatment of the Trinity so uniquely helpful is the attention he devotes to drawing out the connections between this big picture and our personal, daily practice of Christian life. He began with the vignette of an ordinary, simple Christian at prayer and from there moved back to the history of Jesus Christ and the church. Now, after having given due attention to the eternal character of the Trinity, he returns to our experience of that eternal reality. He has shared with us a vision of eternal love in the communion of the Trinity and described it as a kind of drama or dance going on in heaven. "And now," he asks, "what does it all matter?" This allows him to come to his point:

> It matters more than anything else in the world. The whole dance, or drama, or pattern of this three-Personal life is to be played out in each one of us: or (putting it the other way round) each one of us has got to enter that pattern, take his place in that dance. There is no other way to the happiness for which we were made.[27]

There is eternal life going on in the Trinity, and if we are to be saved we must share in that life. Lewis describes our way of access to that Trinitarian life as "good infection," which calls for us to get close enough to the Trinity to catch this communicable life like a healing virus. The triune life is caught, not taught. Good infection is possible, obviously, only because one person of the Trinity, the Son, has united himself with us by becoming human. Proximity to Jesus is the way to come into contact with the eternal life of the Trinity, because Jesus Christ is that life of God incarnate. "If we share in this kind of life we also shall be sons of God. We shall love the Father as He does and the Holy Ghost will arise in us."[28] This brings Lewis's exposition of the Trinity full circle, back to the "ordinary simple Christian at prayer" and the Trinitarian cadence of that prayer.

Lewis takes the Lord's Prayer as the basic, primal Christian prayer and unpacks what it means to say this prayer. To dare to address God as

"Our Father" is to place oneself in the same category as the one person who is absolutely the true Son of God: Jesus Christ. The only reason we dare to do this is that Jesus himself has invited us to pray in this way, and on his authority we find ourselves standing in a place that only he can authentically occupy. There is "the ordinary simple Christian at prayer," praying to the Father, assisted by the Son who makes the prayer possible, and urged on by the Spirit from within. Because Jesus Christ has come and taken our place, we find ourselves included in his place, deep inside the love of the triune God.

C. S. LEWIS'S MERE TRINITARIANISM

This is Lewis's mere Trinitarianism. What is of utmost importance in making his approach so practical is that he keeps his attention fixed on the history of salvation and describes our place in that big history. He finds the Trinity where it really is. By doing so, Lewis makes the doctrine of the Trinity the explanatory key to Christian life. He brings it in to explain, integrate, and illuminate the otherwise obscure and puzzling claims made by Christians. The set of ideas that might otherwise look like an odd assortment of articles of belief turns out to be an organic whole with the Trinity as its unifying center. This doctrine is a description—a kind of map—of God's life with us, and of our life in God.[29] Lewis doesn't need to devise a strategy for making the Trinity relevant; the way he presents the doctrine, it is always already relevant. He doesn't need to bring out any devices to explain it; he uses it to explain everything else. This is to treat the doctrine in the same way as it was originally treated, when it was hammered out in the theology of the Council of Nicaea in the fourth century.

Now we have analyzed what Lewis modestly describes as "first steps in the doctrine of the Trinity." How far do these first steps take us? By way of conclusion, I want to sketch out a little bit of the breadth of Lewis's evangelical Trinitarian vision of the Christian faith.

First of all, it is worth noting that *Mere Christianity* is a book with an evangelistic and apologetic mission and that Lewis gives the doctrine of the Trinity a prominent place in that undertaking. He is Trinitarian, in other words, right there in his evangelism. This strikes me as a refreshingly healthy approach for such a project. Much evangelical preaching and evangelizing betrays a kind of bad conscience when it comes to the doctrine of the Trinity. If we think about it at all, we assume that it is primarily a confounding logical puzzle, about which we should maintain a prudent silence, at least in our initial presentation of Christianity's claims. After all, it's hard enough to persuade someone to believe in God and to win a hearing for the message of Jesus Christ. Why bother them with the Trinity? There's plenty of time to tell them about that sort of thing after they've already converted. The assumption seems to be that we can only expect people to swallow so much at a time, and the Trinity is not an appetizer. In fact, it isn't even the main course; perhaps it's the bitter greens we know we should eat along with the rest of the meal.

I wonder how many people have become Christians and then experienced a little bit of buyer's remorse at discovering that they've committed themselves to believing in such a bewildering doctrine. Anyone who has been helped into the faith by reading C. S. Lewis will not suffer from such a problem.[30] Remember that for Lewis, concentrating on mere Christianity did not mean rounding off the rough edges of what was essential to the faith. The common faith of the church is not an amorphous lump but a distinct form with a few well-defined corners; in this case, three corners: the Father, Son, and Holy Spirit.

The reason Lewis is able to lead with the Trinity is—and this is my second point—that for him the doctrine of salvation is itself the doctrine of the Trinity. He presents the doctrine of God and the way of salvation in the same breath because they are the same thing: the Trinity is the divine mystery of human salvation. Learning the Father's relation to the Son in the Spirit is already the invitation to experience that relationship, to be taken up into it. This is why Lewis's language can cross over from description to invitation so suddenly; he shows us the dance of divine love and indicates that there is room for another dancer to join in.

Thirdly, this presentation of salvation makes a seamless transition into practical instruction in living the Christian life. Our sanctification is a constant reenactment of that same movement, of stepping into the place that the Son of God is holding open for us. There is the famous passage in *Mere Christianity*, in the chapter entitled "Let's Pretend," in which Lewis describes the rationale behind acting as if you are a child of God, or as he says, "dressing up as Christ." It is not a sham, he reminds us, if the reason that we are acting like what we are not yet is because that pretense is the only way to truly become what we are now pretending to be. Lewis has in mind something a little more profound than the Alcoholics Anonymous motto, "Fake it 'til you make it." The relationship is more organic than that. Just as children only become adults by playing at the activities of adulthood, Christians become more like Christ by acting like children of God.

Having established this way of looking at our sanctification, Lewis proceeds to turn it on its head. Although it may look to us as if we are doing all the work, pretending to be Christ, we will eventually become aware that in fact God is the one doing everything:

> In a sense you might even say it is God who does the pretending. The Three-Personal God, so to speak, sees before Him in fact a self-centred, greedy, grumbling, rebellious human animal. But He says "Let us pretend that this is not a mere creature, but our Son. It is like Christ in so far as it is a Man, for He became Man. Let us pretend that it is also like him in Spirit. Let us treat it as if it were what in fact it is not. Let us pretend in order to make that pretence into a reality."[31]

There is no gap here between justification and sanctification, but the two interpenetrate each other as parts of an organic whole that is our life in Christ, our introduction into the love of the Trinity.

Finally, we can indicate the link that Lewis saw between the doctrine of the Trinity and one of his favorite themes, the hope of heaven. In his essay "The Weight of Glory," Lewis searches through the Bible and tries to make sense of the images of heaven that he finds there. He gives particular attention to the idea of a divine accolade, or approval by God:

> The promise of glory is the promise, almost incredible and only possible by the work of Christ, that some of us, that any of us who really chooses . . . shall find approval, shall please God. To please God . . . to be a real ingredient in the divine happiness . . . to be loved by God, not merely pitied, but delighted in as an artist

delights in his work or a father in a son—it seems impossible, a
weight or burden of glory which our thoughts can hardly sustain.
But so it is.[32]

The primal delight that the Father takes in the Son, in the glory that they
shared before the foundation of the world, will in the end be our glorification too. God will be truly pleased with us, and we will be a part of
the mutual delight that is the life of the Trinity. That will be glory, when
we are finally caught up into the heavenly love of the three-personal
God. This is the extent of Lewis's mere Trinitarianism.

Evangelicals tend to ask three questions about the Trinity: Is it
biblical? Does it make sense? and Does it matter? We've seen Lewis's
answers to these questions: yes, it's biblical; it's not explicitly formulated
in the words of the text, but it's woven into the very structure of the history of salvation, which is what the Bible's about. Does it make sense?
Yes, but it also points us beyond what we can conceive of, and Lewis
uses the idea of higher dimensions to make this mystery at least plausible. Finally, however, Lewis is far less interested in these questions than
in the third one: Does the doctrine of the Trinity matter? It matters more
than anything, he says, and he bends all his efforts to demonstrating the
relevance of the unadorned, unabridged doctrine of mere Trinitarianism
in an evangelical mode. These rather humble first steps in the doctrine
of the Trinity are the key to being led further up and further in to the
life of the three-personal God.

Two more remarks about C. S. Lewis are appropriate by way of
conclusion because they are things that have characterized evangelical
Trinitarianism at its best in centuries past and ought to characterize it
more in coming years. First, Lewis had a peculiar genius for hinting or
suggesting the most important things even when he was not directly
talking about them. Owen Barfield said of him, "There was something
in the whole quality and structure of his thinking, something for which
the best label I can find is 'presence of mind.' If I were asked to expand
on that, I could say only that somehow what he thought about everything was secretly present in what he said about anything."[33] This is
the very power we need to cultivate if evangelical Trinitarianism is to
thrive. We do not need so much to talk about the Trinity at all times but

to talk about everything else in a way that our convictions about the Trinity are "somehow . . . secretly present" in everything we say or do. Our words and works need to be supported by a tacit Trinitarianism that distinguishes Christ-centeredness from Father-forgetfulness and Spirit-ignoring.

Finally, Lewis frequently wrote about the demands that God makes on his children for their total devotion and obedience. He once confessed to what he called his "endlessly recurrent temptation: to go down to that Sea (I think St. John of the Cross called God a sea) and there neither dive nor swim nor float, but only dabble and splash, careful not to get out of my depth and holding on to the lifeline which connects me with my things temporal."[34] The great tradition of evangelical Trinitarianism has not dabbled or splashed but has gone deep into the things of the gospel, the deep things of God. Our churches today face the same opportunity and the same "endlessly recurrent temptation." God calls us to the depths, the only place we can find the gospel—the Father, the Son, and the Holy Spirit.

NOTES

INTRODUCTION: EVANGELICALS, THE GOSPEL, AND THE TRINITY

1. This widespread saying is usually introduced with the vague reference, "As somebody has said." I have found a slightly more polite version of it in Harold Lindsell and Charles J. Woodbridge, *A Handbook of Christian Truth* (Westwood, NJ: Revell, 1953), 51–52, though it is surely not original there.

2. This was the view of Emil Brunner, who called the Trinity a "theological doctrine which defends the central faith of the Bible and the Church" but cautioned that it must not be preached or taught to the faithful, lest it present "an artificial stumbling-block." See *The Christian Doctrine of God: Dogmatics* (Philadelphia: Westminster Press, 1949), 1:206, 238.

3. This is another untraceable statement about the Trinity that we keep in circulation via the phrase "As someone has said." I have seen it most recently, introduced thus, in Clifford Pond's keenly gospel-centered little book *This God Is Our God: Enjoying the Trinity* (London: Grace Publications Trust, 2000), 58.

4. Gerald Bray, "The Filioque Clause in History and Theology," *Tyndale Bulletin* 34 (1983): 91–144.

5. "The Glory of the Gospel," *The Works of Thomas Goodwin* (Lafayette, IN: Sovereign Grace, 2000), 4:227–346. Goodwin says this repeatedly, at 238, 272, 281, 288.

6. Echoing Cecil F. Alexander's translation of the Old Irish poem known as "St. Patrick's Breastplate."

7. J. C. Ryle, *Knots Untied: Being Plain Statements on Disputed Points in Religion from the Standpoint of an Evangelical Churchman* (London: William Hunt, 1885), 8. Notice also that Ryle's list has the profile of an experiential grasp of Trinitarianism.

8. *The Fundamentals: A Testimony to the Truth*, vol. 3 (Los Angeles: Bible Institute of Los Angeles, 1917), chap. 12. For more on *The Fundamentals* as a witness to evangelicalism at large and to evangelical Trinitarianism in particular.

9. John Wesley, "Introduction," in The Sermons of John Wesley: The Standard Sermons, ed. Thomas Jackson, 1872 edition.

10. See below, chap. 3, for more on this passage.

11. B. B. Warfield, "Redeemer and Redemption," in *The Person and Work of Christ* (Philadelphia: Presbyterian and Reformed, 1950), 345.

CHAPTER 1: COMPASSED ABOUT BY FATHER, SON, AND HOLY SPIRIT

1. David Wilkerson with John and Elizabeth Sherrill, *The Cross and the Switchblade* (New York: Pyramid, 1963). The book was a best-seller well into the 1970s in the Christian market. It was also the basis of a 1970 movie starring Pat Boone and Erik Estrada, and a 1972 comic book.

2. Nicky Cruz with Jamie Buckingham, *Run Baby Run* (New York: Pyramid, 1968).

3. Nicky Cruz with Charles Paul Conn, *The Magnificent Three* (Old Tappan, NJ: Revell, 1976).

4. Ibid., 9.

5. Ibid., 13.

6. Ibid., 24–25.

7. Ibid., 51.

8. Ibid., 64.

9. Ibid., 103.

10. Ibid., 105.

11. Ibid., 70.

12. Ibid., 18.

13. Ibid., 15.

14. Ibid., 17.

15. Ibid.

16. Millard J. Erickson addresses precisely these questions in his short, incisive book *Making Sense of the Trinity: Three Crucial Questions* (Grand Rapids, MI: Baker Academic, 2000). His title for the third question, which he calls the "So What?" question, is, "Does It Make Any Difference?"

17. Robert Louis Wilken, *The Spirit of Early Christian Thought: Seeking the Face of God* (New Haven: Yale University Press, 2003), xviii.

18. Mark Noll, "The Evangelical Mind Today," *First Things* 146 (October 2004): 34–39.
19. See esp. Bruce D. Marshall's critique of this story in his article "The Trinity," in *The Blackwell Companion to Theology*, ed. Gareth Jones (Oxford: Blackwell, 2004). His warning about exaggerating the importance of Protestant liberalism and Catholic manualism is especially relevant for evangelicals, who were not directly formed by those traditions and so did not directly profit when Barth and Rahner undermined them.
20. Friedrich Schleiermacher, *The Christian Faith*, ed. H. R. MacKintosh and J. S. Stewart (1830; repr. Edinburgh: T&T Clark, 1928).
21. Ibid., 52.
22. Ibid., 123.
23. Ibid., 156.
24. Friedrich Schleiermacher, *On Religion: Speeches to Its Cultured Despisers* (1799; repr. New York: Harper, 1958), 52.
25. Schleiermacher, *Christian Faith*, 747. I have changed the standard translation here and substituted "Protestant" for "Evangelical," which is what Schleiermacher manifestly meant.
26. John Bunyan, "Of the Trinity and a Christian," *The Works of John Bunyan*, ed. W. R. Owens (Oxford: Clarendon Press, 1994), 12:403–5.
27. Bunyan in fact had a much better grasp of the actual dynamics of biblical Trinitarianism than he gave himself credit for. See below (chap. 7) for his Trinitarian definition of prayer. I would even say Bunyan is a typical evangelical in that he is more Trinitarian than he thinks he is.
28. For background, see Philip Dixon, *Nice and Hot Disputes: The Doctrine of the Trinity in the Seventeenth Century* (London: T&T Clark, 2003).
29. This long prayer, entitled "The Author's solemn Address to the great and ever-blessed God on a Review of what he had written in the Trinitarian Controversy," can be found as sec. 21 of "Remnants of Time Employed in Prose and Verse, or Short Essays and Composures on Various Subjects," in *The Works of the Rev. Isaac Watts in Nine Volumes* (London: Longman, Hurst, Rees, Orme and Brown, 1813), 9:505–12. The quotation is from p. 507. These remarks by Watts need to be taken in the total context of his work, in which Trinitarian commitments are evident and, as in the hymns, warmly affirmed.
30. Amanda Smith, *The Story of the Lord's Dealings with Mrs. Amanda Smith, the Colored Evangelist* (Chicago: Meyer and Brother, 1893); repr. from original typesetting in the Schomburg Library of Nineteenth-Century Black Women Writers (New York: Oxford University Press, 1988).
31. Ibid., 141–42.
32. Karl Rahner, *The Trinity* (1967; English trans. New York: Herder and Herder, 1970), 14.
33. Thomas Kuhn, *The Structure of Scientific Revolutions* (Chicago: University of Chicago Press, 1962).
34. Stephen Toulmin, *Cosmopolis: The Hidden Agenda of Modernity* (Chicago: University of Chicago Press, 1990). It is also instructive to recall the work of Hans-Georg Gadamer in philosophy, Alasdair MacIntyre in moral thought, and Imre Lakatos in the philosophy of science, in order to get a sense of the larger context in which Polanyi's work can be meaningfully situated. To associate his project with thinkers like Paul Feyerabend, Bruno Latour, and the "science studies" discipline at large would, however, be going too far and misunderstanding his work.
35. Michael Polanyi, *Personal Knowledge: Toward a Post-Critical Philosophy* (London: Routledge and Kegan Paul, 1958), vii.
36. Ibid., *vii.*
37. Ibid., 266.
38. Thomas F. Torrance, "Notes on Terms and Concepts," *Belief in Science and in Christian Life: The Relevance of Michael Polanyi's Thought for the Christian Faith and Life* (Edinburgh: Handsel Press, 1980), 145.
39. Thomas F. Torrance, *The Christian Doctrine of God: One Being Three Persons* (Edinburgh: T&T Clark, 1996), 89.
40. Gerald Bray, "Evangelicals Losing Their Way: The Doctrine of the Trinity," in *The Compromised Church: The Present Evangelical Crisis*, ed. John Armstrong (Wheaton, IL: Crossway, 1998), 63.
41. Ibid., 64–65.
42. This remark by Unitarian John MacLachlan is reported in Philip Dixon, *Nice and Hot Disputes* (Edinburgh: T&T Clark, 2005), 215.
43. Andrew Louth, *Discerning the Mystery: An Essay on the Nature of Theology* (Oxford: Clarendon Press, 1983).
44. Ibid., 74.
45. Ibid., 75.
46. Ibid., 86.
47. Ibid., 93.

48. Drusilla Scott, *Everyman Revived: The Common Sense of Michael Polanyi* (Grand Rapids, MI: Eerdmans, 1995), 51.

49. Simon Chan, *Spiritual Theology: A Systematic Study of the Christian Life* (Downers Grove, IL: InterVarsity, 1998), chap. 8.

CHAPTER 2: WITHIN THE HAPPY LAND OF THE TRINITY

1. Have you ever stopped to ask, What if there were no hypothetical questions?

2. *Hymns Ancient and Modern* (New York: Pott and Amery, 1870), no. 154.

3. From *A Practical Commentary upon the First Epistle of St. Peter, The Works of Robert Leighton* (London: Longmans, 1870), 3:137. The prophet he quotes is Isaiah (57:15).

4. Scripture does, however, address the question indirectly, leaving plenty of room and guidance for productive biblical mediation. The classic example is Jonathan Edwards's 1765 treatise *The End for Which God Created the World.*

5. Mirabiliter condidisti, mirabilius reformasti is the elegant Latin of this prayer that goes back to at least the seventh century. It became part of the Roman mass, where it is prayed at the mixing of water into the wine.

6. Not to be confused with tipping your waiter 30 percent.

7. From an undated entry, estimated ca. 1711, in Susanna Wesley's devotional journal. *Susanna Wesley: The Complete Writings*, ed. Charles Wallace Jr. (New York: Oxford University Press, 1997), 225.

8. Ibid., "Letter to Mrs. Alice Peard, Tiverton, August 5, 1737," 173.

9. Ibid., 210 (ca. 1710).

10. A. H. Strong, *Systematic Theology: Three Volumes in One* (Valley Forge, PA: Judson Press, 1907), 347.

11. Thomas Manton, *One Hundred and Ninety Sermons on the Hundred and Nineteenth Psalm*, (London: William Brown, 1842), 2:96.

12. Ibid., 98.

13. Ibid., 100.

14. Craig Musseau, "Good to Me" (Mercy/Vineyard, 1990), CCLI #313480.

15. James Denney, *Lectures in Theology* (London: Hodder and Stoughton, 1895), 70. See the 1976 reprint (Baker) for a helpful introduction by David F. Wells to the maverick Denney.

16. Jonathan Edwards, *The Religious Affections* (1746; repr. Carlisle, PA: Banner of Truth, 1961), 167.

17. Ibid., 172.

18. Robert Hawker, "The Personal Testimony of God the Father to the Person, Godhead, and Sonship of God the Son," in *A New Uniform Edition of the Works of the Rev. Robert Hawker, DD* (London: Ebenezer Palmer, 1826), 3:570.

19. Ibid., 567–68.

20. Ibid., 568.

21. Ibid., 569. In the first line, Hawker has "bear" for "bare."

22. G. K. Chesterton, *The Ballad of the White Horse*, bk. 1, lines 209–24.

23. The "someone" who said this was Charles Gore in his 1891 Bampton lectures, which I do not recommend. The line is better out of context than in context, because Gore had a thoroughly kenotic christology and was more interested in the denial than in the affirmation. This is probably why B. B. Warfield quoted the line without naming his source and then amended it to "not so much inculcated as presupposed." See Warfield's 1915 essay "The Biblical Doctrine of the Trinity," reprinted in his *Biblical and Theological Studies* (Philadelphia: Presbyterian and Reformed, 1952), 32.

24. Gerald L. Bray, "Out of the Box: The Christian Experience of God in Trinity," in *God the Holy Trinity: Reflections on Christian Faith and Practice*, ed. Timothy George (Grand Rapids, MI: Baker Academic, 2006), 45.

25. Thomas Traherne, *Centuries* (New York: Harper and Brothers, 1960), 3.

26. William Burkitt, *Expository Notes, with Practical Observations, on the New Testament* (London: James Dinnis, 1832), 2:515.

27. For a brief, accessible explanation of eternal sonship and a refutation of alternative views, see John MacArthur, "Reexamining the Eternal Sonship of Christ," at http://www.gty.org/Resources/Articles/593.

28. The most influential statement of the case for "the fatherhood of God and the infinite value of the human soul" was by Adolf von Harnack, *What Is Christianity?* (New York: Putnam's, 1902). G. E. Ladd refutes the classic liberal case in his "God the Father" article in the *International Standard Bible Encyclopedia, E–J*, ed. Geoffrey Bromiley (Grand Rapids, MI: Eerdmans, 1982), 511.

29. I call it "classic" partly because I could demonstrate that the early church fathers taught it consistently. For a good treatment of the evidence from the early church, see Robert Letham, *The Holy*

Trinity: In Scripture, History, Theology, and Worship (Phillipsburg, NJ: P&R, 2005), 89–200. For my purposes in this book, it is more relevant to show that this has also been the consistent position of evangelical Protestantism, and later chapters will make this abundantly clear. But more important than either of these appeals to tradition and consensus is my claim that the view presented here is the right interpretation of Scripture.

30. John Piper, *Desiring God: Meditations of a Christian Hedonist* (Sisters, OR: Multnomah, 1986), 32.

31. Ibid., 33. Piper is developing ideas from Jonathan Edwards throughout this section.

32. Bill Bright, "Four Spiritual Laws," http://www.campuscrusade.com/four_laws_online.htm.

33. Handley C. G. Moule, *Outlines of Christian Doctrine* (London: Hodder and Stoughton, 1902), 39.

34. From *A Practical Commentary upon the First Epistle of St. Peter*, 149.

CHAPTER 3: SO GREAT SALVATION

1. G. K. Chesterton, *The Everlasting Man* (Garden City, NY: Image, 1955), 1.

2. That is, 202 Greek words. Harold W. Hoehner, *Ephesians: An Exegetical Commentary* (Grand Rapids, MI: Baker Academic, 2002), 153.

3. The other New Testament passage that competes with Ephesians 1 for comprehensiveness and complexity is Romans 8. There too, the effect on the reader is overwhelming, and there too the contour is Trinitarian.

4. It was Eduard Norden who in 1913 called it "the most monstrous sentence conglomeration . . . I have ever met in the Greek language." Markus Barth quoted this remark in his two-volume Anchor Bible Commentary *Ephesians: Introduction, Translation, and Commentary* (New York: Doubleday, 1974), 77. He went on more reverently in his commentary to "make visible the distinctness, the beauty, and the sense of the several limbs of the 'monster.'"

5. Effective communication of the gospel always happens under this Pauline sign: "My speech and my message were not in plausible words of wisdom, but in demonstration of the Spirit and of power" (1 Cor. 2:4).

6. Notice the Father of glory; the Lord Jesus Christ; and the spirit of wisdom, revelation, and knowledge.

7. Barth, *Ephesians*, 34:373.

8. Counting "in him," "in whom," and "in the Beloved," there are 13 occurrences here.

9. *The Works of Thomas Goodwin* (Lafayette, IN: Sovereign Grace, 2000), 1:46.

10. Ibid.

11. A. B. Simpson, *A Larger Christian Life* (New York: Christian Alliance, 1890), 119.

12. *Hymns of the Christian Life* (Harrisburg, PA: Christian Publications, 1978), no. 54.

13. James Denney, cited in John Randolph Taylor, *God Loves Like That! The Theology of James Denney* (Richmond, VA: John Knox Press, 1962), 38.

14. Adolph Saphir, *The Hidden Life: Thoughts on Communion with God* (New York: Carter, 1877), 1.

15. R. A. Torrey, "The Way of Salvation Made as Plain as Day," in *Revival Addresses* (New York: Revell, 1903).

16. John Wesley, *Explanatory Notes upon the New Testament* (London: Epworth Press, 1950), 829–30.

17. John Wesley, "A Plain Account of Christian Perfection," *The Works of John Wesley* (New York: Harper, 1827), 8:11.

18. C. H. Spurgeon, "Salvation to the Uttermost," A Sermon (no. 84) Delivered on Sabbath Evening, June 8, 1856, at Exeter Hall, Strand. http://www.spurgeon.org/sermons/0084.htm.

19. Dallas Willard, *The Divine Conspiracy: Rediscovering Our Hidden Life in God* (San Francisco: HarperOne, 1998).

20. "Health and wealth" preaching of any variety ("prosperity," "name it and claim it," "positive confession") is best considered a blasphemous parody of the evangelical message. These teachers use precisely the "abundance" rhetoric we are examining in this chapter but apply it to their own ends. The more noise they make about abundance and fullness, the more they are constricting the gospel.

21. J. C. Ryle, "Evangelical Religion," *Knots Untied: Being Plain Statements on Disputed Points in Religion from the Standpoint of an Evangelical Churchman* (London: William Hunt, 1885).

22. This book is available in multiple reprint editions. J. I. Packer wrote the introduction to the Christian Focus reprint. It is printed together with all Scougal's extant writings in *The Works of the Rev. Henry Scougal*, ed. Don Kistler (Morgan, PA: Soli Deo Gloria, 2002).

23. Henry Scougal, "The Life of God in the Soul of Man [1667]," *Works of the Rev. Henry Scougal*, 2.

24. I invented this word, but you have my permission to use it.

25. Shirley Carter Hughson, *With Christ in God: A Study of Human Destiny* (London: SPCK, 1947), ix.
26. Thomas C. Oden, *The Transforming Power of Grace* (Nashville: Abingdon, 1993), 33.
27. That is, in the two sentences I have quoted. Oden's book has much to say about grace's conquest of sin. The work is also, by the way, markedly Trinitarian.
28. See above, p. 103.
29. *Works of Thomas Goodwin*, 1:46.
30. Most modern translations prefer "I am your shield, and your reward shall be very great."
31. Dwight L. Moody, "The Eighth Chapter of Romans," in *Moody's Last Sermons: Authorized Edition Printed from Verbatim Reports* (Chicago: Moody Press, n.d.), 43–44. This was the last formal address Moody gave, in the Auditorium at East Northfield, MA, August 12, 1899.
32. F. B. Meyer, *The Exalted Christ and Our Identification with Him in His Exaltation* (London: Wheeler, 1930), 34.
33. "The Glory of the Gospel," in *Works of Thomas Goodwin*, 4:227–346. Goodwin says this repeatedly (238, 272, 281, 288). The sermons titled "The Glory of the Gospel" are on Col. 1:26–27, but Goodwin frequently alludes to and sometimes cites 1 Cor. 2:10.
34. Ibid., 281.
35. "Things" is not strictly present in the original Greek but is provided by the KJV to make sense of "deep" used as a plural noun; "depths of God" is the more common modern translation.
36. Paul is quoting Isa. 40:13 (as he does also in Rom. 11:34), a text which asks, Who has known the mind of Yahweh? Paul answers Isaiah's rhetorical question with the name "Christ." This is one of six New Testament passages where Christ and the name Yahweh are identified. See David B. Capes, *Old Testament Yahweh Texts in Paul's Christology* (Tübingen: Mohr, 1992).
37. *Hymns of the Christian Life*, no. 1.
38. *Cor ad cor loquitur* ("heart speaks to heart") as John Henry Newman's coat of arms said.
39. John Piper, *God Is the Gospel: Meditations on God's Love as the Gift of Himself* (Wheaton, IL: Crossway, 2005).

CHAPTER 4: THE SHAPE OF THE GOSPEL

1. John Owen, "Pneumatologia," in *The Works of John Owen*, 24 vols. ed. William Goold (Edinburgh: Johnstone and Hunter, 1850–53; vols. 1–16 repr. London: Banner of Truth, 1965), 3:23.
2. Most of these words in Ephesians are even built from oik- compounds, echoing the root word of *oikonomia*.
3. The full range of the use of the word economy makes for a fascinating study. For a useful tool that shows all its occurrences but requires no knowledge of Greek, see W. E. Vine, *Vine's Expository Dictionary of Old and New Testament Words* (Old Tappan, NJ: Fleming Revell, 1981), under the entry "dispensation" but also under "stewardship." The word-study method is a rich way of reading the Bible, but there are certain temptations to beware of. Words are not concepts, and etymologies are not meanings. D. A. Carson's book *Exegetical Fallacies*, 2d ed. (Grand Rapids, MI: Baker Academic, 1996) has a helpful section, "Word-Study Fallacies" (27–65). In my use of the word oikonomia here, I have been careful to derive its meaning from Paul's use of it and then to use the "house-law" etymology as a source of illustration. But in its theological usage, *economy* means "history," not "house."
4. Handley C. G. Moule, *Outlines of Christian Theology* (London: Hodder and Stoughton, 1902), 39. For support, Moule points to "John 1:18, 5:20, 17:24, etc." For responsible modern commentary on Jesus' relation to the Father in John's Gospel, see Andreas Köstenberger and Scott Swain, *Father, Son, and Spirit: The Trinity and John's Gospel* (Downers Grove, IL: InterVarsity, 2008), esp. 61–74, 111–33.
5. See Klaus Issler, "Jesus' Example: Prototype of the Dependent, Spirit-Filled Life," in Fred Sanders and Klaus Issler, *Jesus in Trinitarian Perspective: An Introductory Christology* (Nashville: Broadman, 2007), 208–9.
6. R. A. Torrey, *What the Bible Teaches* (New York: Revell, 1898), 287–89.
7. For a concise introduction to the doctrine of God from this point of view, see Dennis F. Kinlaw, *Let's Start with Jesus: A New Way of Doing Theology* (Grand Rapids, MI: Zondervan, 2005), and from the same starting point but with more Trinitarian elaboration, Allen Coppedge, *The God Who Is Triune: Revisioning the Christian Doctrine of God* (Downers Grove, IL: IVP Academic, 2007).
8. Irenaeus, *Haer.*, 4.20.1. He returns to this image in three other places: 5.1.3; 5.6:1; and 5.28.4.
9. Some of the leading ideas here, including the idea of developing two distinct vocabularies or grammars, are from A. A. Van Ruler's essay "Structural Differences Between the Christological and Pneumatological Perspectives," found in his book *Calvinist Trinitarianism and Theocentric Politics: Essays Toward a Public Theology*, trans. and ed. John Bolt (Lewiston, NY: Edwin Mellen Press, 1989), 27–46. A more satisfying exploration of the distinctive ministry of the Spirit can be found in Abraham Kuyper's *The Work of the Holy Spirit* (1900; repr. Chattanooga, TN: AMG, 1995).

10. See John Murray's book of this name, *Redemption Accomplished and Applied*, a classic of its kind.

11. Sermon 5, "Justification by Faith," in Wesley's *52 Standard Sermons*, ed. N. Burwash (Schmul, OH: Schmul, n.d.) 45.

12. This 1657 work has been helpfully republished as *Communion with the Triune God*, ed. Kelly M. Kapic and Justin Taylor (Wheaton, IL: Crossway, 2007).

13. J. I. Packer, *Knowing God* (Downers Grove, IL: InterVarsity, 1973), 15.

14. John Flavel, *The Method of Grace: In the Holy Spirit's Applying to the Souls of Men the Eternal Redemption Contrived by the Father and Accomplished by the Son*, (New York: American Tract Society, 1845), 3. The Method was originally published in the late seventeenth century. Flavel's works have been frequently republished with a variety of changes silently inserted by editors. The edition I am quoting from here is one of the more readable modified versions. Purists will want to seek out the unexpurgated Flavel, which is more decisively Reformed and uses more technical language.

15. Theologians are careful to note that whenever we say a person of the Trinity does something, we should not say this in a way that excludes the others altogether. John Owen gives a simplified description when he says that one of the persons acts "principally, immediately, and by the way of eminency" but never exclusively, in the actions that peculiarly belong to them. See Owen, *Communion with the Triune God*, 104.

16. Flavel, *Method*, 17.

17. Ibid., 16.

18. Ibid., 19.

19. Ibid.

20. See W. H. Griffith-Thomas, "Introductory Note to the Fifth Edition," in Marcus Rainsford, *The Lord's Prayer for Believers: Thoughts on St. John 17, the Lord's Prayer for Believers Throughout All Time*, 5th ed. (London: Thynne, 1904), n.p.

21. Some of these dialogues were published in Marcus Rainsford, *The Fulness of God, and Other Addresses* (London: Partridge, 1898), 236–58. This quotation is from pp. 24–44.

22. Ibid., 255–56.

23. Ibid., 257–58.

24. Owen, "Pneumatologia," 3:23.

25. The great Nazarene theologian H. Orton Wiley inherited this language from an older tradition, but in his three-volume *Christian Theology* he used it with unobjectionable wisdom. "The New Testament does not sanction the thought of an economy of the Spirit apart from that of the Father and the Son except in this sense—that it is the revelation of the Person and work of the Holy Spirit, and therefore the final revelation of the Holy Trinity." See his *Christian Theology* (Kansas City, MO: Beacon Hill Press, 1942), 2:303ff., including the excellent quotations from William Burt Pope.

26. Robert Leighton, cited in T. F. Torrance, *Scottish Theology: From John Knox to John McLeod Campbell* (Edinburgh: T&T Clark, 1996), 172.

27. Owen, "Pneumatologia," 3:23.

28. I apologize for the highly compressed lesson on the incarnation here. For details, see my introductory chapter in *Jesus in Trinitarian Perspective*, 1–41.

29. Austin Farrer, "Incarnation," in *The Brink of Mystery*, ed. Charles C. Conti (London: SPCK, 1976), 20.

30. Ibid.

31. Lesslie Newbigin, *The Relevance of Trinitarian Doctrine for Today's Mission* (Edinburgh: Edinburgh House Press, for the World Council of Churches Commission on World Mission and Evangelism, 1963), 33.

32. Ibid., 32.

33. This four-volume edition, *The Fundamentals: A Testimony to the Truth* (Los Angeles: Bible Institute of Los Angeles, 1917), has been reprinted frequently, most recently by Baker in 2000.

34. What is missing is a capstone article that would assemble the relevant lines of evidence as part of the doctrine of God itself. But numerous articles are devoted to defending elements of Trinitarianism, such as biblical evidence for the deity of Christ and the Spirit. Most telling is the way Trinitarian themes are woven into articles such as Robert E. Speer's "God in Christ the Only Revelation of The Fatherhood of God"; R. A. Torrey's "The Personality and Deity of the Holy Spirit"; and especially Erdman's "The Holy Spirit and the Sons of God." By now, readers of this book should not be surprised that the evangelical Trinitarianism of *The Fundamentals* is powerful, understated, and forgotten.

35. Erdman, "The Holy Spirit," in *Fundamentals*, 2:338.

36. Ibid., 343.

37. Ibid., 338.

38. Heidelberg Catechism, q. 33.

39. From *A Practical Commentary upon the First Epistle of St. Peter*, The Works of Robert Leighton (London: Longmans, 1870), 3:150.
40. Ibid.
41. Sinclair Ferguson, *The Christian Life: A Doctrinal Introduction* (Edinburgh: Banner of Truth, 1981), 96.
42. Rainsford, *The Lord's Prayer for Believers*, 160.
43. James Denney, cited in John Randolph Taylor, *God Loves Like That! The Theology of James Denney* (Richmond, VA: John Knox Press, 1962), 38.
44. Adolph Saphir, *The Hidden Life: Thoughts on Our Communion with God* (New York: Carter and Brothers, 1877), 30. Saphir's five cautions against dangerous tendencies in some mystic writers are very helpful.
45. John Calvin, *Institutes of the Christian Religion* 1.8.1.
46. These verses are usually quoted without attribution. When a source is given, it is usually the name Catesby Paget.
47. Packer, *Knowing God*, 186.
48. Ibid., 187.
49. James Buchanan, *Doctrine of Justification* (Birmingham, AL: Solid Ground, 2006), 276.
50. Packer, *Knowing God*, 194.
51. Adolphe Monod, *Adolphe Monod's Farewell to His Friends and to His Church*, trans. Owen Thomas (London: Banner of Truth, 1962), 114.

CHAPTER 5: INTO THE SAVING LIFE OF CHRIST

1. Billy Graham, *The Holy Spirit: Activating GOD's Power in Your Life* (Waco: Word, 1978), 35–36.
2. Robert Boyd Munger, *My Heart—Christ's Home*, expanded ed. (Downers Grove, IL: InterVarsity, 1986), 3–5.
3. John Calvin, *Institutes of the Christian Religion*, ed. John T. McNeill, trans. Ford Lewis Battles (Philadelphia: Westminster Press, 1960), 1:537.
4. "True Spirituality," in *A Christian Worldview*, The Complete Works of Francis A. Schaeffer, vol. 3 (Wheaton, IL: Crossway, 1985), 264.
5. Ibid.
6. Ibid., 416–17.
7. Ibid., 196.
8. Ibid., 270–71.
9. Ibid., 271.
10. Francis Schaeffer, *A Christian View of the Bible as Truth*, The Complete Works of Francis A. Schaeffer, vol. 2 (Wheaton, IL: Crossway, 1985), 321ff.
11. Ibid., 323.
12. Ibid., 325–26.
13. Ibid., 327.
14. Ibid., 326–27.
15. Ibid., 355.
16. Ibid., 327.
17. Ibid., 360.
18. Schaeffer, *Christian Worldview*, 273.
19. Schaeffer, "True Spirituality," 275.
20. Ibid.
21. Ibid.
22. Schaeffer, *A Christian View of the Bible*, 362.
23. Ibid., 362–63.
24. Schaeffer, *Christian Worldview*, 208.
25. Ibid., 275.
26. Ibid., 269.
27. Ibid., 271.
28. Francis Schaeffer, "The Supernatural Universe," in *Christian Worldview*, 264.
29. Francis Schaeffer, "Two Contents, Two Realities," in *Christian Worldview*, 416–17.
30. *The Complete Works of Oswald Chambers* (Grand Rapids, MI: Discovery, 2000), 18.
31. Ibid., 561.
32. Marcus Rainsford, *The Lord's Prayer for Believers: Thoughts on St. John 17, the Lord's Prayer for Believers Throughout All Time*, 5th ed. (London: Thynne, 1904), 159.
33. Ibid., 161.

CHAPTER 6: HEARING THE VOICE OF GOD IN SCRIPTURE

1. Cited in Morton H. Smith, *Studies in Southern Presbyterian Theology* (Phillipsburg, NJ: P&R, 1987), 224.
2. Adolph Saphir, *The Hidden Life: Thoughts on Our Communion with God* (New York: Carter, 1877).
3. Ibid., 92.
4. Ibid., 93.
5. Ibid.
6. Ibid.
7. Ibid., 97.
8. Ibid., 123.
9. Adolph Saphir, *Christ and the Scriptures* (London: Morgan and Scott, 1884), 124.
10. Ibid., 124–25.
11. Ibid., 125.
12. Ibid., 128.
13. Ibid.
14. Philip Mauro, "Life in the Word," in *The Fundamentals: A Testimony to the Truth* (Los Angeles: Bible Institute of Los Angeles, 1917), 144–208.
15. Ibid., 148.
16. Ibid., 151.
17. Ibid., 188.
18. Ibid., 189.
19. Ibid., 191.
20. G. Campbell Morgan, *The Song Companion to the Scriptures* (London: Morgan & Scott, 1911).
21. Glen G. Scorgie, "Hermeneutics and the Meditative Use of Scripture: The Case for a Baptized Imagination." *Journal of the Evangelical Theological Society* 44 (June 2001): 271–84.
22. Ibid.
23. J. I. Packer, *Keep in Step with the Spirit: Finding Fullness in Our Walk with God* (Old Tappan, NJ: Revell, 1984), 43.

CHAPTER 7: PRAYING WITH THE GRAIN

1. Horatius Bonar, *Light and Truth: or, Bible Thoughts and Themes, The Lesser Epistles* (London: James Nisbet, 1883), 44.
2. John Bunyan, "Discourse on Prayer," in *The Works of That Eminent Servant of Christ, John Bunyan* (Philadelphia: Clarke, 1836), 2:81.
3. Andrew Murray, *Holy in Christ* (London: Nisbet, 1888), 113.
4. "The First Sinner's Prayer in English," with an introduction and commentary by Malcolm Yarnell, *Southwestern Journal of Theology*.
5. Bunyan, "Discourse in Prayer," 85–86.
6. Oswald Chambers, "The Place of Help," in *The Complete Works of Oswald Chambers* (Grand Rapids, MI: Discovery, 2000), 1049.
7. J. C. Ryle, *Knots Untied: Being Plain Statements on Disputed Points in Religion from the Standpoint of an Evangelical Churchman* (London: William Hunt, 1885), 247.
8. Andrew Murray, *With Christ in the School of Prayer: Thoughts on Our Training for the Ministry of Intercession* (New York: Revell, 1895), 132.
9. Ibid., 130–31.
10. Ibid., 131.
11. Ibid., 132.
12. Ibid., 132–33.
13. Ibid., 134.
14. Graham Cole, *Engaging with the Holy Spirit: Real Questions, Practical Answers* (Wheaton, IL: Crossway, 2007), 64.
15. Robert E. Speer, "God in Christ the Only Revelation of the Fatherhood of God," in *The Fundamentals: A Testimony to the Truth* (Los Angeles: Bible Institute of Los Angeles, 1917), 2:235–36.
16. The analogues to God the Son and God the Father are easily identified: in Narnia, they are Aslan and the Great Emperor; in the space trilogy they are Maleldil the Young and the Old One. Aside from allusions to "the Third One," Lewis is content to leave the Holy Spirit in the deep background of his fictional worlds. A striking poetic presentation of Lewis's Trinitarian vision of the world can be found in the hymn on the Great Dance, with which Perelandra concludes. Equal parts Austin Farrer

and Charles Williams, this hymn envisions "all the patterns linked and looped together by the union of a kneeling with a sceptred love. Blessed be He!" *Perelandra* (New York: Collier, 1944), 217.

17. C. S. Lewis, *Mere Christianity*, rev. ed. (New York: Collier, 1952), 141.

18. Ibid., 141.

19. Ibid., 141–42.

20. Ibid., 142.

21. Ibid., 142–43.

22. Ibid., 143.

23. Lewis, who often paraphrased patristic writings without explicitly citing them, is probably intentionally echoing the language of Gregory of Nazianzus's fifth "Theological Oration," sec. 26. Of course he is also drawing on an ancient tradition of summarization that can be found even in the structure of the earliest creeds. For an analysis of this, see Henri de Lubac, *The Christian Faith: An Essay on the Structure of the Apostles' Creed* (San Francisco: Ignatius Press, 1986), 85–131.

24. Chap. 3, "Time and Beyond Time." The discussion of the Son's eternal generation stretches into the following chapter as well.

25. Lewis, *Mere Christianity*, 151.

26. Ibid., 152.

27. Ibid., 153.

28. Ibid.

29. Lewis pursues the metaphor of doctrine as a map in the introduction to Book 4, 135–40.

30. See the remarks by Stephen Williams, "Why Our Evangelism Must Be Trinitarian," *Themelios* 21 (October 1995): 3, and especially his caveat, "That is not to say that in evangelism the word 'Trinity' must be used . . ." But the story must be told, in its full Trinitarian form.

31. Lewis, *Mere Christianity*, 165.

32. C. S. Lewis, *The Weight of Glory and Other Addresses*, rev. and exp. ed. (New York: Collier, 1949), 13.

33. Owen Barfield, "The Five C. S. Lewises," in *Owen Barfield on C. S. Lewis*, ed. G. B. Tennyson (Middletown, CT: Wesleyan University Press, 1989), 121–22.

34. "A Slip of the Tongue," from *The Weight of Glory and Other Addresses* (New York: Harper-Collins, 2001), 187. The sermon was preached on January 29, 1956.

GENERAL INDEX

Abraham, 119, 131

adoption, 157–66; and the claims of sonship, 161–62, 216–17; explanation of in the Heidelberg Catechism, 160; the greatness of divine adoption, 160–61

angels, 39, 67, 107, 122, 130, 137

Anglicanism, evangelical nature of, 14–15

anti-intellectualism, 17, 18, 209

antinomianism, 107

anti-Trinitarianism, 69

Apostles' Creed, 19

Aquinas, Thomas, 24, 118

Aristotle, 68

assurance, 9, 15, 57, 106, 108, 180; and biblical authority, 189; doctrine of, 187–92; and election, 189–90; and faith, 188–89

Athanasius, 24

atheism, 114

atonement, 73, 74, 76, 93, 140, 148, 164

Augustine, 24

baptism, 14, 43, 54–55, 174, 183; infant baptism, 56; of Jesus, 82, 136, 180, 233

Barfield, Owen, 238

Barth, Karl, 38, 242n19

Basic Bible Studies (Schaeffer), 179–80, 181

Bible, the, 12, 15, 16, 17, 21, 25, 28, 35, 65, 73, 77, 85, 95, 153, 169, 179, 193; biblical authority, 189, 194–95; biblical literacy, 20; as the "Blest Book," 204; love songs (hymns) to, 201–9; worship of (Bibliolatry), 197–98. *See also* Bible study

Bible study, 9, 20, 59, 61, 97, 113, 178, 179

Bonar, Horatius, 204–5, 214

Bray, Gerald, 10–11, 21, 52, 55; on the inner life of God, 81

"Break Thou the Bread of Life" (Lathbury), 205

Brunner, Emil, 240n2

Bunyan, John, 41–42, 220, 241n27; definition of true prayer, 214

Burkitt, William, 83

Calvin, John, 163–64, 189; on union with Christ, 172–73

Campus Crusade for Christ, 23

Candlish, Robert S., 161

Chambers, Oswald, 22, 186, 220

Chesterton, G. K., 80, 98

Christ Knocking at the Door of Sinners' Hearts, or, A Solemn Entreaty to Receive the Saviour and His Gospel (Flavel), 170–71

Christian Faith, The (Schleiermacher), 39, 40

Christian and Missionary Alliance, 103

Christian Theology (Wiley), 245n25

Christianity, 14, 22, 39, 54, 87, 97, 107, 109, 114, 229; Christian life and the life of the Trinity, 230–31; evangelical Christianity, 7, 10, 11, 19–20, 21; gospel theology of Christianity's formative period, 36; "heart" Christianity, 115; and the idea of God as a person, 227–28; Trinitarian tradition within, 22–23. *See also* Christians

Christians, 27–28; central reality of (doctrine, behavior, emotions), 112; emotional Christians, 115; evangelical Christians, 34, 209; "hand" Christians, 113–14; "head" Christians, 113; "heart" Christians, 114

Christocentrism, 173, 175

communion, and authority, 193–95

Communion with God the Father, Son, and Holy Ghost (Owen), 142

conversion (to a personal relationship with Jesus), 12, 15–17, 20, 57, 74, 105, 106, 108, 143

"convertive piety," 57

Council of Nicaea, 46, 235

Cowper, William, 206–7

creation, 39, 64, 65–66, 67, 69, 70, 87, 88, 92, 95, 120, 155

cross of Christ, the, 15–16; reductionist nature of emphasizing only the cross in salvation history, 16

Cross and the Switchblade, The (Cruz), 28, 240n1

Cruz, Nicky, 61, 184; difficulty of in understanding the concept of the Trinity, 32–33; on the humanity of Christ, 29; Trinitarian theology of, 28–33; on the work of the Holy Spirit, 30–31

decadence, 110; typical reactions to, 110–11

Denney, James, 74

Desiring God (Piper), 94

Discerning the Mystery: An Essay on the Nature of Theology (Louth), 53–54

"Doctrines That Must Be Emphasized in Successful Evangelism" (Munhall), 15

Munger, Robert Boyd, 170, 171
Munhall, L. W., 15
Murray, Andrew, 215–16; on the eternal
 being of God in its Trinitarian dimension,
 221–23
"My Heart—Christ's Home" (Munger), 170
mystagogy, 55

New Testament, 63, 64, 70, 74, 77, 80, 89,
 96, 120, 134, 153, 165, 169, 179–80;
 New Testament prayers, 224
Newbigin, Lesslie, 153–54
Newton, John, 118, 203
Nicene Creed, 19
No Little People (Schaeffer), 177
Noll, Mark, 37
Notes on the New Testament (J. Wesley), 105

Oden, Thomas, 118–19
oikonomia, 129, 130, 132, 244n3
Old Testament, 63, 64, 70, 119, 131, 179
On Religion (Schleiermacher), 40
orthodoxy, 177, 183
"outward man," the, 113–14
Owen, John, 127, 142, 147, 214, 245n15

Packer, J. I., 22, 142, 210; on adoption, 165
Palmer, Benjamin Morgan, 192, 194
Paul, 18, 83, 85, 101–2, 104, 157–58, 214;
 on the blessings of the gospel, 122–23; on
 God's economy of salvation, 129–33; on
 God's love for us, 121; on Jesus' love for
 believers, 173–74; theme of blessing/prais-
 ing in Ephesians, 99–102; warning to the
 Galatians, 108
Pentecost, 159; role of Calvary and Easter in,
 148–49
Pentecostals, 55
personal belief, and "universal intent," 48
*Personal Knowledge: Toward a Post-Critical
 Philosophy* (Polanyi), 47
Phillips, J. B., 98
Piper, John, 94; "God is the gospel" concept
 of, 125
Polanyi, Michael, 46–49; context of his work,
 241n34; on the nature of knowledge,
 47–48
praise/praising, 101–2; communal praise, 58
prayer, 61, 97; alertness to the Trinity in, 214–
 15; aligning prayer life with spiritual life
 in general, 215–16; as a blessing, 212–13;
 conversational prayer, 20; God's answering of, 221–23; the "grain" of prayer, 212,
 213–14; how prayer works, 211–14; praying like Jesus, 216–20; as tacitly Trinitar-

ian, 212; which member of the Trinity we
 should pray to, 224–26. *See also* Lewis,
 C. S., on the Lord's Prayer; Lewis, C. S.,
 on Trinitarian prayer; Tyndale, William,
 commentary on the Lord's Prayer
"Precious Bible" (Newton), 203
Protestantism, evangelical, 163
Psalms, praise of God in, 119–20

Rahner, Karl, 38, 43–44, 242n19
Rainsford, Marcus, 145–46, 162, 167, 192
rationalism, 199
redemption, 15, 18, 39, 40, 67, 70, 79, 92,
 95–96; accomplishment and application
 of by the Trinity, 141–49; logic of freedom
 and gratitude in, 65–66
Religious Affections, The (Edwards), 77, 78
Run Baby Run (Cruz), 28, 29, 31
Ryle, J. C., 14, 108, 221

salvation, 9, 13, 39, 57, 61, 64, 73, 91, 97–98,
 116, 165, 186; developing a coherent
 doctrine of, 111–12; the economy of
 God's salvation, 128–33, 146–47, 230;
 the economy of God's salvation as the two
 hands of the Father, 136–41; and evangelical theology, 163–64; as an experience of
 conversion, 108; evangelical treatment of,
 107; full salvation (salvation to the "uttermost"), 105–6; propositions and doctrines
 concerning, 107–8; role of Christ's life in,
 16; saving relationship of the believer with
 the triune God, 180–81; and union with
 Christ, 173; what "being saved" means,
 108–9. *See also* assurance, doctrine of;
 salvation history
salvation history, 16, 235; central role of the
 cross in, 15–16; God's presence in, 233–34
sanctification, 39, 43, 74, 106, 145, 180–81,
 216, 236, 237
Saphir, Adolph, 104, 163, 201, 205; approach
 of to Scripture, 195–99; on the charge of
 Bibliolatry, 197–99; on doctrine versus
 the experienced reality of God, 196; on
 Scripture as Trinitarian, 197; on the written Word of the past and the living Word
 of the present, 196–97
Schaeffer, Edith, 177
Schaeffer, Francis, 22, 167; on accepting
 Christ as our Savior, 182–83; on "relationship" with God, 182; on sanctification,
 181; soteriology of, 178, 180–81; Trinitarian theology of, 175–84
Schleiermacher, Friedrich, 38–39
Scorgie, Glen, 209

SCRIPTURE INDEX